THE POLITICS OF CURRICULAR CHANGE

Studies in the Postmodern Theory of Education

Joe L. Kincheloe and Shirley R. Steinberg
General Editors

Vol. 131

PETER LANG
New York • Washington, D.C./Baltimore • Bern
Frankfurt am Main • Berlin • Brussels • Vienna • Oxford

THE POLITICS OF CURRICULAR CHANGE

Race, Hegemony, and Power in Education

EDITED BY
M. Christopher Brown II and Roderic R. Land

WITH A FOREWORD BY
Lisa Delpit

PETER LANG
New York • Washington, D.C./Baltimore • Bern
Frankfurt am Main • Berlin • Brussels • Vienna • Oxford

Library of Congress Cataloging-in-Publication Data
The politics of curricular change: race, hegemony, and power in
education / [edited by] M. Christopher Brown II, Roderic R. Land.
p. cm. — (Counterpoints; vol. 131)
Includes bibliographical references and index.
1. Education—Curricula—United States. 2. Curriculum change—
United States. 3. Politics and education—United States.
4. Multiculturalism—United States. I. Brown, M. Christopher.
II. Land, Roderic R. III. Series: Counterpoints (New York, N.Y.); v. 131.
LB1570.P58   375'.006—dc22   2003022444
ISBN 0-8204-4863-X
ISSN 1058-1634

Bibliographic information published by Die Deutsche Bibliothek.
Die Deutsche Bibliothek lists this publication in the "Deutsche
Nationalbibliografie"; detailed bibliographic data is available
on the Internet at http://dnb.ddb.de/.

Cover design by Dutton & Sherman Design

© 2005 Peter Lang Publishing, Inc., New York
275 Seventh Avenue, 28th Floor, New York, NY 10001
www.peterlangusa.com

All rights reserved.
Reprint or reproduction, even partially, in all forms such as microfilm,
xerography, microfiche, microcard, and offset strictly prohibited.

To Steven P. Thomas
who taught me that the only limit
to the possibility of change
is the will to create it;
to Anthony A. Pittman
who has most supported my right to change;
and to Nigel P. Pierce for suffering
through my changes and endeavoring to do the same.

—mcb2

To my entire family
for their unwavering support;
to my academic fathers – David L. Eanes,
William A. Smith (B.P.), William T. Trent,
Laurence Parker, and James Anderson; and
most importantly to my biological father,
James E. Land (Ben),
who is reading this from above.
Love and miss you always.

—rrl

TABLE OF CONTENTS

Foreword ix
Lisa Delpit

1. **Telling the Truth...AGAIN: Another Introduction**................1
   M. Christopher Brown II

PART ONE: PARADIGM POWER: THE UNCHANGING PREMISE OF RACE

2. **A Sociological Treatise on the Racialized Context of American Education**..15
   David M. Stovall

3. **Learning in Spite of Opposition: African Americans and their History of Education Exclusion in Antebellum America**...26
   Christopher M. Span

4. **Toward the Study of Blackness: The Development of a Field of Inquiry**...............................54
   Roderic R. Land

5. **Reflecting Black: Maintaining a Politics of Opposition in Academe**.................76
   Marvin Lynn

6. **Racialized Technology: Computers, Commodification, and "Cyber-race"**..................91
   Jamel K. Donnor

PART TWO: CURRICULAR HEGEMONY: THE POLITICS OF
EDUCATION AND SCHOOLING

7. Wounded (Soul)diers in the Classroom:
Qualifying the Black Teacher's Experience.........................105
Roderic R. Land

8. Weaving a Womanist Discourse
to Unravel White Male Privilege in the Classroom...............128
Dianne Smith

9. Practicing Multicultural Education:
Answering Recurring Questions
About What It Is (Not)..143
André J. Branch

10. African American Students
in the Desegregated P–16 Pipeline:
Opportunities, Outcomes, and Value-Based Ideologies..........162
M. Christopher Brown II and RoSusan D. Bartee

11. School Mathematics and African American Students:
The Need to Revisit
Opportunity-to-Learn Standards.......................................178
William F. Tate

12. Race and Change in Education:
Toward a Semiotics of Curriculum....................................211
Garrett A. Duncan

Epilogue:
"The Struggle Continues"..231
Geneva Gay

About the Editors..253

OREWORD

Lisa Delpit

Rereading the book, *The Politics of Curricular Change: Race, Hegemony, and Power in Education*, has brought to mind a story I have frequently shared. I was helping a 6th grader learn multiplication, which she had somehow failed to master in her earlier educational history. In the middle of an explanation she looked up at me in exasperation and demanded, "Miss Lisa, why you trying to teach me this? Multiplication is for white people; black people just add and subtract!" While her response inspires a bit of a chuckle, when thinking more deeply about her remark one is left more pensive than amused. Where did she get this idea? What has she learned in the society she lives in, the schools she has attended, and the curriculum she's been exposed to that could leave this young woman believing that people who look like her are so inferior to white people that they cannot be expected to perform one of the most elementary of mathematical operations? Moreover, that it is not something they might even consider utilizing as a tool in their everyday lives?

The answers to these questions are the reason for this book. What must be done to educate a child who is the victim of a society whose belief system—social and academic—declares her to be inferior? From founding father Thomas Jefferson, who declared in the 1700s that people of African descent were "dull, tasteless, and anomalous" to renowned Harvard professor and scientist, Louis Agassiz who, in the mid-1890s wrote exhaustively about the intellectual and physical inferiority of the Negroes who "are incapable of living on a footing of social equality with whites" (quoted in Gould, 1981, p. 48), and should only be educated to use their hands, while the white man is educated to use his mind.

Throughout the history of this country, numerous "scholars" of varying disciplines have reiterated the inferiority treatise. More recently, authors of

The Bell Curve have received standing ovations in middle-class white communities with their portrayals of the genetic basis for black intellectual inferiority, and their policy recommendations suggesting that some individuals are not worth enough to our society to justify the cost of their education. Furthermore, the book's authors argue that since blacks have inferior intelligence, the government should not support unwed mothers with food stamps or money, and their children should be put in permanent government-run nurseries (Herrnstein & Murray, 1994).

Not only have "scientists" proffered theories of black inferiority, our federal government has supported such theories as well. After a 1967 article entitled, "The Role of Brain Disease in Riots and Urban Violence" in the *Journal of the American Medical Association*, two of the authors received National Institute of Mental Health monies for experiments in psychosurgery for violence control in urban communities (Breggin & Breggin, 1998). The NIMH and the Department of Justice have also funded projects that can supposedly identify "violence-prone" African American pre-schoolers and elementary students and use experimental drugs to "treat" them without fully disclosing the purpose of the "treatment" to their parents. A major initiative of such a project was halted in the 1990's, only when protesters brought the project to public scrutiny (Breggin & Breggin, 1998).

Surrounded with such unrelenting assaults to her intellectual and social integrity, could it be surprising that the young girl I tutored could find it so hard to believe that she could learn to multiply? And she is not alone. Millions of other young people of African descent have internalized similar negative views of themselves. And, of course, their beliefs about themselves can only be reinforced by the similar beliefs held by those who are not of African descent. All who live in the United States of America have appropriated, consciously or unconsciously, belief systems that cast doubt on the intellectual and social worthiness of black people. As Angela Davis said in a recent lecture, "When we think we are thinking, we are actually being thought by the discourses that shape us" (Davis, 2003).

Because the discourse of black inferiority is so embedded in the American psyche, it is important that this discourse be laid bare and examined. Doing so is not easy, for just as those who live in Los Angeles are unconscious "smog breathers, "those who live in the United States are "racism breathers" (Tatum, 1997). It is only after we become explicitly aware of the racism permeating the very air we breathe that we can consider strategies to eradicate it.

The authors of this volume attempt to do both – to describe the racially charged nature of being black in a white intellectual world, and to examine those demeaning realities with the goal of considering humanizing alternatives. M. Christopher Brown ends his introduction with the words, "Our only hope is that this will be the last time we have to detail how the roles of race and power hinder educational opportunity and outcomes for so many students (p. 10). I cannot predict what effect this book will have upon its readers, but I can guarantee that Dr. Brown's hope will not be fulfilled. Given the history of this country, one can only predict that each new generation of scholars-of-color will find the need to make explicit, once again, the pervasive nature of racialized thinking in America.

References

Breggin, P., & Breggin, G. (1998). *The war against children of color.* Monroe, Maine: Common Courage Press.
Davis, A. Y. (2003). Slavery and the prison industrial complex. 5th Annual Eric E. Williams Memorial Lecture, Florida International University.
Gould, S. J. (1981). *The mismeasure of man.* New York: W.W. Norton.
Herrnstein, R., & Murray, C. (1994). *The bell curve: Intelligence and class structure in American life.* New York: The Free Press.
Tatum, B. (1997). *"Why are all the black kids sitting together in the cafeteria?" and other conversations about race.* New York: HarperCollins Publishers.

Telling the Truth...Again: Another Introduction

M. Christopher Brown II

Another Introduction

Here we go again trying to explain why another treatment of race in education is important. The reality is that despite increasing discourses about class and forms of capital (i.e., cultural, social, economic, and human), there is nothing more permanent to social interactions than race. Inasmuch as the delivery of educational services is a function that occurs in the social/public space, education is bedeviled by the realities of race–race bias, race privilege, race effects, and racism.

The U.S. has undergone different conceptions of education as different and significant peoples have joined the population. Without question, educating everyone in the twenty-first century will require curricular change. Hence, cultural/racial difference, both as a hallmark of American society and as an aspect of the higher-education curriculum, will continue to excite debate and conceptual confusion. This conscious acknowledgment of race in an idyllically named colorblind society fodders a dialectic between power, race, and hegemony that contours the definition, purpose, content, and pedagogy of primary schools and secondary institutions, not to mention colleges and universities.

Although assimilationist policies and blended multiculturalist ideologies are regarded as outmoded, injurious, and, most importantly, a failure in the contemporary research community within the U.S., there remains a recognizable cohort of academics who continue to favor the "melting pot" notion that all who come to America are welcome as long as they surrender their individual cultures and become part of the larger or dominant society. These pseudo-progressives adopt multicultural phraseology as an expedient response when interacting with the ever-growing number and size of ethnic and racial groups within American society. For such researchers, curricular theorists, and educators, the goals of assimilation can be pursued without denying cultural rights to minorities by adopting what the academics presume to be the language of multiculturalism. As such, the discourse on education is confounded by the recognition that society is comprised of intricately intertwined networks and frameworks of race (i.e., communal culture), hegemony (i.e., dominance and leadership), and power (i.e., the politics of policy). The aggregation of these myriad social histories, informal language patterns, and familial traditions makes it difficult to create one definition of an inclusive curriculum.

Like society writ large, education within the U.S. must respond to the swelling population of students from myriad backgrounds and experiences. Consequently, the educational structure must also engage the complex nuances of multiple cultures, languages, and contexts within and without the classroom. The attempts to create a broad system of education that includes all persons have created visions of a culture in which many marginalized and oppressed groups are visible. Given the multiple dialogues from underrepresented groups, the mandate requires curricular changes which can unite all of the voices, and that will move society closer to the reality of "liberty and justice for all" (Kincheloe & Steinberg, 1997). The truth, however, is that the U.S. is not a nation comprised of persons with cultural differences. The U.S. is a culture of difference.

Given that culture, it becomes clear that the totality of public and educational policy should not highlight each and every culture and/or language. Rather, educational and social planning and visioning must be centered on the multiple contexts in which all cultures and languages interact and intersect. A multiple-context approach to education allows for all cultures, regardless of their respective uniqueness, to find themselves and be validated within the collective society without needing particularistic attention. It is within this multiple context that "Culture, rather than a homogeneous entity, becomes a site of production and contestation not only over the goals in which we are engaged, but also over the processes we take to achieve these goals. Indeed, the processes exist in a dialectal relationship with goals so that the discourses we use to talk about our goals, and the relationships we establish to make decisions also determine what decisions are made" (Tierney, 1993, p. 29).

In the effort to acknowledge these myriad contexts, one must raise a series of critical questions to demystify the candor of a highly politicized system of education. In whose interest are students of color being educated? To whose culture are they being indoctrinated? And, most importantly, are they being schooled into "miseducation"? Much like the U.S., the institution of education was founded on a cultural hegemony that assigned privilege to the white patriarch while relegating non-whites and women to the margins. Not only has education served as a system for legitimating domination, but it has also been one that fosters the reproduction of racialized, cultural, and economic structures/hierarchies.

As such, the task of theorizing race, hegemony, and education requires educators to critically examine egocentric and allocentric positionalities through race in a society. This is particularly important when race is the agency in which oppression is ascertained, as well as the agency in which the oppressed struggle for their liberation. Furthermore, we must be mindful that the institutional praxis that (in)formed the foundation of colonization and the ability to rule other people monopolized the ability to know—in the sense of being able to name, analyze, judge, study, illustrate, and discipline—colonized people (Said, 1979). Because the demographics of the students in our schools, colleges, and universities are changing, the way of knowing must change. It is necessary to develop a new frame of reference that transcends the limits of existing concepts, theories, and ideologies. Reality has been conceptualized, by and large, in terms of a limited perspective from the dominant social forms that reside in western populations. Educators must challenge the constructions of truth operating in prevailing educational discourses that perpetuate dominant social structure and power relations (Gordon, 1997).

Thus, the call for more racially and ideologically diverse voices in the construction of knowledge that informs the curriculum must be answered.

Curricular change not only affects students, but it also affects how teachers come to know what they know and the epistemological methods that are used to inform their instructional knowledge base. Given that large proportions of our teachers at each level of education are white, and the demographic changes within the student population, the teachers' race becomes significant. A psychological view of racism assumes that if we can alter the mentality of white teachers, this in turn will create changes in institutions and their discourse. A Foucauldian understanding of discourse draws an important connection between discourses and power within social relations. Power is not conceptualized as a possession that one individual exerts over another; rather, it is a circulatory force that operates through knowledge as individuals enact, take up, or resist the practices and social positions that particular forms of knowledge make available (Duesterberg, 1999). Subjectivity and identity is produced in and through this discourse.

In sum, an inclusive curriculum (and the politics involved) must acknowledge and utilize various racial, ethnic, political, economic, and linguistic groups in addition to the dominant majority in order to support and maintain diversity, tolerance, and ultimately community. This struggle over race, hegemony, and power will continue to loom large as long as the dominant group seeks to maintain schools as exclusive enclaves of superiority for which underrepresented and marginalized groups must entreat access and equality of opportunity. Race affects, informs, and dominates the educational experience. So, why is it that we refuse to tell the truth about race in the curriculum?

Race Rules: The Colorful Concepts of the Contract

The myriad conceptualizations of race have consistently influenced the relationship between blacks and others in the known world. Mills (1997) argues that these two primary groups have therefore either involuntarily or voluntarily entered into an agreement that proffers non-blacks as superior and blacks as inferior. Non-blacks become beneficiaries and parishioners of their race while blacks are victimized and prisoners within their own skin.

The contract is laden with unfair connotations and unjust results that inherently signify political and moral innuendoes behind "racialized color." Two important questions emerge from within this literature: (1) What created this racial divide? And (2) how has "racialized color" affected the larger society?

Bederman (1995) argues that the division between the races is an ideological juxtaposition of the various interpretations of civilization. These seemingly polar positions on human existence emerged during the late nineteenth century or the post-Civil War era. While these positions depict the meaning of civilization very differently, in many ways all racialized human beings become accustomed to similar roles and results. The connotations of race vividly construct images of the vestiges of "white-skin" superiority and racial hatred that existed for blacks throughout the Diaspora. The distinction between these two primary clusters of people consequently appears clear. While this is the appearance, the reality of how and whether race shapes phenomena has paradigmatic implications for role performance among students, teachers, and the curriculum. Race becomes a perceived proxy for ideology, as well as the schema for the epistemological context of education.

Race matters penetrate the core of human emotions, schooling practices, and societal fabric. This unacknowledged "content" (rather than context) implies perceptional and policy differences regarding the status of persons based on race. In fact, much of the racial ambiguity and conflict emerges from the extant conceptualizations of race and how the effects of race construct institutionalized prejudice and discrimination. Within these systemic operations resonate power and privileges that significantly impact the larger society and its ability to forge social justice and distribute equality and equity to American citizens.

Further, a critical examination of race illuminates the manner in which all individuals conceptualize the stratification of humanity. Mills (1997) acknowledges the significance of race by exploring its role of fostering and sustaining a hierarchical society. Needless to say, race is an observable characteristic. Race cannot be concealed or disregarded simply because of its controversial implications. Race cannot be masked because it brings forth feelings of discomfort, confusion, and fear. The proposed solution, however, has been to silence discussions of race. This attempt suggests that the world should engage in the notion of colorblindness. It is assumed that to be colorblind is to be impartial, fair, and objective (Brown, 2000b; Nieto, 1996). On the contrary: Colorblindness is a race-conscious ideology—one simply chooses not to acknowledge race. Race is a mandate of difference that bestows rights of power and privilege. It is in reality a colorful mark of inevitable separation that distinguishes the have and have-nots and ultimately the oppressor and the oppressed in a positional space. Race is an element of education that cannot and should not be ignored. "Race continues to preoccupy the public mind, a reminder of a past that cannot be willed away" (Hacker, 1992, p. 4). Education must correct the fallacy of colorblindness, and declare that the positionality of each individual is subjective, significant, and colored by race.

A Word on Education and Schooling by Whom and for What

Like the historical ground from which they grow, schools and classrooms are not raceless, nor have they ever been. They are the sites where the rules of race are taught and reinforced. There is a struggle in the realm of education that centers on education's function. Much of this struggle also involves a need to distinguish between education and schooling. Schooling has as one of its goals to teach students about the ways of society so that they might be able to understand and participate in that society. This often leads to the perpetuation of inequalities of race (much less class or gender).

Education, unlike schooling, usually involves a liberating quality that challenges the status quo, and thus can serve to liberate persons from hegemonic structures that oppress. These oppressions may be based on race, gender, class, age, and/or other characteristics. Combining the liberating quality of education with morality requires one to challenge those structures in society that have served to exploit some and to privilege others. Questioning the "rightness" of past and present acts against peoples is a requirement of a liberating education. Without a morality that is rooted in what is good and humane to all persons, education cannot liberate. The alternative is then a perpetuation of those structures that endow more power (although not legitimate power) to those who are already powerful.

Before expounding on some of the politically based discrepancies within schools, there must be some consensus on the purpose of education and school. Underwood states that school "must prepare you to be a rational, reflective, and critical thinker. It should provide truthful knowledge about who you are and how you become a productive member of society" (2000, p. 44). Being a rational, reflective, and critical thinker can be complex and require a solid base of knowledge about a subject. However, if most schools concentrate on a curriculum that centers on non-black students, how can the students be expected to relate to the subject, let alone think critically about its content?

The curriculum is primarily concentrated on European-American ideologies and perspectives. Rarely do black students attend a public school that has a curriculum focused on their cultures and histories. This lack of a "relevant" education could perpetuate low academic achievement by this cohort of learners, because many of these students may not see the relevance or importance of schooling. Far too many teachers then view these students as underachievers or learning disabled. This is not true (see Brown & Davis, 2000).

Most policymakers fail to recognize the correlation between race and education. Meaningful policy change must start with a dialogue on the curriculum. Dialogue, which uses words to name the world and transform it, imposes itself as the way humans achieve significance. Through words, men and women are able to change, or *name*, the world. Freire (1993) has explained the dimensions and the importance of the word. The word is the essential instrument in dialogue. But, more importantly, it is both reflective and active by nature. Moreover, there can be no true word without both its reflective and active dimensions. In order to have true education, dialogue must exist. Brown (2000a) refers to the "Word" as the sum total of our lived experiences identifiable as real and intellectual. These experiences are lessons of empowerment and liberation. The word maximizes human possibility to change current conditions in society.

Given the importance of the word in naming the world and the importance of dialogue in determining human significance, it seems evident that the words used in dialogue determine the success of the dialogue and ultimately the success of education. However, racial dialogue does not represent true dialogue. Racial dialogue lacks the active and reflective involvement of all persons, and is often contaminated by the infusion of white-skin privilege in determining the direction of the conversation. This phenomenon is accomplished by confusing individuals who candidly talk about race with those individuals who are in fact racist. By discussing issues, race relations are disturbed in our colorblind society. Macedo (1994) refers to actions of this nature as "discourse sanitation."

The dominance of white-skin privilege, in addition to determining who may actively participate in dialogue, also determines the language used in the dialogue. Terms that label the dominant culture (note: this term is used instead of "oppressor" in the spirit of political correctness) tend to be viewed as harmless euphemisms (Macedo, 1994). For example, the term "disenfranchised" is preferred over "oppressed" because it prevents the ascription of blame to the dominant culture. Macedo (1994) identifies a number of euphemisms that allow the dominant culture to be seen as harmless. Such terms include "ethnic cleansing," which is used to redefine the genocide experienced by the Jews in Nazi Germany and Bosnian Muslims in Serbia. The disheartening phrase suggests that the Germans and the Serbs were acting in a manner that would "cleanse" or "purify" the their respective regions of the ethnic "filth" that resided among them.

More importantly, this assignment of euphemisms can be witnessed in education as well. The term "at-risk" is used to classify urban students who are in danger of dropping out of school and encountering legal problems, when instead terms such as "at-promise" could be attached to these students to affirm that all students can learn irrespective of background. By using the term "at-risk," teachers and administrators are relieved of the blame for these students' lack of success. The educational system uses similar other euphemisms ad nauseam.

If positive change is to occur in schools and educational settings, open and race-conscious dialogue must occur. This volume is the first step in that dialogue. The experiences of blacks must be included and valued in the racial dialogue for real progress to occur. This book fills a void in the literature regarding the relationship of curricular change to race, hegemony, and power as independent and correlative constructs. Further, the volume evinces how these constructs, situated within their own contexts, serve as facilitators of curricular change.

Don't Say We Didn't Tell You

The pages that follow will illustrate how the systems of education and schooling in the U.S. contribute to the racial affairs between peoples. Without intervention, these institutions will continue to hinder the liberation and the emancipation of both the minds and lives of persons subjectified, commodified, and stratified by the rules of race, discrimination, and inequity. True education provides a means of confronting, understanding, and remedying the roots and the effects of the racial contract. Informed and enlightened educators have not only the opportunity but also the obligation to apply their lessons, scholarship, and positions to redressing racial discrimination and to widening the circle of inclusion.

If education is to become the truly great liberating tool it is capable of being, all humans must be allowed to participate. We cannot allow one group to dictate the conversation by determining what is and is not acceptable for discussion. We cannot allow the discomfort of some to prevent the liberation of others. One cannot truly be educated unless dialogue occurs. It is imperative that issues of race be both acknowledged and addressed in the classroom. The educational systems must not silence discussions of race, but rather use race as a learning tool to bring positive change. Doing so will allow students to recognize and appreciate cultural differences.

Race must be kept as a central focus in education programs. Issues of race and racism are consciously and unconsciously embedded in topics relating to culture, ethnicity, and class. By adding more culturally sensitive and accurate information to the curriculum and examining race as a social construct, educational settings can be more successful in preparing students to teach in racially diverse schools. Educational policies and practices must be consciously developed and implemented to avoid the perpetuation of those ideologies that we seek to remedy. In order to facilitate a sound educational environment in the schools, there needs to be a revision of all subject-matter curricula (especially social studies and history). The curricula should be infused with learning situations and contexts that are culturally relevant.

These are the first steps in disrupting the hegemonic overlay of race and power in the educational curriculum. Each of the chapters that follow will proffer other insights, guidance, and recommendations for enacting curricular change. In this volume we each tell the truth, the whole truth, and nothing but the truth. Our only hope is that this will be the last time we have to detail how the role of race and power hinder educational opportunity and outcomes for far too many students. Many scholars are wearying of telling the same stories, the same statistics, and the same truths to people who apparently have not been listening. So please, pay close attention.

References

Bederman, G. (1995). *Manliness & civilization: A cultural history of gender and race in the United States, 1880–1917.* Chicago: University of Chicago Press.

Brown, M. C. (1999). *The quest to define collegiate desegregation: Black colleges, Title VI compliance, and post-Adams litigation.* Westport, CT: Bergin & Garvey.

Brown, M. C. (2000a). Prophets of power in the professoriate: A sermon for cultural workers. In M. C. Brown & J. E. Davis (Eds.), *Black sons to mothers: Compliments, critiques, and challenges for cultural workers in education* (pp. 219–234). New York: Peter Lang.

Brown, M. C. (2000b). Seeing the invisible color black: Race-ing the collegiate desegregation discourse. *Race, Ethnicity and Education, 3,* 259–270.

Brown, M. C. (Ed.). (2002). *Equity and access in higher education: Changing the definition of educational opportunity.* (Readings on Equal Education, Vol. 18). New York: AMS Press.

Brown, M. C., & Davis, J. E. (Eds.). (2000). *Black sons to mothers: Compliments, critiques, and challenges for cultural workers in education.* New York: Peter Lang.

Duesterberg, L. M. (1999). Theorizing race in the context of learning to teach. *Teachers College Record, 100* (4), 751–775.

Freire, P. (1993). *Pedagogy of the oppressed.* New York: Continuum.

Gordon, B. M. (1997). Curriculum, policy, and African American cultural knowledge: Challenges and possibilities for the year 2000 and beyond. *Educational Policy, 11* (2), 227–242.

Hacker, A. (1992). *Two nations: Black and white, separate, hostile, unequal.*

New York: Macmillan.
Kincheloe, J. L., & Steinberg, S. R. (1997). *Changing multiculturalism*. Bristol, PA: Open University.
Macedo, D. (1994). *Literacies of power*. Boulder, CO: Westview.
Mills, C. W. (1997). *The racial contract*. Ithaca, NY: Cornell University Press.
Nieto, S. (1996). *Affirming diversity*. White Plains, NY: Longman.
Patterson, O. (2000, January 10). Race over. *The New Republic, 222* (2), 6.
Said, E. W. (1979). *Orientalism*. New York: Vintage Books.
Tierney, W. G. (1993). *Building communities of difference: Higher education in the twenty-first century*. Westport, CT: Bergin & Garvey.
Underwood, E. (2000). From son to mother? Intellectualizing the personal. In M. C. Brown & J. E. Davis (Eds.), *Black sons to mothers: Compliments, critiques, and challenges for cultural workers in education* (pp. 35–49). New York: Peter Lang.

PART ONE

 ARADIGM POWER:
THE UNCHANGING
PREMISE OF RACE

A Sociological Treatise on the Racialized Context of American Education

David M. Stovall

Author's Note: The following should not be read as an attempt to skew the accepted tenets of qualitative sociology. As a "treatise," the responsibility is to systematically analyze the permanence of a racialized system of education. Because I am often chided in the academic community for not adhering to the "formal" rules of sociological analysis, I would like to thank the editors for considering my attempt.

Education is not a neutral concept. As a systemic agent of stratification and oppression, education has contributed greatly to the creation and maintenance of hegemonic oppression. High-stakes testing, special education evaluations, vouchers, and school choice are often posed as solutions but further exacerbate inequality. In conjunction with the numerous works identifying racism's legal, historical, political, and social importance in education (Anderson, 1988; Watkins, Lewis, & Chou 2001; McCarthy, 1993; Weiss & Fine, 2000), the goal here is to describe a racialized context of urban education. When we speak of "racialized," we are operating from the definition of racialization as "any process or situation wherein the idea of 'race' is introduced to define and give meaning to some particular population, its characteristics and actions" (Miles in Hatcher & Troyna in McCarthy & Crichlow, 1993, p. 109). The purpose of this account is to identify, problematize, and emphasize the importance of reconstructing a paradigm enabling youth to determine themselves as important to the educational process. Because the current educational system complicates the means by which to achieve this paradigm, the process can be difficult for both teacher and student. Nevertheless, through analysis and evaluation researchers and practitioners can enable such praxis to flourish.

As a "treatise," the following should be read as an attempt to systemically account for a living history widely misinterpreted within mainstream multicultural ideology. Instead of solely engaging the surrounding literature and empirical data on the state of urban education, I decided to use an alternative methodology based on my own experience as a high school social studies teacher. Students, as directly affected by policy implementation, were able to provide critical analysis of those policies. By documenting my interactions with students, I was able to provide an analysis of educational policy through the intersection of teacher, student, and school policy.

Currently, popular public education policies have been placed under the moniker "No Child Left Behind" (U.S. Department of Education, 2000). Macedo and Bartolome identify an alternative context to the former, disguised in the language of diversity and tolerance:

> ...promising the "other" a dose of tolerance so we can get along, not only eclipses real opportunities for the development of mutual respect and cultural solidarity but also hides the privilege and paternalism inscribed in the proposition "I will tolerate you even though your culture is repugnant." It is the same paternalism that is often encoded as: "We need to empower minorities" or "we need to give them voice." First of all, we need to become keenly aware that voice is not something to be given by those in power. Voice requires struggle and the understanding of both possibilities and limitations. The most educators can do is to create structures that would enable submerged voices to emerge. It is not a gift. Voice is a human right. (1999, p. 39)

The following is an attempt to document a story of the often ignored, and bring new voices to light.

Setting

The project took place at a high school located on Chicago's South Side. Recently removed from a mandatory probation for graduation rates and test scores, the school has divided itself into four "small schools" with foci in art, science, business, and technical training. Because the school is listed in the registry of Chicago schools as a neighborhood school, youth from the surrounding area have first priority of enrollment and cannot be refused admission. The school currently serves 2,500 African American students, an overwhelming majority of which are labeled "low income" or "at-risk." Both categories are specific to African American and Latino students in current policy language.

Students were enrolled in a social studies course titled "Education and Inequality." The format was a team-taught exchange model where two instructors were responsible for the development of classroom projects, field trips, and discussion. While one instructor was responsible for conducting class for another group in California, my responsibility was supervising the Chicago component. The course ended with an exchange program where the Chicago students traveled to California to observe the other participating high school. In turn, the California students traveled to Chicago for a week to observe the Chicago school. At the end of the two-week period, students gathered for three days of discussion and exchange.

Designed as a ten-week course, the program is usually intended for students in advanced placement (AP) courses. However, the guidance counselor purposely selected a mixed group of students to participate in the project, ranging from those in AP courses to those who would be considered "middle-tier" students, receiving mostly 'B's and 'C's on their grade report.

This account will focus on the classroom component of the Chicago group. In developing a treatise on the racialized context of American education, classroom activities provide the best model to address the problem. From the design of the course to the students' participation, the project develops a means for young people to deconstruct the master narratives that influence their lives.

Methodology and Framework

The development of a concrete methodology that includes students of color is rooted in acknowledging a culture of resistance. The methodology must enable student analysis and input through a combination of life experiences and classroom readings. Because synergy is often difficult between the two, we utilized an array of alternative and postmodern texts based on new approaches to educating African American students. In addition, we utilized participant observation and action-research as a hands-on research approach to working with young people. The point was not to engage in an "objective" fact-finding mission. Instead, I chose to engage participants as a participant myself. From this vantage point an enriched knowledge is gained of a population underserved in current sociological and policy analysis.

Over the ten-week period, we used field notes and videotape transcriptions to develop the context for the study, and coordinated the class with assistance from the cooperating teacher at the California site. Both groups engaged in the same course, while coordinators conferred in weekly phone conversations on the direction of the class and coordination of student readings. We wrote field notes at the end of each session and compiled them in a log. At the termination of both classes, we analyzed the field notes and videotapes to develop this account.

In order to develop a treatise, the information gathered in the ten-week period is coupled with historical, sociological, and educational entries. Moreover, the juxtaposition of the voices of high school students and school policy connects the "lives of individuals to society" (Foster, 1997, p. xxi), and reveals tensions often cited in ethnographic accounts, but rarely referenced in policy analysis. It is clear that student perception and involvement has an effect on the entire educational process. If students do not want to be there, they will demonstrate their dissatisfaction (often to the dismay of the teacher). Although the study is limited in scope (only one school is examined), its analysis of school policy and student observation provides important insights.

The observations of Macedo and Bartolome were integral to supervising and directing the course:

> By refocusing on learning instead of teaching, educators will be able to develop a lucid clarity regarding the interrelationship between learning and teaching in order to realize that there is no teaching without learning and that learning ultimately determines and shapes teaching. (1999, p. 119)

We took the pedagogical stance that learning is demonstrated in the ability to apply gathered information to everyday life. From lived experience, new knowledge is created through feedback and the ability to communicate the information to others. In short, a good way to display what you are learning is through a creative process (e.g., narrative, projects, writing exercises). Although many students do not like to write or complete projects, the combination of the two provided students a form of expression that was to their liking.

Instead of mainstream textbooks, the class used a course packet of readings that problematized educational inequality and racism. The selection of readings included popular periodicals such as *Time*, *Newsweek*, and *The New Yorker*), song lyrics (e.g., KRS-ONE, Black Star, Lauryn Hill, Jill Scott), postmodern critique (e.g., Hall, Foucault, Arendt, Gramsci, Freire), sociology (e.g., Omi and Winant, Martin), history (e.g., Anderson, Watkins, Sittle-Walker), and literature (e.g., Baldwin, Neale Hurston, Morrison).

Using the course packet, class members were required to complete a video project and writing assignment based on questions concerning their lives. The first question was, "Where does society expect you to be in ten years?" The second asked, "Where do you expect to be in the next ten years?" Though these questions we were able to discuss societal influences and juxtapose them with what students were actively trying to do in their lives.

Based on the field notes from classroom discussions, the debriefing, and exchanges with high-school administrators we compiled a report, which was developed into a narrative. Similar to the concept of narrative in critical race theory, it is held that

> ...most of social reality is constructed. We decide what is, and, almost simultaneously, what ought to be. Narrative habits, patterns of seeing, shape what we see and that to which we aspire. These patterns of perception become habitual, tempting us to believe the way the things are is inevitable, or the best that can be in an imperfect world. Alternative visions of reality are not explored, or, if they are, rejected as extreme or implausible. (Delgado, 1995, p. 66)

For the students, what would be viewed by the mainstream as "extreme" or "implausible" is part of their daily reality. Creating an instructional space for their daily concerns to be analyzed allows them to address what is "real" to them and "overreaction" to others.

The Racialized Classroom

Many would find it strange to have a class on race in an entirely African American classroom. Some argue there is nothing to be discussed in terms of how students see themselves as racialized beings in a school with a homogenous population. Hooks (1998) would remind us of the ever-present internal class issues with racial and ethnic groups, but the majority of students in this high school are recognized as low-income. Given that racism is "ordinary" and not "exceptional" (Delgado, 1995), one of the aims of the classroom was to identify racism as an ordinary phenomenon, and analyze the many issues and concerns related to it.

Two key components of the class were inequality and the video project. The inequality discussion emphasized common aspects of the public school system (school finance, state budgets, etc.). Our video project attempted to create a visual representation of student's perception of themselves in the context of school and the larger society. Concluding the process was a debriefing session where students evaluated the program's strengths and weaknesses, and suggested improvements.

Inequality

To place a face on structural inequality in education, one of the first exercises was to take a tour of the school building and to observe what the problems were. I first inquired about the plants in the foyer of the building. Students informed me that they had been left there from when the mayor came to visit. They continued by informing me of all the preparations for the mayor's visit and how those same duties are not performed on a daily basis. When I asked what these duties were, they described tasks like sweeping and mopping the floors, placing toilet tissue in the bathrooms, unlocking the bathroom doors, and shoveling snow from the walkways. All of the students recognized it as a "bogus attempt to impress somebody that doesn't care anyway."

As they walked through the building, they began to identify problems with the physical structure. Class members identified cracked windows, broken pipes, lack of heat, and ragged classroom furniture as the most noticeable problems. As we engaged the issue further, students began to talk about structural problems in the office, such as the lack of supplies for the administrative staff, broken copy machines, and the difficulty in contacting an administrator during school hours. This conversation lasted the entire class period.

Subsequent sessions discussed the readings from the course packet, with topics ranging from stereotype threat to Freire's *Pedagogy of the Oppressed*. We discussed how students saw themselves in the context of educational inequality, and addressed their concerns with the readings through their stories and writing assignments. A favorite quote was an excerpt from Baldwin's "A Talk to Teachers."

> The paradox of education is precisely this—that as one begins to become conscious one begins to examine the society in which he is being educated. The purpose of education, finally, is to create in a person the ability to look at the world for himself, to make his own decisions...To ask questions of the universe, and then to learn to live with those questions, is the way he achieves his own identity. But no society is really anxious to have that kind of person around. What societies really, ideally, want is a citizenry which will simply obey the rules of society. If a society succeeds in this, that society is about to perish. (Baldwin, 1985, p. 326)

Baldwin believes the responsibility of education is to give a person the ability to analyze, process, and change one's reality, and students upheld the idea through discussion and writing projects. The latter exercise equipped students with information to move to the next stage of the course.

Video Project

The video project was guided by a curricular exercise titled "Predestined Me." Initially the work was to incorporate the narrative reflections of students through visual media. Students were required to complete the following focus question:

> Based on the overwhelming influence of the societal messages that exist about you as a [insert your present race/ethnicity, gender, sexual orientation, socioeconomic status here] kid, who are you predestined to be in 2011?

When "low-income African American" completed the phrase, students began to discuss what it meant to them to have such labels. Many began to discuss classroom experiences where teachers would tell them outright "they would never make it" and how the teachers would "never send their children to this school." Despite the irony of not wanting to send their children to a school they teach in, larger questions abounded. Currently minimal attention is paid to the idea that many children continue to attend these types of schools.

As part of the project, students were required to create a timeline documenting the next ten years of their life. Students then created an individual video presentation reflecting that timeline. The first segment included a visual presentation of what they felt society expected them to be in the next ten years. Following a fade out, the second segment would present where they expected themselves to be in the next ten years in spite of society's expectations. Students were allowed to incorporate props and use other students to aid in the creation of the video.

Several themes were examined in the creation of the video. In the first segment, some students portrayed themselves as pregnant mothers unable to care for their children, gang members, and drug addicts. Others portrayed themselves as uncaring fathers, prostitutes, drug dealers, and thieves. Regardless of these stereotypical inner-city characters, many students made specific commentary in their presentation on common feelings of rejection from the school and society at large. For example, a male student presented a fictitious account of a drug-dealer. Within the presentation he explained to the camera that he did not want to be in the situation, but "he had to do what he had to do." When asked why such phrasing was used in the portrayal, he replied that some of his friends reply to him in a similar manner in conversations about why they participate in illegal activity. He replied, "It's not like my guys grow up and instantly decide they want to be drug dealers." Other students chimed in that they understood that such behaviors are harmful, but the reality of the situation was that there were few options available without a high school diploma or college degree. You could obtain employment in the menial sense but it would be "impossible" to survive working full time (forty hours per week) on minimum wage ($5.15 per hour).

Many of the portrayals in the second segment discussed what they would do in their lives *despite* popular stereotypes of young African American adults. Students chose occupations and activities across a broad scale. Many were multi-faceted descriptions of their lives in terms of occupation, family commitment, and educational attainment. Instead of single occupations, students engaged in a portrayal of a person involved in numerous activities, demonstrating what they felt to be a "well-rounded" person. When asked what a "well-rounded" person was, many replied that it was someone who "succeeded" despite the barriers society has placed on their lives.

The Treatise: Limitations and Conclusions

As a "treatise" on the racialized context of American education, the previous sections may initially be viewed as underdeveloped. However, the objective was to replace conventional sociological policy analysis with narrative. We echo the sentiments of Diaute:

> The value of narrative social consciousness work is that it engages young people and adults who listen to them in thinking complexly—recognizing and cultivating abilities to see the world in diverse ways at the same time. Literature of social justice is thus a narrative genre that can have an impact on young people's development of social consciousness...We have much to learn from young people in U.S. cities—about social understanding, reality, action, tolerance and hope—if we provide them with spaces, support, leadership, and assessments in which reconstruction is encouraged and celebrated. (Diaute in Fine & Weiss, 2000, p. 233)

Because the account is undersized in terms of providing broad-based policy analysis, the hope was to challenge policy analysts to engage ethnographic data as a resource in the development of school policy. Current trends in policy archaeology (Scheurich, 1994) have begun to address the need to include qualitative data in policy analysis, but few accounts explain why its exclusion has been problematic.

Nevertheless, the examples used in this account are short and do not demonstrate the full interaction of the conversations held in class. Thus, this study should be considered an introductory work in the development of qualitative policy analysis. In addition, it is the hope of the author that empirical data can be fused with similar studies to include populations that may "slip" through conventional policy conversations. Examples of projects making such attempts are the Small Schools Workshop and the Umoja Leadership Institute. Both have engaged the development of small group instruction, discussion, and reflection. In the process, fewer students are excluded, and safe spaces are developed for students to create.

An effective policy must take into account student reflection and value the input of all students, as opposed to empty surveys and conversations with the "brightest" students. Our efforts cannot end with problematizing inequality in public schools. Instead, we must continue to work toward the development of new approaches that challenge hegemonic ideology and praxis in public schooling.[i]

References

Andersen, A., & Hill, C. P. (Eds.). (2001). *Race class and gender: An anthology*. Stamford, CT: Wadsworth Learning.

Baldwin, J. (1985). *The price of the ticket: Collected nonfiction 1948-1985*. New York: St. Martin's Press.

Bulmer, M., & Solomos, J. (Eds.). (1999). *Racism*. Oxford: Oxford University Press.

Delgado, R. (Ed.). (1995). *Critical race theory: The cutting edge*. Philadelphia: Temple University Press.

Feagin, J. (2001). *Racist America: Roots, current realities, and future reparations*. New York: Routledge Press.

Foster, M. (1997). *Black teachers on teaching*. New York: The New Press.

Ladson-Billings, G. (1994). *The dreamkeepers: Successful teachers of African American children*. San Francisco: Jossey-Bass.

Lipsky, S. (2000). *Internalized racism*. Seattle: Rational Island Publishers.

Lynn, M. (1999). Toward a critical race pedagogy: A research note. *Urban Education, 33* (5), 606–627.

Macedo, D., & Bartolome, L. (1999). *Dancing with bigotry: Beyond the politics of tolerance.* New York: St. Martin's Press.

McCarthy, C., & Crichlow, W. (1993). *Race, identity, and representation in education.* New York: Routledge Press.

Scheurich, J. J. (1994). Policy archaeology: A new policy studies methodology. *Journal of Educational Policy, 9* (4), 297–316.

Watkins, W., Lewis, J., & Chou, V. (Eds.). (2001). *Race and education: The roles of history and society in educating African American students.* Needham Heights, MA: Ally and Bacon.

Weiss, L., & Fine, M. (Eds.). (2000). *Construction sites: Excavating race, class, and gender among urban youth.* New York: Teachers College Press.

Woodson, C. G. (2000). *The mis-education of the Negro.* Trenton, NJ: Africa World Press.

Zavarzadeh, M., & Morton, D. (1994). Theory as resistance: Politics and culture

---

[i] The author would like to thank Lisa Arrastia for her contribution to the project.

EARNING IN SPITE OF OPPOSITION: AFRICAN AMERICANS AND THEIR HISTORY OF EDUCATIONAL EXCLUSION IN ANTEBELLUM AMERICA

Christopher M. Span

For nearly four centuries, learning in spite of opposition has been a recurring theme in the educational history of African Americans. No example better demonstrates this contention than the denied or restricted educational opportunities for free and enslaved African Americans during the antebellum, or pre-Civil War, era. Their continuous and oftentimes deleterious quest to acquire some level of education epitomized African Americans' legacy of perseverance amid overtly oppressive and extremely hostile conditions. In some instances, free and enslaved African Americans' efforts to acquire the rudiments of learning during this time period were ingenious; in others—given the insurmountable odds and conditions—they were heroic. Despite the societal conditions or restrictions imposed upon them, free and enslaved African Americans' sheer determination in acquiring an education illustrated the group's historic fortitude, ability, and appreciation of learning, freedom, and universal self-improvement. For contemporary educators, the educational history of antebellum African Americans represents an alternative ontology to consider when discussing American slavery, the African American response to this "peculiar institution," and the unrelenting reverence African Americans—enslaved or free—maintained toward literacy and schools.

Ideology, the Law, and Pre-Civil War Opposition to African American Education

From its earliest beginnings, the educational history of African Americans was characterized by struggle and strife. For approximately the first 250 years of the African American experience (1619–1865) every American colony and later state prohibited or stridently restricted teaching free and enslaved African Americans the rudiments of literacy—the skills of reading and writing. Accordingly, by the end of the Civil War the overwhelming majority of enslaved African Americans were illiterate and few formal educational opportunities existed for freeborn or manumitted African American children.

This assessment was especially accurate in the nation's southern colonies and later states. South Carolina and Georgia were two of the first colonies to legally forbid the teaching of African Americans. In 1740, South Carolina's colonial legislation passed the first compulsory illiteracy laws, thus making it a crime to teach enslaved African Americans (Raffel, 1998, p. xiii). Thirty years later, colonial Georgia followed South Carolina's precedent, ratifying a law forbidding the teaching of slaves to read or write (Cornelius, 1991, p. 18). By 1830, Georgia—as a state—imposed fines, public whippings, and/or imprisonments to anyone caught teaching enslaved or free African Americans these prohibited skills. In that same year, North Carolina, Virginia, and Louisiana also enforced such punishments on persons willing to teach the rudiments of literacy to enslaved African Americans. In 1832, Alabama's *Digest of Laws* prohibited under fine the teaching of enslaved African Americans, but this measure was not codified until 1852. During these antebellum years, anti-black literacy laws were exceptionally repressive in South Carolina, a state that possessed a high free black populace and where enslaved African Americans outnumbered whites three to one. In 1834, three years after Nat Turner led a slave revolt in Virginia's Southampton County, South Carolina enacted legislation that sternly punished and imprisoned every person caught teaching African Americans—enslaved or free. Mississippi, Missouri, and Maryland never adopted such legal restrictions against African American education or statutorily penalized persons engaged in such endeavors. Rather, they barred public assemblages of African Americans for educational purposes and strongly discouraged whites from assisting blacks in acquiring the rudiments of learning (Cornelius, 1991, pp. 32–33).

North of slavery, the educational opportunities of African Americans fared somewhat better. Still, in northern states, segregation, by law and/or cultural practice, overwhelmingly determined the educational opportunities of the region's free blacks. Practically every northern state providing common schooling for its free citizenry established a segregated or dual school system for its white and "colored" residents. Prejudice and discrimination served as the guidepost for free blacks' blatant educational exclusion or segregation. At the beginning of the nineteenth century, as noted by historian Leon Litwack, local school committees throughout the New England region frequently assigned African American children "to separate institutions, regardless of the district in which they resided" (Litwack, 1961, p. 114). Colonial and antebellum Connecticut, for example, "forbade, without the approval of civil authorities, the establishment of any educational institutions for the instruction" of nonresident African Americans (Litwack, 1961, p. 70). A secondary purpose of this statute was to control the possible influx of runaway or migrating African Americans to Connecticut. Similarly, colonial and antebellum New York authorized its school districts to provide for the segregation of black and white children (Litwack, 1961, p. 114). In 1789, African Americans in New York City responded to the state's limited and discriminatory educational initiatives toward them by establishing a small number of private schools known as African Free Schools. Not until 1824 did the state's common council openly support these private black schools established to address the educational concerns and interests of the city's black residents (Rury, 1983, p. 187).

There were exceptions to these deliberate exclusions and inconveniences regarding African American education in the New England region, however. The 1789 Massachusetts Education Act provided for the schooling of its educable children irrespective of gender or race. Following the American Revolution, Massachusetts, accordingly, became the first American province to enact legislation in support of the public education of African American children. Notwithstanding, by 1798, African Americans in Boston—because of persistent acts of local discrimination—petitioned the city legislature for a separate school. African American residents firmly believed their children were receiving, in comparison to their white counterparts, "no benefit from the free schools" provided by the city (Schultz, 1973, p. 116). When their petition was denied, Boston's African American community responded by commencing a private school in the home of Primus Hall, a prominent free black and abolitionist (Woodson, 1998, p. 58). Two years later, and again in 1806, sixty-six of Boston's leading African American residents would resubmit—to no avail—their request for separate school facilities; thereafter, Boston's school committee agreed to establish a permanent black school and until 1855 adhered to a de facto segregated school system.[i]

Pennsylvania and Ohio, like Massachusetts, provided public schooling for all children. Yet, even these pro-abolitionist states adhered to the unwritten rule of requiring district school directors to establish—whenever possible—separate educational facilities for African American children (Litwack, 1961, p. 114). "Michigan and Wisconsin," according to historian John Hope Franklin, "adopted more democratic policies," but even free blacks here had to wait until after the Civil War to benefit from the state's educational initiatives (2000, p. 178-179). Other Midwestern states were not as liberal. As late as 1860, Indiana, Illinois, and even the newly admitted state of Kansas passed similar legislation barring and/or circumscribing free blacks' formal educational opportunities. Indiana legislation determined that "Negroes and mulattoes [sic] were not liable to school taxes, nor entitled to the benefit of school funds" (Hooker, 1876, p. 14). An Illinois statute established that "persons of color were to have no other interest in the common school taxes except such amount as they paid themselves" (Hooker, 1876, p. 14). Similarly, Kansas law—until 1872—altogether excluded African Americans from any of the state's public school initiatives (Hooker, 1876, p. 15). Accordingly, well before the Civil War, in fact by the 1830s as Litwack estimated, "statute or custom" purposefully placed African American children in "separate schools in nearly every northern community" or excluded them altogether (1961, p. 115).

Notwithstanding, a relatively small, but significant, number of antebellum whites—North and South, slave owning or not—staunchly opposed these legal and ideological restrictions shaping the educational opportunities of African Americans, but more so with regard to slave literacy than public school segregation. Their reasons were primarily religious: They believed that even enslaved persons had the right to read and personally comprehend the Bible for their own salvation. However, their rhetoric, complaints, and in some cases petitions had little impact on the nation's entrenched ideological consensus supportive of black inferiority theories, slavery, segregation, and the overall subjugation of African Americans. These dominant views complemented the growing number of laws banning or constricting black literacy. The views "proved" that African Americans—enslaved or free—were inherently incapable of learning, that attempting to teach African Americans would incite slave insurrections or escape attempts, and that schools for African Americans or a literate slave population piercingly conflicted with the relative success of a national political economy overwhelming by dependent upon slave labor.

In *Notes on the State of Virginia* (1781) Thomas Jefferson's racialized views on black intelligence and education embodied the nation's perspective on slavery, black inferiority, and the futility of educating enslaved or free African Americans. Jefferson was utterly convinced that people of African descent, because of biological or racial characteristics, were mentally inferior in reason and imagination to whites. "I think one could scarcely be found," decreed Jefferson, "capable of tracing and comprehending the investigations of Euclid; and that in imagination they are dull, tasteless, and anomalous…" (1999, pp. 146-147). Jefferson concluded enslavement aided rather than impeded blacks' overall development, and that social reforms or educational initiatives directly aimed at the overall improvement of African Americans would do little to change their status in a country that despised their very existence even as slave property.

In 1831, Elias B. Caldwell, acting secretary of the American Colonization Society, articulated a very similar argument.[ii] To Caldwell, enslaved and free blacks would be best kept "in the lowest state of degradation and ignorance" to avoid their unfruitful aspirations of wanting "privileges which they can never attain" (Litwack, 1961, p. 23). Three years earlier, the Colonization Society of Connecticut seemed to have served as the forerunner to Caldwell's contention. The society was convinced that schooling and education would be a waste of time and a disservice to African Americans.

> Educate him [the African or African American] and you have added little or nothing to his happiness—you have unfitted him for the society and sympathies of his degraded kindred, and yet you have not procured for him, and cannot procure for

him, any admission into the society and sympathy of white men. (Colonization Society of Connecticut, 1828, p. 5)

Mutually, the American Colonization Society and its Connecticut subsidiary sincerely believed that they were offering antebellum African Americans a just and humane solution by restricting their existing educational opportunities and advocating their near-immediate relocation to continental Africa. It was perceived that such measures would alleviate the problems free and enslaved African Americans endured in a nation hostile to their very existence.

By contrast, both enslaved and free African Americans during the antebellum era responded to these varying forms of discrimination and recalled with great clarity how such ideology and legal restrictions excluded them from learning even the rudiments of literacy. From their testimony it appeared that legislative acts of exclusion or restriction were less of a problem than local sentiment and opposition. For instance, Maryland-born slave Charles Ball was certain that "the cotton planters have always been most careful to prevent the slaves from learning to read" (1837, p. 164). "They fear," he continued, "that they [slaves] may be imbibed with the notions of equality and liberty" from such teachings (1837, p. 164). Wilson Armistead drew the same conclusion, arguing further that the foremost culprit to the blatant exclusion of African Americans from the learning process was slavery and its intended outcome. "The tendency of Slavery," said Armistead, "is to keep down, at nearly the level of brutes, beings who might be brightened into intellectual and moral beauty" by education (1848, p. 38).

Similar to Armistead, Francis Fedric, a runaway slave from Kentucky, staunchly challenged the prevailing views about African Americans' inherent incapacity to learn and their designated place as subjugated people in America. His position perhaps best summarized the opinions of most antebellum African Americans cognizant of how denigrating and misinformed beliefs, the law, and the institution of slavery adversely affected African Americans' chances for an education:

> It cannot be pretended for one moment, truthfully, that we are not capable of understanding if we were taught. I myself am a living witness against such an absurdity; after fifty years of age I have learnt to read and write. No, no. It is not our

stupidity, but the slave owners' lust of power and gain which makes them directly oppose the precepts of our Lord...It is only by keeping the poor slaves in brutish ignorance that they can uphold slavery. Let the slaves have the same opportunity as the freemen to learn to read and write, and nothing could prevent their rising, and freeing themselves. (1863, pp. 53–54)

Ideology and law aside, some enslaved African Americans knew personally the horrors imposed upon a slave able to secretly acquire a rudimentary education. Ex-slave and postbellum African Methodist Episcopal (AME) Bishop William Heard witnessed firsthand from his childhood the harsh reality that awaited any enslaved person caught reading and/or writing. "It was against the law for any person to teach any slave to read," stated Heard, "and any slave caught writing suffered the penalty of having his forefinger cut from his right hand" (1924, p. 31). Disfigurement was to ensure that a literate slave never wrote again, because a slave able to write could literally write his or her own pass to freedom. Still, despite the severity of the punishment, as Heard concluded, there were some among him "who could read and write" (1924, p. 31). Enslaved on a cotton plantation in Macon, Georgia, Lucindy Jurdon was keenly aware of Heard's stark recollection. When asked many years later if she ever learned how to read and/or write, Jurdon reiterated Heard's remembrance to her interviewer: "Ef us tried to learn to read or write, dey would cut your forefingers off" (Rawick, 1972, Alabama, p. 14). Even at the age of one hundred Ferebe Rogers also remembered this severe punishment reserved for educationally ambitious or literate slaves, despite the imprecise particulars of her recollection. When prodded to answer if she, or anyone she knew while enslaved, learned to read or write, Rogers ardently responded, "I'd had my right arm cut off at de elbow if I'd a-done dat. If dey foun' an nigger what could read and write, dey'd cut yo' arn off at de elbow, or sometimes at de shoulder" (Rawick, 1972, Georgia, p. 215).

Alabama native Louis Meadows quickly shrugged off his interviewer's question regarding his possible acquisition of literacy during enslavement. "Mistus," he bluntly stated, "us was whooped if us even looked into a book. Us couldn't read a line, you know, but if us even looked in at de pictures, it was jest too bad" (Rawick, 1972, Alabama, p. 255). Ex-slave and Tuscumbia, Alabama native Mary Ella Grandberry agreed. "De white folks," she commented, "didn't 'low us to even look at a book. Dey would stol' an' sometimes whup us iffen dey caught us wid our head in a book" (Rawick, 1972, Alabama, p. 160). Former slave William J. Anderson well understood Meadows's and Grandberry's remembrances and was convinced that "slaveholders' laws" were "positively opposed to the slave learning anything more than to handle the axe, plough and hoe" (1857, p. 6). "I had no schooling," Anderson insisted, "except what I stole by fire and moon light, with a little Sabbath light. And oftentimes...I was whipped for trying to read my Bible" (1857, p. 6). Still, the aforementioned repercussions or opposition, while present, seemed secondary to Enoch Golden of Baldwin County, Georgia in his pursuit of learning how to read and write. He escaped penalty and kept secret his acquired learning—and soon thereafter covert teachings—in the slave quarters. However, his initiatives caused great harm to many of his fellow bondsmen. On his deathbed, Golden declared with both pride and regret that "he been de death o' many a nigger 'cause he taught so many to read and write" (Rawick, 1972, Georgia, p. 212).

Free blacks—North and South—desiring a formal education in their communities also recognized the legal and ideological ramifications associated with achieving this outcome. As a group, their existence and varying successes proved to be an anomaly in a nation premised upon a white supremacist ideology and the hereditary and lifelong enslavement of blacks. In some locales, especially in the South, they barely maintained a quasi-free status and, consequently, fared little better than their enslaved brethren. Such fate was all too familiar to the Reverend William Troy, who left his birth state for Canada when he and his family could no longer endure life in the U.S. Born free in Essex County, Virginia, Troy recalled the immense difficulty he had in procuring an education for himself and his family. "Personally, I have suffered on account of my color in regard to education. I was not allowed to go to school publicly, had to learn privately...Further, I could not educate my children there, and make them feel as women and men ought—for, under those oppressive laws, they would feel a degradation not intended by Him who made of one blood all the people of the earth" (Drew, 1856, p. 355). Freeborn black Thomas Hedgebeth suffered a similar outcome in Halifax County, North Carolina. "The law," he reasoned, "there does not favor colored people...A free-born man in North Carolina is as much oppressed, in one sense, as the slave. I was not allowed to go to school...and I think it an outrageous sin and shame, that a free colored man could not be taught" (Drew, 1856, p. 276).

Some free blacks—especially those in the North—were very outspoken about their blatant exclusion from the growing array of opportunities throughout the nation and the hypocrisy of living in a segregated, slave-sanctioning democracy. For example, David Walker, born in 1789 a free black in North Carolina, was an extremely outspoken person on the continuous subjugation and enslavement of African Americans. In the early 1820s, Walker moved to Boston and soon thereafter became a contributor for the nation's first black newspaper, *Freedom's Journal,* and the author of *Walker's Appeal* (1829). Prior to his death in 1830, Walker's publications directly challenged the nation's position on slavery, the historic exclusion of African Americans from a quality education, and the various colonization movements aimed to transport free blacks to Africa. Educationally, Walker maintained, whites intentionally kept African Americans from receiving any significant amount of learning. He cited the countless laws and restrictions in the South that prohibited the teaching of blacks. He also detailed the inadequate and inferior education that African American children in the North received in comparison to white children (Walker, 1969).

Walker was not alone in expressing such politically charged convictions. Expatriate Armistead, in his immense volume *A Tribute to the Negro* (1848), also blasted his birth country for its incessant regard of African American education as a crime and its perpetual inhumane treatment of "Africa's progeny":

> The great doctrine, that God hath "created all men equal, and endowed them with certain inalienable rights," and that amongst these are "life, liberty, and the pursuit of happiness," is affirmed in the American Declaration of Independence, and justified in the theory of its constitutional laws. But there is a stain upon its glory; Slavery, in its most abject and revolting form, pollutes its soil; the wailings of Slaves mingle with its songs of liberty; and the clank of their chain is heard, in horrid discord, with the chorus of their triumphs. The records of the States are not less distinguished by their wise provisions for securing the order and maintaining the institutions of the country, than by their ingenious devices for riveting the chain, and perpetuating the degradation of, their Coloured brethren;—*their education is branded as a crime,*—their freedom is dreaded as a blasting pestilence;—the bare suggestion of their emancipation is proscribed as a treason to the cause of American independence. (pp. 94–95, emphasis added)

Armistead, like Walker, voiced his demand for slavery's immediate abolition and greater opportunities for the nation's African American populace. Together they articulated the opinions of countless antebellum free blacks that invariably saw their prospective opportunities, self-interests, education, and even existence, uncontrollably linked to the future of American slavery.

Education and Its Value Among African Americans in Antebellum America

In both the free black and slave communities education was valued for a myriad of reasons. Among free blacks, in particular, education was perceived as a primary vehicle to combat racism and second-class citizenship (Williams, 1985, p. 3). According to Dorothy Porter (1995), northern and southern free black leaders recognized the necessity and expediency of education given the group's limited and insecure existence in the American social order. Throughout the nation, various welfare, temperance, Bible, moral reform, and educational societies—established by and for free blacks—catered to the group's educational expectations at a time when the nation was withdrawing or restricting its efforts regarding African American education. For more than employment purposes, education was to render free blacks "useful to society and acceptable to God," eradicate the notion of them as "indolent and shiftless" people, and "replace idleness and intemperance" with "good taste and manners" (Porter, 1995, pp. 79–80). In 1834, the Reverend Joseph M. Corr of Philadelphia affirmed this sentiment in his Fourth of July oration before the Humane Mechanic's Society of Philadelphia. Corr regarded education as the "means whereby the shackles of ignorance may be unrivetted, and man be qualified for usefulness in all the pursuits of life; for knowledge is light—knowledge is power" (p. 3).

Free blacks expected their antebellum educational opportunities to serve as the foundation for the race's societal advancement. Schools were intended to be institutions that informed African American youth of their precarious societal statuses; they were to assist freeborn African American children in learning the literacy skills necessary for combating discrimination, segregation, and slavery in adulthood; and they were expected to aid African Americans in acquiring equality, or at least some degree of social mobility.

Education was perceived as the primary tool for free blacks to prove their humanity, merit, and capabilities in an American society that regarded them as slaves or inferior people.

To free black William Watkins, a Baltimore native, such emphasis on education was deemed absolutely essential and could only be achieved through the collective resources and support of free blacks throughout the country. Only a people with a good education, Watkins believed, could effectively counter the many challenges antebellum African American children were to face when they came of age in a slave-sanctioning and race-based society. "A good education," argued Watkins, "was the most valuable blessing that we [free blacks], as a people, can bestow upon the rising generation" (1836, p. 2). He concluded, "give them this and they cease to grovel; give them this and they emerge from their degradation, though crushed beneath a mountain weight of prejudice; give them this and they will command respect and consideration from all whose good opinions are worth having" (1836, p. 11).

Similar sentiment toward education and its transformative potential was expressed in the antebellum slave community. Despite the legal restrictions and harsh punishments for seeking a rudimentary education, countless enslaved African Americans seemed willing to risk "life or limb" in order to acquire some degree of literacy. By the close of the American Revolution, for example, it appeared that enslaved African Americans already had a distinct respect for literacy inherent in their culture's value system. If we accept the testimony of former slaves interviewed by the Works Progress Administration (WPA) between 1936 and 1938, the majority of slaves sought to become literate during slavery in order to read the Bible for personal salvation or personal liberation.[iii]

In comparison to the antebellum educational experiences of free blacks, contemporary historians have offered much more speculation on the quest for and value of literacy in the antebellum slave community. For example, Carter G. Woodson (1921), Henry Bullock (1967), Thomas Webber (1978), and Janet Duitsman Cornelius (1991) each agree that the acquired skills of reading and/or writing were viewed as a very practical means of empowerment, autonomy, and freedom to enslaved African Americans. Without question, literacy meant freedom to Thomas Johnson and his family. "As soon as I was old enough" he explained, "my mother taught me the difference between the condition of the coloured and white people...She told me that if I would learn how to read and write, some day I might be able to get my freedom; but all that would have to be kept a secret" (1909, p. 3). Rooted in this life lesson, as Johnson recalled, was his mother's recognition of the power of literacy and its potential usefulness in obtaining freedom.

In her work, Cornelius acknowledges the optimistic attitude toward learning in the testimonial exchange between Johnson and his mother, and affirms that literacy reinforced an image of self-worth and community empowerment among enslaved African Americans. She characterizes slave literacy as "a communal act" and "a political demonstration of resistance to oppression and of self-determination for the black community...through literacy the slave could obtain skills valuable in the white world...and could use those skills for special privileges or to gain freedom" (1991, p. 3). Susan Boggs, like Johnson's mother, provides another excellent illustration of enslaved African Americans' perception of literacy as a form of personal and communal resistance. Boggs consciously sacrificed her own ambition of acquiring some degree of literacy so her son could learn to read and write in a secret school held on a nearby farm. Her hope was that he would be able to use his acquired learning to escape enslavement and help others eager to do the same (Blassingame, 1977, pp. 420–421).

Similar to Cornelius, Webber offers an interesting perspective on enslaved African Americans' proactive demeanor toward learning. Webber reasons:

> To understand the nature of education in the slave quarter community is to come to grips with the paradox of the "free slave." Though the chains with which whites controlled black bodies were very real, try as they might, whites could not control black minds. These were molded from birth in an educational process created and managed by the quarter community...While still legally slaves, the black men, women, and children of the quarter community successfully protected their psychological freedom and celebrated their human dignity. (1978, pp. 261–262)

Historian James Olney concurred with Webber's thesis, and added that enslaved African Americans saw literacy as a "mechanism for forming an identity," and the freedom of becoming a person, even a citizen, in American society (1985, p. 153). Similarly, literacy in the antebellum slave community, according to historian Vincent P. Franklin, signified an additional skill to protect and assist enslaved African Americans in surviving the immeasurable vices of American slavery. Franklin writes, "Education and literacy were greatly valued among Afro-Americans enslaved in the United States because they saw in their day-to-day experiences—from one generation to the next—that knowledge and information helped one to survive in a hostile environment" (1984, p. 164). Accordingly, enslaved African Americans saw education as an additional arsenal for enduring slave life and possibly escaping enslavement and earning freedom for themselves, family members, and/or friends.

Ivan McDougle's early twentieth-century publication on runaway slaves strongly supports the contention that enslaved African Americans used their secretly gained literacy skills to earn freedom. McDougle cites that 20.2 percent, or seventy-one of the 350 advertised runaways in antebellum Kentucky were listed as being able to read. Thirty-seven or 10.5 percent of the total number of runaways in antebellum Kentucky were also reported as being able to write (1918). Similarly, almost 9 percent of the 625 runaway slaves interviewed in William Still's *The Underground Railroad* (approximately fifty-six escapees) were recorded as knowing how to read and/or write (1872). While these figures may be perceived as low or inconsequential in the greater analysis, they serve as excellent examples of literate and semiliterate African Americans in the antebellum slave community. Moreover, they illustrate that enslaved African Americans desired—and sometimes used—these skills to challenge their status and increase their chances of obtaining freedom. Such ambition—whether gained or not—was passed down for generations until freedom universally came to enslaved African Americans with the end of the Civil War.

Unsurprisingly, one of the primary initiatives of formerly enslaved African Americans following the Civil War was the establishment of schools for their own personal and professional improvement (Anderson, 1988; Butchart, 1980; Jones, 1980; Morris, 1982; Span, 2001, 2002). Former slave John Quincy Adams of Richmond, Virginia, characterized the beliefs and assumptions of newly freed blacks throughout the postwar South. As a slave child unable to acquire any formal instruction he considered "going to school to get knowledge…one of the greatest privileges" that a person could enjoy (1872, p. 14). "That was the reason," he presumed, "the South fought against the colored people learning to read and write" (p. 14) and continued to challenge their educational pursuits as freed people in slavery's aftermath.

The African American Response to Educational Exclusion in Antebellum America

The proactive attitude of enslaved and free antebellum African Americans toward learning demonstrated their profound respect for literacy, irrespective of the legal restraints or severe repercussions they confronted daily. As evident from the previous discussion, throughout the antebellum era a small minority of enslaved African Americans ingeniously acquired some degree of literacy, and free blacks built schools for themselves despite the opposition. Still, much debate exists regarding the approximate percentage of literate slaves in this era. For example, in 1916, the "father of black history" Carter G. Woodson estimated that at least 10 percent of the nation's adult enslaved population "had the rudiments of education in 1860" (1998, p. 139). "But the proportion," he concluded "was much less than it was near the close of the era of better beginnings about 1825" (1998, p. 139). Woodson also estimated that slave literacy rates declined by almost one half after the 1820s, given the series of strict legal measures aimed at deterring the teaching of enslaved African Americans. Nineteen years later, the noted historian and sociologist W. E. B. DuBois (1935), primarily assessing the educational and governmental activities of ex-slaves in the postbellum era, estimated that approximately 5 percent of the nation's enslaved population was literate on the eve of the Civil War.

Approximately sixty-five years later contemporary historian Janet Duitsman Cornelius offered her own assessment, which supported Woodson's higher estimate. She reviewed the testimony of ex-slaves interviewed between 1936 and 1938 by the Works Progress Administration (WPA) and the more than two hundred autobiographical narratives of formerly enslaved African Americans. Cornelius concluded that more enslaved African Americans learned to read and/or write after 1825 than Woodson or DuBois could have known when they proffered their assessments. At least 5 percent of the ex-slaves interviewed by the WPA explicitly stated that they learned to read and/or write during enslavement

(Cornelius, 1991). Given the fact that these interviews were conducted approximately sixty-five years after slavery's abolition, virtually all ex-slaves acknowledging their acquisition of some degree of literacy during enslavement had to have attained these skills post-1825. Notwithstanding, Cornelius forewarns "there can never be exact measurements of the extent of literacy among enslaved African Americans just as these are impossible in other cultures of the past" (p. 8).

While Cornelius's final remarks prove to be true, the fact that enslaved African Americans acquired the skills of reading and writing, despite their blatant exclusion from the process, truly characterizes the group's historic fortitude and determination to learn. With few options for instruction, minimal resources—pencils, paper, books, and so on—and under the most constraining circumstances, numerous enslaved African Americans, haphazardly and defiantly, acquired an elementary education.

Frederick Douglass's evolution from illiteracy to literacy represented both contexts: education by circumstance and education for liberation. At about the age of eight or ten, Douglass's curiosity about his mistress's ability to read the Bible gave him the incentive to ask her to teach him this skill. She obliged, and "in an incredibly short time, by her kind assistance" Douglass "had mastered the alphabet and could spell words of three or four letters" (Douglass, 1881, p. 70). Upon her husband's discovery of Douglass's newly gained ability, he forbade his wife from teaching Douglass another lesson. Before Douglass, he scolded her stating, "If you give a nigger an inch he will take an ell. Learning will spoil the best nigger in the world. If he learns to read the Bible it will forever unfit him to be a slave. He should know nothing but the will of his master, and learn to obey it" (1881, p. 70). These expressions had a profound effect on Douglass's future considerations regarding slavery, literacy, and freedom, especially since Douglass aspired to learn to read out of curiosity, not resistance. In retrospect, Douglass surmised:

"His iron sentences, cold and harsh, sunk like heavy weights deep into my heart, and stirred up within me a rebellion not soon to be allayed...he underrated my comprehension, and had little idea of the use to which I was capable of putting the impressive lesson he was giving to his wife. He wanted me to be a slave; I had already voted against that on the home plantation of Col. Lloyd. That which he most loved I most hated; and the very determination which he expressed to keep me in ignorance only rendered me the more resolute to seek intelligence. In learning to read, therefore, I am not sure that I do not owe quite as much to the opposition of my master as to the kindly assistance of my amiable mistress. (1881, pp. 70–71)

Thenceforth, attempting to learn how to read and later write was an obsession for young Douglass. Filled with the determination to learn to read at any cost, and unable to rely anymore on his mistress as a potential resource, Douglass sought out differing avenues to develop his new ability. One opportunity that repeatedly seemed available involved the support of his white plantation playmates. "I used to carry almost constantly a copy of Webster's spelling-book in my pocket," Douglass recalled, "and when sent of errands, or when play-time was allowed me, I would step aside with my young friends and take a lesson in spelling" (1881, p. 74). He learned to write in much the same manner. While working Douglass very cautiously sketched the various words he identified on the barrels he loaded, and in the evenings or on Sundays he coaxed his unsuspecting white playmates into competitive games involving the alphabet and writing. "With play-mates for my teachers, fences and pavements for my copy-books, and chalk for my pen and ink," Douglass proudly recollected, "I learned to write" (1881, p. 86).

Douglass's informal educational attainment typified the earliest learning opportunities for the majority of enslaved blacks who obtained some degree of literacy. Despite the law, most accounts indicate that they learned to read before the age of twelve, with some assistance from whites, and well before they learned—if at all—to write. Learning to read before writing should not come as a surprise since writing required the mastery and acquisition of special equipment. According to Cornelius, "writing was harder to learn than reading, and presented the challenge of finding or making materials in a mostly rural society which had little use for these tools" (1991, p. 61). Nonetheless, enslaved blacks made the most of their chances to learn to read or write when such opportunities arose, whether at work or home, publicly or secretly. A great example was Benjamin Holmes. As an apprentice tailor in Charleston, South Carolina, Holmes "studied all the signs and names on the doors" of his employment. Thereafter, he would ask people to tell him—one or two at a time—the words he observed on the signs and doors. Remarkably, by the age of twelve he discovered that he could read newspapers (Cornelius, 1991, p. 69).

Another common characteristic associated with slave literacy was the exchanging of goods for instructional lessons. Many slave children, for example, bartered trinkets, fruits, and other goods to their white peers to secure a rudimentary education. Young Richard Parker, for example, exchanged marbles to any youth willing to teach him the alphabet (Blassingame, 1977, p. 465). Tabb Gross learned to read by promising his eight-year-old master an orange every time he taught him the alphabet (Blassingame, 1977, pp. 347–348). John Quincy Adams's brother Robert acquired his first reading lessons in similar fashion. As a child "he would get all the nice fruit he could," stated Adams, "and bartered it off in the evening and on Sundays to any white child willing to teach him from a book he secretly possessed" (Adams, 1872, pp. 9–10). Adams recalled, "That is the way many poor slaves learned to read and write" (1872, p. 10).

Virginia-born Louis Hughes was somewhat of an exception to these aforementioned characteristics. Like Douglass, Hughes recalled "learning off the wall"; however, he was not a child, but a young adult when he obtained his first reading lessons. Moreover, a fellow adult slave, Tom, who was the coachman for the plantation, taught him his first lessons. Tom secretly acquired his learning from some neighboring plasterers and workmen. According to Hughes, "they saw that he was so anxious to learn that they promised to teach him every evening if he would slip out to their house" (Hughes, 1896, p. 100). Hughes was also anxious to learn, but being a house servant he could not get away as easily. Tom recognized Hughes's inconvenience and ambitions and in secrecy taught him by writing numerals and the alphabet on the side of a barn for Hughes to copy (Hughes, 1896, p. 100). These lessons lasted for months before the plantation overseers finally discovered and put an end to them. Notwithstanding, Hughes had already learned the basics of reading and writing.

The ingenious methods used by educationally ambitious slaves to acquire some degree of literacy are recognizable in other ways as well. In his autobiography, Lucius Holsey recalled selling old rags for books. He sold so many that he was able to buy five books: two Webster's "blue-back" spellers, a school dictionary, Milton's *Paradise Lost*, and the Bible. These books "constituted his 'full stock of literary possessions,'" a library, boasted

Holsey, "more precious than gold" to him (Holsey, 1898, p. 17). He acknowledged that some white children and a black man taught him the alphabet. "After which," he relayed,

> I fought my way unaided through the depths of my ponderous library. Day by day I took a leaf from one of the spelling books, and so folded it that one or two of the lessons were on the outside as if printed on a card. This I put in the pocket of my vest or coat, and when I was sitting on the carriage, walking the yard or streets, or using hoe or spade, or in the dining room, I would take out my spelling leaf, catch a word and commit it to memory. When one side of the spelling leaf was finished by this process, I would refold it again with a new lesson on the outside. When night came, I went to my little room, and with chips of fat pine, and pine roots...I would kindle a little blaze in the fire-place and turn my head toward it while lying flat on my back so as to get the most of the light on the leaves of the book...I reviewed the lessons of the day from the unnamed book. By these means I learned to read and write a little in six months. Besides, I would catch words from the white people and retain them in memory until I could get to my dictionary. Then I would spell and define the words, until they became perfectly impressed upon my memory. (1898, pp. 17–18)

Holsey was fortunate that it only took him six months to master the art of reading. For most semiliterate or literate enslaved blacks, given their restricted circumstances, such attainment was a laborious, extremely dangerous, and time-consuming process. For even the most determined slave it oftentimes took years of clandestine self-instruction in order to comprehend the written English well enough to claim the right of knowing how to read. Holsey's and other enslaved blacks' determination and raw intellectual capabilities to acquire an elementary education are incontestably impressive, given the little time and guidance they had, and the stresses and penalties of slave life. As Cornelius affirms, "with fragmented time, few teacher guides, and limited vocabulary...[it is] no wonder it could take even a determined slave years to read. Add the physical threats to other obstacles and the process becomes heroic" (1991, p. 68).

Some enslaved blacks, however, did not have to go through the trouble of self-education in secrecy or in fear of severe punishment. According to John Hope Franklin, schools for enslaved blacks are known to have existed—despite the law or public sentiment—in Savannah, Georgia; Charleston, South Carolina; Fayetteville, New Bern, and Raleigh, North

Carolina; Lexington and Louisville, Kentucky; Fredericksburg and Norfolk, Virginia; "and various other cities in Florida, Tennessee, and Louisiana" (2000, p. 155). The same was true on the private dwellings of some slave owners who demonstrated the subjectivity of slave and anti-literacy laws. For example, Aaron Robinson recalled how his owner *required* the latter's own children teach Robinson how to read to avoid taking them rabbit hunting (Blassingame, 1977, p. 498). Mississippi native Smart Walker learned to read by his master's son, who had asked his father if he could teach Walker his school lessons (Blassingame, 1977, p. 517). Similarly, Thomas Johnson's mother hired and paid a free black man fifty cents to teach her son to read and write, with the permission from Johnson's slave owner. These lessons only lasted one month, because Johnson's owner soon became disapproving of them; nonetheless, this scenario illustrates the ambiguity regarding the slaveholding response to some slaves acquiring a rudimentary education (Johnson, 1909, p. 14). Johnson's learning, however, did not stop. In secrecy he appropriated a Bible and "pored over it in his spare time, beginning with Genesis and calling out the letters of each word he could not understand" (Cornelius, 1991, p. 59). In addition, he convinced his master's son to read aloud a chapter from the New Testament every evening. Afterward, Johnson would attempt to find these words in his Bible. "I got to understand a little about the Bible, and at the same time I was learning to spell" (Cornelius, 1991, p. 59). Before permanently escaping slavery, Johnson would also teach himself how to write both in print and cursive.

Like their enslaved counterparts, southern-born free blacks desiring a formal education experienced similar difficulties. Their anomaly status in the slave South severely circumscribed their opportunities of acquiring a formal education. As previously noted, virtually every southern state challenged southern-born free blacks' privilege to acquire an education by passing laws making it illegal to instruct blacks—enslaved or free. Moreover, and irrespective of race, the antebellum South exhibited only the slightest public interest in supporting a system of public schools until almost a full decade after the Civil War (Span, 2001, p. 153). With regard to the education of free blacks it was believed that schooling in general would foster seditious and incendiary rhetoric against their designated societal position and American slavery. Consequently, most freeborn southern blacks bore the responsibility of personally and privately educating their youth. They nonetheless responded to the task. In numerous southern locales a surprisingly significant number of southern free blacks acquired a rudimentary education through their own resources and efforts. In Baltimore alone, for example, "there were almost 200 adult blacks studying in 1820" and several private schools sprang up throughout the state of Maryland during this time period (Franklin, 2000, p. 179).

Southern free black children also received private school instruction from whites in many locales including the District of Columbia; Raleigh, North Carolina; Fredericksburg, Virginia; and New Orleans, Louisiana. For those able to afford it and gain local consensus, private schooling embodied freeborn southern blacks' formal schooling opportunities during the antebellum era. For instance, wealthy free blacks in New Orleans and Charleston throughout the time period hired private tutors and established very elaborate private schools for their children. In numerous instances, they extended their generosity to free blacks unable to make such accommodations for their children, demonstrating the value they placed on education. One noteworthy example occurred in 1840 upon the death of a wealthy free woman of color in New Orleans. Strongly valuing the need for education among the most destitute of the city's free black residents, she entrusted a large endowment for the creation and maintenance of the *Ecoles des Orphelins Indigents* (The School for Indigent Orphans). During the years prior to the Civil War, the school served as one of the primary places of instruction for countless poor free black children in New Orleans (Dunbar-Nelson, 1917, p. 16).

Some well-to-do southern free blacks were able to challenge their locales' discriminatory schooling practices by sending their children to a public or private school outside of their own state. For instance, in 1838 Virginia's free black populace, as a group, sought permission from the state legislature to send their children to school out of the state (Franklin, 2000, p. 180). Their collective effort, while unsuccessful, challenged Virginia's law that staunchly prohibited the teaching of state blacks. Notwithstanding, the majority of free blacks in the South capable of receiving a rudimentary education did so in the comforts of their respective churches. From the days of slavery well into the twentieth century, the black church served as the chief agency and edifice of instruction for free—and later freed—southern blacks. While there is no way to determine the type or extent of schooling in these institutions during the antebellum era, most historians view the southern black church as a self-serving entity, and agree that it served the dual purpose of preparing free and freed black families for life in the hostile, segregated, slave South (Franklin, 1984).

North of slavery, free blacks concomitantly contested their blatant educational exclusion. Private schooling and the black church played as significant a role as they did in the South, but the struggle against northern freeborn blacks' blatant educational exclusion also carried over into the arena of public schooling. Carter G. Woodson best summarized the persistent struggle of northern blacks attempting to be part of the nation's antebellum educational efforts. He documented the extent to which these blacks—despite being blatantly marginalized from local school initiatives—zealously sought an education and invested tremendous time and resources in establishing their own system of schools (Woodson, 1921). At the forefront of these independent school efforts were Philadelphia's free blacks. During the late 1820s and under the leadership of Philadelphia clergyman Richard Allen and businessman William Whipper, Philadelphia's free blacks organized a number of educational literary societies to promote the necessity of free blacks supporting the concept of education. By 1837, black Philadelphians—whose population was approximately 25,000 in this year—had established at least twenty-one schools for black youth and seventeen Sabbath schools. The city's black residents had also established three literary societies, three debating societies, one moral-reform society, and four temperance societies for their overall self-improvement (Porter, 1995, p. 212).

Similarly, antebellum free blacks in the cities of Buffalo and Troy, New York, and Boston, Massachusetts, achieved comparable educational successes. In 1837, the five hundred black residents in the abolitionist city of Buffalo had two churches and two private schools to accommodate their educational needs. They too had a literary and debating society, and collectively these black residents had a net worth of approximately $100,000 in property and other assets (Porter, 1995, pp. 212–213). Also in this year, Troy's 990 free black residents independently maintained three churches, two private schools, two Sabbath schools, one literary society, one debating society, four moral-reform societies, and two temperance societies (Porter, 1995, pp. 212–213).[iv] Likewise, free blacks in segregated Boston also showed their resiliency in educating their children despite the ideology and law restricting their opportunities. By 1850, for example, of the 2,038 free blacks in the city, almost 1,500 were in school; and as in Philadelphia, Buffalo, and other major cities in which free blacks resided, Boston blacks established their own literary and moral-reform societies to promote their educational, personal, and professional interests. Like antebellum free blacks throughout the nation, they took it upon themselves to forthrightly insure that their interests and needs as a people were met despite the nation's continual neglect or resistance to their educational progression or to African Americans in general.

Conclusion

Despite the societal conditions, laws, or varying restrictions imposed upon them, free, freed, and enslaved African Americans managed to acquire some degree of learning during the antebellum era. Literacy had specific purposes in antebellum black communities. North of slavery, free blacks perceived literacy or an education as a chief means to challenge their societal status, slavery, segregation, and the myriad of inferiority theories circulating about them throughout the nation. Segregation, by law or cultural practice, restricted or denied many of their educational opportunities as citizens, but it did not discourage them from establishing their own schools and services for the betterment of themselves, their communities, and their race. Southern freeborn blacks also viewed education as a means of social mobility and protection from the vices burdening them in a racialized society. In spite of the countless laws and ideological persuasions against them being taught or learning, they too—although to a lesser degree than northern blacks—established a network of schooling opportunities for themselves and their children.

The determination of enslaved African Americans to educate themselves was just as impressive. Their efforts and fortitude provided the most profound examples of the value antebellum blacks placed on literacy. Despite the slave codes and harsh repercussions associated with a slave acquiring some degree of literacy, countless enslaved blacks were willing to endure severe punishments, maiming, and even the possibility of losing their lives, to acquire a rudimentary education. Literacy equaled empowerment: the power to determine individual identity and to challenge their enslaved status. Together, the educational ambitions and initiatives of free and enslaved antebellum blacks epitomized their historic determination to persevere in spite of their society's efforts to subjugate and enslave them. Their focus on acquiring some degree of learning challenged the nation's ideologies and practices regarding black education, demonstrated antebellum blacks' collective high regard for learning, and served as a model of perseverance or "learning in spite of" for contemporary educators to consider.

References

Adams, J. Q. (1872). *Narrative of the life of John Quincy Adams, when in slavery, and now as a freeman.* Harrisburg, PA: Sieg Printer and Stationer.

Albert, O., & Rogers, V. (1890). *The house of bondage or Charlotte Brooks and other slaves original and life-like, as they appeared in the old plantation and city slave life; Together with pen-pictures of the peculiar institution with sights and insights into their new relations as freedmen, freemen, and citizens.* New York: Hunt & Eaton.

Anderson, J. D. (1988). *The education of blacks in the South, 1860--1935.* Chapel Hill: University of North Carolina Press.

Anderson, W. J. (1857). *Life and narrative of William J. Anderson, twenty-four years a slave; sold eight times! In jail sixty times!! Whipped three hundred times!!! Or the dark deeds of American slavery revealed. Containing scriptural views of the origin of the black and of the white man. Also, a simple and easy plan to abolish slavery in the United States. Together with an account of the services of colored men in the Revolutionary War—day and date, and interesting facts.* Chicago: Daily Tribune Book and Job Printing Office.

Armistead, W. (1848). *A tribute for the Negro: Being a vindication of the moral, intellectual, and religious capabilities of the coloured portion of mankind; with particular reference to the African race.* Philadelphia: William Irwin.

Ball, C. (1837). *Slavery in the United States: A narrative of the life and adventures of Charles Ball, a black man, who lived forty years in Maryland, South Carolina, and Georgia, as a slave, under various masters, and was one year in the navy with commodore Barney, during the late war.* New York: John S. Taylor.

Blassingame, J. (1979). *The slave community: Plantation life in the antebellum South.* (Rev. ed.). New York: Oxford University Press.

Blassingame, J. (Ed.). (1977). *Slave testimony: two centuries of letters, speeches, interviews, and autobiographies.* Baton Rouge: Louisiana State University Press.

Bullock, H. (1967). *A history of Negro education in the South from 1619 to the present.* Cambridge: Harvard University Press.

Colonization Society of Connecticut (1828). *An address to the public by the managers of the Colonization Society of Connecticut.* New Haven: Colonization Society of Connecticut.

Cornelius, J. (1983). We slipped and learned to read: Slaves and the literacy process, 1830–1865. *Phylon, 44,* 171–186.

Cornelius, J. (1991). *When I can read my title clear: Literacy, slavery, and religion in the antebellum South.* Columbia: University of South Carolina Press.

Corr, J. (1834). *Address delivered before the Humane Mechanics' Society on the 4th of July, 1834.* Philadelphia: Humane Mechanics' Society.

Davis, C., & Gates, Jr., H. L. (1985). *The slave's narrative.* New York: Oxford University Press.

Douglass, F. (1881). *Life and times of Frederick Douglass, written by himself.* Hartford, CT: Park.

Drew, B. (1856). *A north-side view of slavery. The refugee: Or the narratives of fugitive slaves in Canada related by themselves.* Boston: J. P. Jewett.

DuBois, W. E. B. (1935). *Black reconstruction: An essay toward a history of the part which black folk played in the attempt to reconstruct democracy in America.* New York: Harcourt.

Dunbar-Nelson, A. (1917). People of color in Louisiana: Part II. *Journal of Negro History, 2,* 51–78.

Franklin, J. H. (1994). *From slavery to freedom.* (7th ed.). New York: Mcgraw-hill.

Franklin, V. P. (1984). *Black self-determination: A cultural history of the faith of the fathers.* Westport, CT: Lawrence Hill.

Fredic, F. (1863). *Slave life in Virginia and Kentucky; or, fifty years of slavery in the southern states of America.* London: Wertheim, Macintosh, and Hunt.

Genovese, E. (1974). *Roll, Jordan, roll: The world the slaves made.* New York: Pantheon Books.

Heard, W. (1924). *From slavery to the bishopric in the A.M.E. church.* New York: Arno Press.

Holsey, L. (1898). *Autobiographies, sermons, addresses and essays.* Atlanta: Franklin Printing and Publication Co.

Hooker, C. E. (1876). *On the relation between the White and colored people of the South: A speech of Hon. Chas. E. Hooker of Mississippi delivered in the United States House of Representatives, June 15, 1876.* Washington, DC: U.S. Governmental Printing Office.

Hughes, L. (1896). *Thirty years a slave.* Milwaukee, WI: South Side Printing Co.

Jefferson, T. (1999). *Notes on the state of Virginia.* New York: Penguin.

Johnson, T. (1909). *Twenty-eight years a slave.* Bournemouth, England: W. Mate & Sons.

Jones, J. (1980). *Soldiers of light and love: Northern teachers and Georgia blacks, 1865–1873.* Chapel Hill: University of North Carolina Press.

Litwack, L. (1962). *North of slavery.* Chicago: University of Chicago Press.

McDougle, I. (1918). Slavery in Kentucky. *Journal of Negro History, 3,* 211–328.

Morris, R. C. (1982). *Reading, 'riting, and reconstruction: The education of freedmen in the South, 1861-1870.* Chicago: University of Chicago Press.

Olney, J. (1985). 'I was born': Slave narratives, their status as autobiography and literature. In Davis, C., & Gates, Jr., H. L. (Eds.), *The slave's narrative.* New York: Oxford University Press.

Porter, D. (1995). *Early Negro writing, 1760–1837.* Baltimore, MD: Black Classic Press.

Raffel, J. (1998). *Historical dictionary of school segregation and desegregation: The American experience.* New Haven, CT: Greenwood.

Rawick, G. (1972). *The American slave: A composite autobiography.* (19 vols.). Westport, CT: Greenwood.

Rury, J. (1983). The New York African free school, 1827–1836: Conflict over community control of Black education. *Phylon, 44,* 187–197.

Schultz, S. (1973). *The culture factory: Boston public schools, 1789–1860.* New York: Oxford University Press.

Simmons, W. J. (1968). *Men of mark: Eminent, progressive, and rising.* New York: Arno Press.

Span, C. M. (2001). *Citizen or laborer?: The social purposes of black schooling in reconstruction Mississippi, 1862-1875.* Urbana-Champaign: University of Illinois, Unpublished doctoral dissertation.

Span, C. M. (2002). 'I must learn now or not at all': Social and cultural capital in the educational initiatives of formerly enslaved African Americans in Mississippi, 1862–1869. *Journal of African American History, 87,* 196–205.

Still, W. (1872). *The underground railroad.* Philadelphia: Porter & Coates.

Walker, D. (1969). *Walker's appeal in four articles.* New York: Arno Press.

Watkins, W. (1836). *Address delivered before the Moral Reform Society in Philadelphia, August 8, 1838.* Philadelphia: Merrihew and Gunn, Printers.

Webber, T. (1978). *Deep like the rivers: Education in the slave quarter community, 1831–1865.* New York: Norton.

Williams, L. (1985). Community educational activities and the liberation of black Buffalo. *Journal of Negro Education, 54,* 174–188.

Woodson, C. G. (1998). *The education of the Negro prior to 1861.* New York: A+B Publisher Group.

---

[i] The second time African American residents in Boston were denied their request for a separate school they employed two men from Harvard College as instructors. Thereafter, Prince Saunders, an experienced diplomatic official of Emperor Christopher of Haiti (then spelled "Hayti"), and John B. Russworm, a graduate of Amherst and Bowdoin colleges, respectively, and later governor of the colony of Gape Palmas in southern Liberia, would serve as instructors for this school (Woodson, 1998, p. 58–59). Russworm would go on to co-

found the nation's first black newspaper, *Freedom's Journal*, with Samuel Cornish in 1827 (Franklin, 1994, p. 164). By the mid 1830s, Boston blacks began challenging their predecessors' decision to petition for separate schools. The separate schools established for Boston's black children offered few advantages in comparison to the better-funded and staffed white schools. They argued for the reintegration of the city's schools, which were over time segregated by personal sentiment and cultural practice, not law. Boston's school officials, however, refused to accommodate this request. They declared the city's black and white schools as "separate but equal" institutions. In 1849, Benjamin F. Roberts, on behalf of his five-year-old daughter Sara, disagreed and sued the city of Boston for perpetuating a system of unequal segregated schools. Sara Roberts had to walk past five white elementary schools to attend Smith School, a dilapidated educational facility for the area's black children. Roberts argued the Smith School was vastly inferior to the five white schools his daughter had to walk past, and requested his daughter be allowed to attend one of them to accommodate her educational needs. This case went before the Massachusetts Supreme Court, and it was the first legal suit against school segregation in the country. Roberts's lawyers, abolitionist Charles Sumner and Boston's first black attorney, Robert Morris, argued that all persons were equal before Massachusetts law and that race-based distinctions were not permissible in the state. They further argued that racial segregation characterized all African Americans as inferior and that a segregated black school could not equal a segregated white school because of the "stigma associated with segregation." The Massachusetts Supreme Court rejected their argument. Their ruling permitted segregated schools as long as they were equally provided for. Roberts, however, was not dismayed by the decision. He continued his pursuit on behalf of his daughter, and in 1855, amid the nation's struggle to settle the boundaries and future of slavery, Massachusetts legislature passed a law prohibiting race-based schooling. Still, as desegregation scholar Jeffrey A. Raffel notes, *Roberts v. City of Boston* (1849) "was the first use of the separate but equal doctrine." This case was cited in the *Plessy v. Ferguson* decision (1896) as support for the segregation ruling, "for if even in Massachusetts, where the rights of blacks had been enforced, segregation was considered legal, surely it would be legal in the South" (Raffel, 1998, p. 221).

[ii] In 1817, the American Colonization Society (ACS) was organized to interest emancipated or free blacks in migrating to Africa, in particular the American colony of Liberia. The society's greatest success came in its first ten years. By 1831, abolitionists, led by William Lloyd Garrison, publicly opposed the ACS, arguing that its purpose was to rid the nation of its free black population to cater to the interest of slaveholders. In total, approximately 12,000 blacks would migrate to Africa because of the efforts of this organization (Franklin, 2000, pp. 188–190).

[iii] From 1936 to 1938, Federal Writers' Project (FWP) writers and journalists under the aegis of the Works Progress Administration (WPA) interviewed over 2,300 former slaves from across the American South. These former slaves, most born in the concluding years of slavery or during the Civil War, provided firsthand accounts of their experiences. These narratives remain an unrivaled resource for understanding the lives of America's four million slaves. The narratives are collected in a forty-one-volume series edited by George Rawick entitled *The American Slave: A Composite Autobiography* (Greenwood Press, 1972–1979). However, the interviews themselves present some problems as historical data and have been a persistent source of contention for historians debating their validity and usefulness in understanding American slavery and the slave's worldview. Age, dependency, the inexperience and race of the interviewer, and regional biases all played crucial roles in the responses offered by ex-slaves. Yet, as Charles T. Davis and Henry Louis Gates, Jr. properly insist, such shortcomings

should not dismiss the tremendous value these interviews have as resources on the American slave experience (Davis & Gates, 1985, p. xvi).

[iv] Dorothy Porter has done the most extensive work on antebellum free black literary societies. Her work demonstrates the extent that free blacks—north and south—valued literacy and how they attempted to educate themselves at a time when the nation was restricting or ignoring their educational demands. Here is an abbreviated listing of the literary societies that Porter had identified between 1820 and 1850. Negro Literary Societies in Philadelphia, Pennsylvania: Demonsthenian Institute (1837), Edgeworth Society (1837), Female Literary Society (1831), Gilbert Lyceum (1841), Library Company of Colored Persons (1833), Minerva Literary Association (1834), Reading Room Society (1828), Rush Library and Debating Society (1836); in Pittsburgh, Pennsylvania: Theban Literary Society (1831), Young Men's Literary and Moral Reform Society (1837); in New York City: Female Literary Society (1836), Ladies Literary Society (1834), New York African Clarkson Society (1829), New York Garrison Literary Association (1834), New York Philomathean Society (1830), Phoenix Society (1833); in Albany, New York: two literary societies (before 1843); in Buffalo, New York: Debating Society (before 1837), Young Ladies Literary Society (before 1837); Rochester, New York: Debating Society (before 1843), Ladies Literary and Dorcas Society (1833); in Troy, New York: Debating Society (before 1837), Literary Society (before 1837), Mental and Moral Improvement Society (before 1837); in Boston, Massachusetts: Adelphic Union for the Promotion of Literature and Science (1836), Afric-American Female Intelligence Society (before 1835), Thompson Literary and Debating Society (before 1835), Young Men's Literary Society (before 1845); in New Bedford, Massachusetts: Debating Society (1837); in Hartford, Connecticut: Literary and Religious Institution (1834); in Providence, Rhode Island: Literary Society (1833), Debating Society (before 1837); in Newark, New Jersey: Tyro and Literary Association (1832); in Baltimore, Maryland: Young Men's Mental Improvement Society (before 1835), Phoenix Society (before 1835); in Washington, DC: Debating Society (before 1837), Literary Society (before 1837), Washington Conventional Society (1834); in Cincinnati, Ohio: Literary Society (before 1843); in Columbus, Ohio: Literary Society (before 1843); in Detroit, Michigan: Young Men's Lyceum and Debating Society (before 1846) (Porter, 1936, pp. 557–558).

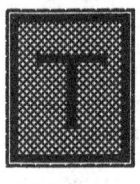oward the Study of Blackness: The Development of a Field of Inquiry

Roderic R. Land

> ...we must first redefine ourselves. Our basic need is to reclaim our history and our identity from what must be called cultural terrorism, from the depredation of self-justifying white guilt. We shall have to struggle for the right to create our own terms through which to define ourselves and our relationship to the society, and to have these terms recognized. This is the first necessity of a free people, and the first right that any oppressor must suspend.
>
> —K. Ture and C. V. Hamilton

There has been and continues to be a vexing problem that plagues the African American community. It encompasses self-expression, self-reliance, self-efficacy, and the ability to define oneself. It is the result of cultural hegemony imposed by Western values, beliefs, behaviors, philosophies, ideologies, and epistemologies. As we sit 156 years after the controversial signing of the Emancipation Proclamation, African Americans still struggle to have a legitimate voice in academia for their interpretation and perspective on their historical and contemporary experiences in Africa, the Diaspora, and America. Not only have their voices been absent, but also the history of African Americans' experiences and contributions to America has historically and systematically been missing from the texts and the curricula.

Thus, black studies supplements the traditional academic disciplines relative to the African experience. According to Anderson (1990) some educators and social integrationists might view the establishing of black studies as a distinct and separate discipline as less than ideal. The question is, to what extent would Africans' contributions and experiences be taught and learned if black studies did not exist? Black studies is based on the implicit notion that the black experience has been ignored and/or has not been accurately portrayed in academia or popular culture. From the earliest period of black studies to the present, this movement has had two main objectives. The first is to combat the deleterious effects of white colonialism, hegemony, and racism. The second is to generate a stronger sense of black identity and community as a way of increasing the group's leverage in the struggle for liberation.

European colonialism and imperialism stretched across most of the world and thus created a world racist system that still operates to date. Colonialism in all its forms and stages has and continues to use race as a construct for the ideological justification of the domination and oppression of "inferior" groups. Audrey Smedley argues, "Race was, from its inception, a folk classification, a product of popular beliefs about human differences that evolved from the sixteenth through the nineteenth centuries" (1993). Racist ideologies associated the different biological characteristics of races with different "racial values," and were designed to maintain the privilege, advantage, and power that whites enjoyed over subordinate groups. Key factors in the colonization and enslavement of Africans were the denouncement of their human status, total deterioration of their cultural identity, complete denial of political rights, and an indoctrination of a belief system that justified their status.

This, indeed, creates the necessity to move toward the study of blackness: a field of inquiry focusing on the accomplishments, contributions, and experiences of people of African descent, as well as their health, political, social, economic, and spiritual situations. A field of inquiry designed to deconstruct and demystify racist regimes, institutions, structures, ideologies, and practices cloaked in concepts of objectivity and meritocracy. A field of inquiry that gives voice to the voiceless, brings the marginalized to the center, and most importantly inspires and aids in the struggle for the liberation of the African mind.

Black Mask, Black Soul: Whiteness Undefined

For the people of African descent, blackness is antithetical to the identity whites have assigned them and is a way of being human under regimes of white supremacy. Furthermore, blackness is a tool of resistance to white hegemonic forces and the logic of slavery and colonialism. According to DuBois, blackness serves the function of attaining a better and truer self than the one revealed to blacks by whiteness; that the general assertion of the manhood rights of the Negro was the source of main reliance. This first manifestation of blackness occurred as a resistance to the constant bombardment of white values, principles, behaviors, and ideologies. The foundations for the emergence of a self-conscious concept of blackness as a proxy to whiteness was not developed in Africa, but was shaped in the Americas by performative acts of liberation by blacks through Western arts, religion, literature, science, and revolution (Diawara, 1990).

Blackness insists on a discourse of difference which enables it to combat "the image of the Black as an aberration of Whiteness," and, by undermining white privilege over aesthetics, economics, and law, to posit relativistic aesthetics and the aesthetics of relativity (Diawara, 1990). Thus, blackness calls to question the monolithic craving of modernist theories to assert the "superior" subject of whiteness.

Blackness as a discourse adds to the literature what has historically and systematically been omitted. It is an initiative to tackle the problem of perspective. It implies that fields of study such as literature, psychology, sociology, and religion in and of themselves do not adequately address issues relative to people of African descent in America and the Diaspora. This field of inquiry harbors compound words like black literature, black psychology, black sociology, black education, black economics, and black religion to bring light to the black experiences, accomplishments, and conditions. The development of blackness in America and throughout the Western world empowers itself with "Africanism," i.e., African traditions, cultural values, norms, history, and languages. Thus, blackness is the reflexive movement of modernity that empowers the elements of freedom, revolution, identity formation, and resistance to tyranny (Diawara, 1990).

Defining the Field

Since the genesis of black studies, the discipline has been struggling to properly identify and label itself. John H. Clarke (1980) prefers the term "Africana Studies" to "black studies." He believes that while "black" is an honorable word, it has its limitations. Black, or blackness, tells you how you look without stating precisely who you are, whereas Africa, or Africana, relates you to land, history, and culture.

Most institutions prefer using titles like "Afro-American," "African and Afro-American," or "Africana" studies. Those who insist on the term "Africana Studies" maintain that "Afro-American Studies" is too limiting. The latter term implies that the primary focus of teaching and research is the historical, cultural, and political development of Afro-Americans living within the boundaries of North America (Clark, 1980; Hine, 1990). Furthermore, "African and Afro-American Studies" tends to neglect the Caribbean and other parts of the Americas. "Africana Studies" encompasses a broader geographical, if not disciplinary, reach, spanning North and South America, the Caribbean, the African continent, and the African Diaspora (Clark, 1980; Hine, 1990). "Black studies," however, as Abdul Alkalimat (1986) contends, is more comprehensive and universally accepted. In this essay, the term "black studies" will be employed.

Much like the nomenclature of black studies, defining it has also presented a challenge. Black studies cannot easily be reduced to a single explanatory formula; the field is presently defined and practiced in myriad ways. However, it can generally be characterized as a multidisciplinary field that analyzes the conditions that have affected people of African descent in America, the Diaspora, and Africa in various aspects of their lives (Clark, 1970; Gordon, 1981; Alkalimat, 1990; Anderson, 1990; Harris, 1990; Karenga, 1991).[i] Black studies examines people of African ancestry wherever they may be found, and derives many of its themes from the historical position of African people in relation to Western societies. These themes include slavery, oppression, colonization, imperialism, emancipation, self-determination, liberation, and socioeconomic and political development.

Anderson (1990) defines black studies as "an interdisciplinary field of study or discipline that systematically treats the past and present culture, characteristics, achievements, issues and problems of the Black race and in a context that interacts relevantly with other peoples of the world." For the purpose of this essay, we are defining black studies as a conglomeration of the definitions noted above.

Karenga, in his book *Introduction to Black Studies*, outlines several objectives that black studies seeks to achieve. These basic objectives are presented in Table 1 (Karenga, 1991).

Table 1. (Karenga, 1991)

Basic Objectives of Black Studies

- To teach what is called the black experience in its historical and current unfolding.
- To assemble and create a body of knowledge that contributes to intellectual and political emancipation.
- To create a body of black intellectuals who are dedicated to community service and development rather than vulgar careerism.
- To advocate the cultivation, maintenance, and continuous expansion of a mutually beneficial relationship between the campus and the community.
- To establish black studies as a legitimate, respected, and permanent discipline.

These objectives have served as the rhetorical backdrop for the discipline since its evolvement in the 1970s. The discipline has been greatly scrutinized and challenged by many academicians about its objectives and relevancy. Karenga (1990) notes that as a result of the struggle to achieve and refine the aforementioned objectives, fundamental and undeniable grounds of relevance for black studies have been established which clearly define the field's academic and social contributions. Those grounds of relevance are outlined in Table 2 (Karanga, 1991).

Table 2. (Karenga, 1991)

Relevance of Black Studies
- It is a definitive contribution to humanity's understanding of self.
- Contributes to the U.S. society's understanding of itself.
- Contributes to the university's realization of its claim and challenge to teach the whole truth, or something as close to it as humanly possible.
- Contributes to the rescue and reconstruction of black history and humanity.
- A critical contribution to a new social science and humanities that will not only benefit blacks, but also the U.S. and the world.
- Contributes to the development of a black intelligentsia and professional stratum whose knowledge, social competence, and commitment furthers the liberation and development of the black community and thus society as a whole.
- Contributes to the critique, resistance, and reversal of the progressive Europeanization of human consciousness and culture, which is one of the major problems of our times.

Black studies challenges the cultural content and definition of what is called "Western" and argues for a multicultural interpretation of the western hemisphere rather than a Eurocentric one. Furthermore, as aforementioned, black studies is interdisciplinary. It has its earliest roots in history, sociology, literature, and the arts. Black studies' most important concepts, methods, and findings to date are centered within these disciplines.

Historical Overview

It is argued that as early as the Colonial period, black studies has been in existence. The way in which the slaves and free blacks acquired and transmitted knowledge of their history and culture was significant. Some gained the information in a piecemeal fashion, and others through a formal education process such as Sabbath schools and true-bands. Furthermore, according to Crouchett (1971), the more literate blacks communicated to their fellow men all they knew of Africa, African heritage, and the ways in which blacks were being exploited and oppressed in America. Teaching a form of Ethiopianism, Christian mythology, and Egyptian history became a primary tool to counter exploitation and enslavement. These teaching forums were held in secret classrooms that consisted of the fields, work groups, restricted social gatherings, and black churches (Crouchett, 1971; Stuckey, 1987; Franklin, 1974).

In the early eighteenth century, the first known organized black studies course came from Hicksite Quaker educators. Although this was a small portion of the education for blacks, their efforts served to inspire the developing interest in Africans and blacks in American history and culture. As early as 1713, a movement to distribute knowledge about black history, culture, and contributions appeared when the Pennsylvania Quakers devised a program for educating free blacks to serve as missionaries on the African continent. The Quakers sought to resettle freed slaves in Africa and often urged the teaching of black history to the free blacks. They hoped that this education would stimulate the free blacks to see their humiliation and oppression, become disenchanted with America, and welcome migration back to Africa.

After the abolishment of slavery in the north, freedmen began to organize themselves as communities. One of the earliest organizations was the African Union, which was established in 1780 in Rhode Island before slavery had ended there. This organization carried out a census of the black community and expressed the collective opinion of the community. The Free African Society of Philadelphia was established in 1787. This society was interested in the collective welfare of blacks and gave rise to free African societies in Boston, Newark, New Jersey, and many other places by the 1820s. A more significant society, established in 1826, was the Massachusetts General Colored Association, devoted to the abolition and elevation of blacks. David Walker, a noted intellectual, was the centerpiece for the organization during this time.

Walker highlighted the greatness of Africa in *Appeals*, published in 1829. This document was an assessment of the political and religious habits and behaviors of blacks, free and in bondage. *Appeals* constituted the first black political document that brought about a direct political response from the slave government.

By the early 1830s, in New York and Philadelphia, Africans established library societies which emphasized the involvement of Africans and blacks in the Revolution and War of 1812. In conjunction with the development of these libraries, the bulk of the "off-campus" black education in the 1830s was to be found in the black convention movement. From that time on, black conventions were earmarked by a concern for developing reliable data about the status of blacks.[ii] Sociological and statistical assessments on the status of blacks continued well into the 1840s. These activists were interested in applying known social data to political and social problems they confronted in their daily lives.

Prior to the Fugitive Slave Laws of 1850, the Council of Colored Men was proposed under the auspices of Frederick Douglass. The council had a component entitled "Committee on Publication." This committee was designed to collect all facts, statistics, statements, laws, historical records, and biographies related to blacks, as well as all books by black authors. In 1850, Douglass, an ex-slave, and David Ruggles and Charlotte Forten, two free blacks, all spoke about the necessity of both black and white understanding of the cultural and historical contributions of black Americans. The next generation, which spanned from Reconstruction to the Harlem Renaissance has been coined the "Negro History Era." This era is marked by the publication *History of the Negro Race in America*, by George W. Williams, published in 1882 and 1883. This two-volume text was accompanied by E. A. Johnson's work, *School History of the Negro Race*, published in 1893. Other significant pieces published during this time that contributed to the study of blacks were *The Suppression of the African Slave-Trade to the United States of America*, published in 1896 by W. E. B. DuBois, and *Story of the Negro* by Booker T. Washington, published in 1909.

The Atlanta University Conferences, held from 1898–1914 under the auspices of DuBois, marked the inauguration of the first scientific study of the conditions of blacks. The conferences covered important aspects of life, such as health, homes, economic development, higher education, common schools, artisans, the church, crime, and suffrage. It was during this period that black studies was formally introduced to the university, and black academics initiated research studies.

One of the important goals of the scholars of this period was to counteract the negative images and representations of blacks that were institutionalized within academia and society. This was in response to the major tenet of social science research at this time, according to which blacks were genetically inferior to whites and Africa was a "dark continent" that lacked civilization (Caldwell, 1830; Ripley, 1899). The American Negro Academy, founded in 1896, set as one of its major goals to assist, by publications, the vindication of the race from vicious assaults, in all areas of learning and truth. Later, in 1899, Dubois published a sociological study, *The Philadelphia Negro*. This landmark study highlighted the conditions of blacks in Philadelphia in the Seventh Ward. The study investigated the black experience as reflected in business, public education, religion, voluntary associations, and public health.

In 1915 the founding of the Association for the Study of Negro Life and History (ASNLH) by Carter G. Woodson marked the beginning of a new era in black studies. The purpose of the ASNLH involved promoting historical research, publishing books on black life and history, promoting the study of blacks through clubs and schools, and bringing harmony between the races by interpreting the one to the other. In 1916, Woodson founded the *Journal of Negro History* and served as its editor until his death. This was perhaps one of Woodson's greatest contributions to the area of black studies.

In 1921, Woodson started Associated Publishers, a division of the ASNLH. This company was established to publish scholarly books on African Americans. The ASNLH's goal was to raise consciousness regarding the portrayal of blacks in American history.

Just five years later, in 1926, Woodson and his colleagues launched Negro History Week. This event, which later evolved into a whole month, was not intended to be the only time of the year in which Negro history was to be celebrated and taught. He and his colleagues viewed this as a time to highlight the ongoing study of black history that was to take place throughout the year.

It was during this time that Historically Black Colleges and Universities (HBCUs) began to respond to the scholarly activities in history and social science. It was becoming ever so clear that black education should conform to the social conditions of blacks. Black colleges began to augment their curricula with courses in black history. Consequently, black college students began to call for a culturally relevant curriculum, a theme that reoccurs later with greater political influence.

Prior to HBCUs offering black history courses as a part of their curriculum, Woodson issued the first report on black studies courses offered in northern colleges in 1919. He reported the following sites that offered a course in black studies:

1. Ohio State University—*Slavery Struggles in the United States*
2. Nebraska University—*The Negro Problem Under Slavery and Freedom*
3. Stanford University—*Immigration and the Race Problem*
4. University of Oklahoma—*Modern Race Problems*
5. University of Missouri—*The Negro in America*
6. University of Chicago—*The Negro in America*
7. University of Minnesota—*The American Negro*
8. Harvard University—*American Population Problems: Immigration and the Negro*

Furthermore, Woodson reported that a small number of black colleges were offering courses in sociology and history pertaining to the Negro experience. Crouchett (1971) cites Woodson, stating that in spite of the lack of trained teachers, Tuskeegee, Atlanta University, Fisk, Wilberforce, and Howard offered such courses, even at the risk of their becoming expressions of opinions without the necessary data to support them.

In spite of the dominant paradigm that the inferiority of blacks was an indisputable scientific fact backed by evolutionary theory and intelligence testing, the 1920s produced a heightened interest in black life and culture. Literary and artistic expressions played as much of a role in black studies as did history and the social sciences. As a self-conscious cultural movement, the Negro Renaissance produced voices regarding black life that never emerged before. Committed to self-expression, these black artists produced literary and artistic contributions that would prompt new criticism. Blacks began to develop an aesthetic and critical tradition that would influence black intellectual customs. Howard University philosopher Alain Locke aided in the integration of black aesthetics into black studies. Moreover, several of the Renaissance leaders owed their first publicity to DuBois as the editor of *The Crisis* and Charles S. Johnson as editor of the *Opportunity* and founder of the Race Relations Institute at Fisk University.

Yet another era of black studies, focusing on history and social science, lasted from approximately 1940 to the mid or late 1960s. Franklin (1986) posits that this period was characterized by an increasing legitimacy of the field and an increasing number of white scholars. Prior to this time, black scholars did the majority of the research. Gunnar Myrdal's *An American Dilemma: The Negro Problem and Modern Democracy*, published in 1944, was the most expensive and comprehensive study of race relations in the U.S. Although Myrdal did direct the study, it must be mentioned that he drew heavily on the works of DuBois, Frazier, and Bunche (Bailey, 1973).

Two other white scholars that made great contributions to the field were anthropologist Franz Boas and sociologist Robert Park. Boas was known for leading the charge against the prevailing paradigm that some races were subordinate or inferior to others and that the environment had very little influence on heredity. Thus, African American studies began to take a more interdisciplinary shape. Rather than being merely historiography, there would be an additional focus on critical interpretations (Woodyard, 1991). As a result of Robert Park's research methodology, a new breed of social theorists educated during the 1940s and 1950s began to understand African American life in a causal relationship with racial prejudice and discrimination and emphasized that scientific research could help to solve race problems (Woodyard, 1991; Bailey, 1973). The objectivity and detachment that is a key component in scientific research was evident in the works of Park's protégés,[iii] who eventually began to search for a truer form of social science research (Woodyard, 1991).

Key historical works published by white scholars during this era included, but were not limited to, *The Peculiar Institution: Slavery in the Ante-Bellum South* by Kenneth Stampp (1956), *Slavery: A Problem in American Institutional and Intellectual Life* by Stanley Elkins (1959), and *Negro Thought in America, 1880–1915* by August Meier (1963). While white scholars became increasingly interested in African American history and studies and began to produce work in this area, blacks continued to produce seminal pieces as well. Among the latter works are *The Negro in the American Revolution* (1961) and *Lincoln and the Negro* (1962) by Benjamin Quarles; *The Emancipation Proclamation* (1963) and the first edition of *From Slavery to Freedom: A History of Negro Americans* (1947) by John Hope Franklin; and *What the Negro Wants* (1944) by Rayford Logan.

Black studies departments were created in a confrontational environment with the rejection of traditional curricula content (Adams, 1996; Karenga, 1993; Banks, 1996). Mainstream university support for black studies emerged in the late 1960s. This was done in conjunction with the protests of the Civil Rights Movement, the Black Power movement, and the admission of a massive influx of black students into predominantly white institutions.

The preconditions for the growth of black studies were demographic, social, and political. Between 1945 and 1965, over three million blacks left the south and migrated to the northeast, north central, and western states. The Black Freedom Movement, in the Civil Rights phase (1955–1965) and the Black Power component (1966–1975), fostered the desegregation of whites and blacks and the empowerment of blacks within previously all-white institutions. The racial composition of U.S. colleges dramatically changed. For example, according to Marable (2000), approximately 75,000 blacks were enrolled in colleges and universities in 1950. In the 1960s three quarters of all black students attended HBCUs. By 1970, approximately 700,000 blacks were enrolled, three quarters of which were in predominantly white institutions.

The student strike of 1968–1969, held at San Francisco State University (SFSU), forced the establishment of the Division of Ethnic Studies and the departments of black, Asian, Chicano, and Native American studies. The Black Student Union at SFSU drafted a political statement, "The Justification for Black Studies," which would become the main document for developing black studies departments at more than sixty universities. The demands and objectives were included within this document included: (1) the opposition of the "Liberal-Fascist" ideology that was rampant on campus (college administrations had attempted to pacify the Black Student Union's demands for systemic curriculum by offering one or two courses in black history and literature); (2) to prepare black students for direct participation in the black community struggles, and to define themselves as responsible to and for the future successes of that community; (3) to reinforce the position that blacks in Africa and the Diaspora deserve democratic rights, self-determination, and liberation; and (4) to oppose the dominant ideology of capitalism, world imperialism, and white supremacy.

During this period, Nathan Hare was employed at SFSU. He and Jimmy Garrett collaborated to put together the first black studies program in the country. Instead of searching for equality of education, the premise of black education, as noted by Hare (1972), was that there can be no equality of education in a racist society. The type of education conceived and perpetrated by the white oppressor is essentially an education for oppression, and black education must be education for liberation, or at least for change. In this respect, black education was to prepare black students to become the catalyst for a black cultural revolution. Black education would thus become the instrument for change (Hare, 1972).

From 1968 to 1971, hundreds of black studies departments and programs were developed. Allen (1974) estimated there were approximately five hundred colleges and universities that provided full-scale black studies programs by 1971. Up to 1,300 institutions offered at least one course in black studies as of 1974. Some estimates place the number of black studies programs reaching its peak at eight hundred in the early 1970s and declining to about 375, due to the lack of resources and support, by the mid 1990s.

The current phase of Afro-American Studies has been developing as a result of a radical social movement in opposition to institutional racism in U.S. higher education. According to Alkalimat (1986), the black studies movement has gone through four main stages of development: innovation, experimentation, crisis, and institutionalization.

Innovation. The origin of the movement came through social protest and disruption of the university. Blacks sought to attack and to change the policies and practices of institutional racism.

Experimentation. The initial protestors for black studies sought to bring the general rhetorical orientation of the national movement within local campus administrative and cultural style. Many different types of academic structures and programs were developed on a trial-and-error basis.

Crisis. When the post-1960s fiscal and demographical shift hit higher education (less money and fewer students), Afro-American studies was challenged for immediate results. It was faced with the prospects of diminished status and decreased resources.

Institutionalization. The strategic orientation for Afro-American Studies was developed in 1977 as "Academic Excellence and Social Responsibility." Under this banner, a set of professional standards began to put the field on a permanent academic foundation.

Black studies has withstood and continues to endure criticism as a viable field of inquiry. Although many colleges and universities throughout the U.S. and abroad have formally adopted it, whether as a department or a program, black studies continues to struggle for its legitimacy.

Some academicians question the integrity, theory, and objectivity of the field. And some continue to raise the questions of why there is a need and whom it is for.

Why Study Black Studies?

The development of black studies from the very outset compelled blacks to evaluate the largely racist nature of established education in America. Due to the problem of cultural hegemony, blacks and Africans in the Diaspora have found the issue of perspective to be perennially problematic. Africans were stripped of their cultural foundations due to the cataclysmic experience of chattel slavery—the basis for cultural hegemony. This in turn produced historical discontinuity and preempted normative culture building through a decentering process. Although the experience of oppression and exploitation required movement away from an African center, it was this experience that produced the conditions for the (re)emergence of an African-centered consciousness. Thus, the problem of perspective emerged as the black intellectual tradition.

Considering the conventional roles of American education and its institutionalized discriminations, exploitations, rejections, and particularizations, blacks in many sectors reached the conclusion that educators occupy one of two positions: oppressors or liberators. As a result, many blacks began to consider black education as having a special assignment: to challenge and eventually replace white education because it was deficient and corrupt. They also realized that education is undeniably political and that black education can scarcely afford to be anything less.

Many black scholars have been busy with the task of developing black studies as a major liberating force: one that enables blacks to take control of their own lives and share their history and experiences from their own perspective. Prior to black studies, the study of blacks' modes of thought was based almost entirely on the paradigmatic orientations of white scholars. A mode of thought is a framework in which research is conducted, curriculums are designed, and public policy developed (Alkalimat, 1990). Furthermore, it is viewed as a set of assumptions that defines the consensus of an intellectual community. In 1969, anthropologist St. Clair Drake voiced this perspective that the very use of the term black studies inherently an indictment of western scholarship and its claim to objectivity. Europeans and whites, in general have benefited from the distortion of world history and the monopolization of the construction of knowledge and/or truth. It is clear that they know more about history and the power that constructing knowledge and truth yields than they are prepared to admit. The power to construct knowledge and control history can be viewed as a two-edged sword that can be used both as an instrument of liberation and as a weapon of enslavement. History, like a gun, is neutral—it will serve anyone who uses it effectively.

As many postmodernist theorists have contended, knowledge is socially constructed and reflects human interests, values, and action. The knowledge that people create is heavily influenced by their interpretations of their experiences and their positions within particular social, economic, and political systems. Scheurich and Young (1997) contend that epistemologies we typically use in educational research are often racially biased. Thus, schools can be and are used to control others by distributing knowledge that builds allegiance to ruling elites and convinces individuals to accept their subordinate position in society and in existing power relations. Moreover, the interests of the oppressors lie in "changing the consciousness of the oppressed, not the situation which oppresses them" (Scheurich & Young, 1997). The more the oppressed can be led to adapt to that situation, the more easily they can be dominated.

White researchers have defined the behavior of blacks through ideological concepts. Social theories that were developed to explain the race problem have not adequately dealt with the daily functioning of black social systems or specified the nature of the political and economic oppression to which blacks are subjected. We often hear of the problems that blacks encounter but seldom do we engage in dialogue about the pathology of white racism.

The objectification of knowledge is a matter of privilege and power. Consequently, the privileged and elite subset of the population uses knowledge as a way of interpreting reality and imposing its will on others through the control of major institutions such as the media, schooling, and legislation. In particular, the objectification of social-science knowledge has invalidated the unique ethno-culturalism of racial "minorities" (Stanfield, 1985). Thus, it is mandatory that we develop a new frame of reference which transcends the concepts historically defined for and by whites.

In Western societies, science is primarily concerned with the creation and use of ideas and theories designed to acquire power. Power, today, is defined by the creation of ideas and the ability to have people respond to one's ideas as if these ideas represented the respondent's reality (Semaj, 1981). Wade Nobles (1978) reiterates this point, stating that Western science and particularly social science are, like economic and political institutions, instruments designed to reflect the culture of the oppressor and allow for more efficient domination.

According to Spight it is virtually impossible to separate science as it has evolved in Western society from Western culture itself. He contends that science is characterized in three ways: (1) a body of knowledge, a set of ordered facts, an artifact of culture, an object defined by its constancy; (2) a methodology, a process, a dynamic phenomenon, an object defined by its historicity; and (3) a social activity, a human expression, an object defined by its subjectivity (Spight, 1974).

Gordon et al. (1990) contend that the problem is not that the methods of science are dysfunctional for the research and scholarly efforts of ethnic minorities. The problem is cultural and methodological hegemony, which favors too narrow a range of perspectives and investigative techniques. Stanfield (1985) posits that social sciences are ethno-cultural institutions that are microcosms of the hegemonic social privileges of Euro-Americans. Furthermore, all knowledge is relative to the context in which it is manifested and experienced. Thus, we perceive and conceive of the world and its events in terms that either fit or are adjusted to the context that we know.

Thus, the task for black studies is to describe the nature and limitations of "classical" social science and develop a framework within which a "modern" social science can develop and flourish (Clark, 1972). The main objective of this field of inquiry should consist of nothing less than the liberation of the black mind. The methodology and ideology of black studies should be grounded in the uniqueness of black life and emphasis should not be on neutrality but on development and utilization of concepts and theories of social change (Semaj, 1996).

Many racial and ethnic groups struggled to survive in these United States of America. Those who achieved a meaningful measure of freedom wisely maintained their ancestral roots. Thus, the liberation of the African Mind, Body, and Spirit can only be achieved and maintained through African-centered thinking, philosophy worldview, and value systems. Furthermore, an African-centered education that emphasizes the successes and failures of the past is of the highest priority.

Afrocentricity is African genius and African values created, reconstructed, and derived from our history and experiences in our best interest. According to Asante (1990), Afrocentricism as a framework for black studies treats African people as subjects rather than as objects of study. Asante suggest that centrism is the placement of one's own historical experiences, concepts, paradigms, theories, and methods of the core question is significant.

Consequently, Afrocentricity asserts that the life experiences of all people of African descent must be the focal point of Afrocentric knowledge. It emphasizes an analysis rooted in the historical and contemporary realities of blacks without negating or minimizing the experiences of other groups. Afrocentricity emphasizes the particular and distinct experiences of people of African descent that have helped shape black reality.

The psychology of the African American without an African-centered foundation is a matter of great concern. As opposed to looking out from one's own center, the non-Afrocentric person operates in a manner that is negatively predictable and "their images, symbols, lifestyles, and manners are contradictory and destructive to personal and collective growth and development" (Asante, 1988, 1996). Becoming African-centered in one's thinking necessarily involves a critical analysis of the social order and a historical understanding of one's position in it.

This centering process entails the deconstruction of socially constructed versions of reality. However, the deconstruction of social realities that validate European-centered hegemony is a necessary but not sufficient condition for African-centered personal transformation. There must also be a process of reconstructing social reality—both objectively and subjectively—based on one's understanding of African cultural history and perception of one's place in it (Shujaa, 1994). This process involves learning about African and African American cultural history and critically reinterpreting what one has been (mis)taught to believe.

Table 3 outlines a brief comparison of Afrocentric and Eurocentric worldviews. In short, we must move from an individual-based philosophy to a more collective one—"I am because we are, and because we are, I am."

Table 3

Afrocentric vs. Eurocentric Worldview

Afrocentric	Eurocentric
(1) Groupness	Individuality
(2) Sameness	Uniqueness
(3) Commonality	Differences
(4) Cooperation	Competition
(5) Collective responsibility	Individual rights
(6) Cooperativeness and depending on one another	Separateness/independence
(7) Survival of the tribe	Survival of the fittest
(8) One with nature	Control over nature

Young and Hardiman (1983) offer a method for the reclamation of an African-centered worldview. Their method consists of five phases. The first phase is reclamation. Reclamation consists of the documentation of evidence verifying the true African historical record. Phase two entails emotional and intellectual identification in which participants conduct their own personally relevant investigations, raising questions and answering them.

The third phase for the reclamation of the African mind is demystification. Emphasis is placed on defining and clarifying structural elements, form, content, and other devices. In the fourth phase, understanding, participants focus on integrating, synthesizing, internalizing, and reflecting what they have learned through analysis of Western orthodox work. Finally, the fifth phase, mastery, requires that students demonstrate their understanding by applying the information in a product of their own creation for future generations of humankind and thereby take their place in African legacy. This method for the reclamation of an African-centered worldview is a transformative power that allows people of African descent to define their own reality; critically dissect racist societal structures, practices, policies, and institutions that impede their progress; and empower themselves with the knowledge to combat the Novocain effect of white hegemonic forces.

Conclusion

As discussed in this chapter, it is imperative to first note the dominance of white racism in developing the context in which black social inquiry has been conducted. This racist ideology has greatly impacted black social research by influencing questions asked, determining modes of analysis, and shaping conclusions. Neither black nor white scholars have escaped this phenomenon. As stated by Carter G. Woodson (1933),

> When a Negro has finished his education in our schools, then, he has been equipped to begin the life of an Americanized or Europeanized white man, but before he steps from the threshold of his alma mater he is told by his teachers that he must go back to his own people from whom he has been estranged by a vision of ideals which in his disillusionment he will realize that he cannot attain. (p. 5)

> Taught from books of the same bias, trained by Caucasians of the same prejudices or by Negroes of enslaved minds, one generation of Negro teachers after another have served for no higher purpose than to do what they are told. (p. 23)

The full exposition and understanding of this dim reality will illuminate much detail about the true nature of the problems faced by blacks then, now, and if things do not change, the future.

Thus, the development of such a field of inquiry shall prove itself to be antithetical to white modes of thought and the racist epitaphs that get labeled as knowledge. If blacks are to win this war against white supremacy, they must develop their own field of inquiry to inform, build, and reinforce their educational institutions. To paraphrase J. Carruthers (1999), in order to liberate the African mind, blacks must take the world and then reorganize it according to their worldview. Only then will mankind be able to live in harmony with the universe. Only then will blacks truly be free.

References

Adams, R. L. (1977). Black studies perspectives. *Journal of Negro Education, 46*(2), 99–117.
Alkalimat, A. (1990). *Paradigms in Black Studies.* Chicago, IL: Twenty-First Century Books and Publications.
Anderson, T. (1990). *Black studies: Theory, method, and cultural perspectives.* Pullman: Washington State University Press.
Asante, M. (1988). *Afrocentricity.* Trenton, NJ: Africa World Press, Inc.
Asante, M. (1990). *Kemte, Afrocentricity and Kkowledge.* Trenton, NJ: Africa World Press.
Bailey, R. (1973). Black studies in historical perspective. *Journal of Social Issues 29* (1), 97–108.
Banks, J. (1993). The canon debate, knowledge construction, and multicultural education. *Educational Researcher* (June-July 1993).
Carruthers, J. (1999). *Intellectual warfare.* Chicago: Third World Press.
Clark, H. (1970). *Black studies and the study of black people.* Unpublished manuscript. Stanford University.
Clark, C. (1972). Black studies or the study of black people? In R. Jones (Ed.) *Black psychology,* New York: Harper & Row.
Clarke, J. H. (1984). Africana Studies: A Decade of Change, Challenge and Conflict. In J. E. Turner (Ed.), *The next decade: Theoretical and research issues in africana studies.* Ithica, New York: African Studies and Reseach Center Cornell University.
Colon, A. K. (1980). *Historical foundations for black studies: An overview of social and intellectual considerations.,* Unpublished doctoral, Stanford University, California.
Crouchett, L. (1971). Early black studies movements. *Journal of Black Studies,* 2(2), 189-200.
Diawara, M. (1990). English and Blackness: Cricket as discourse on colonialism. *Callaloo 13* (4), 830-844.
Franklin, J. H. (1986). On the Evolution of Scholarship in Afro-American History. In D. C. Hine (Ed.), *The State of Afro-American History: Past, Present, and Future.* Baton Rouge, LA.
Freire, P. (1970). *The pedagogy of the oppressed.* New York: The Continuum Publishing Company.

Garrett, J. P. (1998). Black/Africana/Pan-African studies: From radical to reaction to reform?--Its role and relevance in the era of global capitalism in the new millenium. *Journal of Pan-African Studies, 1*(1).

Gordon, E., Miller, F., & Rollock, D. (1990). Coping with communicentric bias in knowledge production in the social sciences. *Educational Researcher 19* (3), 14–19.

Gordon, V. (1981). The coming of age of black Studies. The Western Journal of Black Studies. Vol. 5, (3) p. 231.

Hare, N. (1972). The Battle for Black Studies. *The Black Scholar,* May, 1972, 32-47.

Harris, R. L. (1990). The Intellectual and Institutional Development of Africana Studies. In D. C. H. Robert L. Harris, & Nellie McKay (Ed.), *Three essays black studies in the united states.* New York: Ford Foundation.

Karenga, M. (1991). *Introduction to black studies* (pp.13–15). (2nd ed.). Los Angeles: The University of Sankore Press.

Kershaw, T. (1989). The Emerging Paradigm in Black Studies. *Western journal of black studies, 13*(1), 45-51.

Marable, M. (2000). *Dispatches for the ebony tower.* New York: Columbia University Press.

McClendon, W. H. (1974). Black Studies: Education for Liberation. *The black scholar, 6,* 15-25.

Moss, A. A. (1981). *The american negro academy: Voice of the talented tenth.* Baton Rouge, LA: Southern University.

Nobles, W. (1978). African consciousness and liberation struggles: implications for the development and construction of scientific paradigms. Paper presented to the Fanon Research Development Conference, February, Port of Spain, Trinidad.

Semaj, L (1981). Race and identity and children of the african diaspora: Contributions of Rastafari. *Studia Africana, 1* (4), 412-419.

Semaj, L. (1996). Towards a Cultural Science. In D. Azibo (Ed.) African psychology in historical perspective and related commentary. Trenton, NJ: Africa World Press.

Semmes, C. E. (1981). Foundations of an Afrocentric Social Science: Implications for curriculum building, theory, and research in black studies. *Journal of Black Studies, 12,* 3-17.

Semmes, C. E. (1992). *Cultural hegemony and African American development.* Westport, CT: Praeger Publishers.

Shujaa, M. J. (1994). *Too Much Schooling, Too Little Education*. Trenton, NJ: Africa World Press.
Smedley, A. (1993). Race in North America
Spight, C. (1974). Towards a black science and technology. *Black Books Bulletin 56*, (3), 6-11, 49.
Stanfield, J (1985). The ethnocentric bias of social science knowledge production. *Review of Research in Education, 12*, pp. 387-415
Stuckey, S. (1987). *Slave culture*. New York: Oxford University Press.
Turner, J., & McGann, C. S. (1980). Black Studies as an integral tradition in African American intellectual history. *Journal of Negro Education, 49*, 52–59.
Woodson, C. G. (1919). Negro life and history in our schools. *Journal of Negro History, 4*.
Woodson, C. G. (1933). The Mis-education of the Negro. Trenton, NJ: Africa World Press.
Woodyard, J. L. (1991). Evolution of a discipline: Intellectual antecedents of African American studies. *Journal of Black Studies, 22*(2), 239-251.

---

[i] The various components of life that is being analyzed are the social, political, economic, education, psychological, legal, and moral status.

[ii] Data consisted of the number of churches, ministers, day schools, teachers, sabbath schools, Sunday School teachers, Bible classes, literary societies, debating societies, mutual relief societies, temperance societies, mechanics, real estate, taxes paid, and the black population of the states listed.

[iii] Park's protégés included Charles S. Johnston, E. Franklin Frazier, St. Clair Drake, Horace Cayton, and Bertram W. Doyle.

EFLECTING BLACK: MAINTAINING A POLITICS OF OPPOSITION IN ACADEME

Marvin Lynn

> *In this essay, the author uses his schooling experience as a backdrop for discussing the ways in which academic institutions attempt to confiscate the minds and souls of African Americans who seek to find success within its walls. Juxtaposing plantation life in the South with life in academe, the author draws a parallel between the life of the slave and the life of the academic—arguing chiefly that physical slavery and material depravity has been replaced by another more insidious form of mental slavery. This discussion is brought to life as the author describes in detail his experience as a doctoral student at a prestigious and "liberal" institution of higher learning on the West Coast.*

In this chapter, I intend to discuss, in some detail, my career as an undergrad student, which will lead directly into a more analytical discussion regarding my experience as a graduate student. After describing my graduate school experience, I will discuss the theoretical explanations for why and how schools work, and then propose a research typology that both encapsulates the current conditions in academe and demands that we move beyond these conditions to the possibility of a future that more highly regards the political nature of academic and social life.

From Good Boy to Rebel:
The Difference Between Education and Schooling

Like many African American males in the U.S., I grew up in the slums of a large metropolis. I spent the first half of my childhood in an all-black community on the South Side of Chicago that was and is still known for having one of the highest crime rates in the city. This infamous area is known as the Notorious Englewood Community. Because of various political, social, and economic factors, the majority of blacks that inhabit the city live on the South Side. To that extent, the South Side of Chicago has—since the first migrants came from Mississippi and surrounding areas in the early and mid 1900s—experienced a great deal of social and economic dislocation. This is especially true when you compare the Southside to the Northside—where the majority of the city's white residents dwell. This "Ghetto Poverty Census Tract," as William Julius Wilson would call it, was replete with all of the problems and issues that confront urban areas where there are high poverty rates. Life was not easy. However, school was enjoyable. From kindergarten through the beginning of fourth grade, I attended Jesse Sherwood Elementary school—an all-black K–5 school just behind our apartment on the other side of the park district's recreational center. I remember vividly many of my experiences there.

As Vanessa Siddle Walker has documented again and again in her work on black schools in the segregated South, I found that my school was too a caring one: one that pushed me to excel and rewarded me handsomely when I did. I remember being recognized before the entire school for participating in a book contest over the summer. At the encouragement of one of my teachers, I read fifteen books and wrote short reports on each of them during the summer after kindergarten or first grade! I also remember what happened to me when I did work that was less than excellent. Suffice it to say that any behavior or attitude that was unbecoming was quickly and swiftly dealt with. For the most part, I enjoyed my life as a student in this quaint little school on the corner. The report from all my teachers confirmed this.

At the age of about ten, my family moved to the other side of town: the Northside. This new area presented a different set of challenges. However, like the school I had attended previously, the majority of children—including myself—received free lunches and benefited greatly from state aid. While the second grade school I attended was far more diverse, there were very few white students in the school. As a matter of fact, I can remember having only one white classmate: Michael, an overweight but jovial kid who surprisingly got along well with almost everyone. Like the rest of his black and Latino (most Puerto Rican and some Mexican) peers, he excelled in the art of "casing" as we called it. This activity would extend for several minutes at a time, in or out of class, depending on who was running the show. While I was often the recipient of these attacks, it didn't happen to me any more than it did to others. So, while I initially felt isolated and alone, I soon began to feel more comfortable. Because I enjoyed school and took special care not to cause trouble, I was well liked by most of my teachers and graduated from grade school at the top of my class. I continued to excel in high school.

The high school I attended was a typical American public urban high school in that it was an extremely large institution that struggled to maintain a modicum of control over what was often an unwieldy population of students, most of whom were poor and working-class African Americans and Latinos. At this particular school, there were also a number of poor immigrant children from Southeast Asia. Once again, I got along well with most of my teachers and managed to be one of few blacks allowed into the honors program. At the time, I did not view tracking as unjust. I have since learned through firsthand experience and through the research on tracking of the negative impact that this practice has on the schooling experiences of most students of color (Oakes, 1990). Even though I had not come into contact with the research literature on the unfair practice of tracking, I was very much aware that the education that I was receiving was far superior to that of most of those who looked like me, including my own brother who was pushed into the remedial track. As a result, he barely made it through high school. College was never a consideration. Unlike my brother, I was encouraged to go to college. So I did. It was at that point that I became acutely aware of my own marginalization as a working-class African American in a racist and classist society.

Being thrust into a nearly all-white environment provided me with a great deal of motivation for developing a consciousness about the nature of social inequality. In addition to that, I had the good fortune of taking a class with a well-known black professor concerned with issues of race, class, and gender in American education. This was the beginning of my awakening. At that point, I immediately became involved in black student organizations and contributed rather frequently to the school newspaper's political op-ed section. I then went on to graduate school and full-time elementary school teaching in New York City. While in New York, I began to contemplate the relationship between theory and life experience. As I began to read about the nature of radical pedagogy and the experiences of teachers of color, I began to see a relationship between my practices, my experiences, and what I was reading. It was then that I developed a thirst for utilizing research as a way in which to dismantle structures of oppression.

When I began my search for a Ph.D. program after four years of frustration in elementary schools on the East Coast and in the Midwest, I was determined to enter into a doctoral program that would help me develop the necessary skills for doing research aimed at liberating the oppressed. Fortunately (so I thought), I was able to find a liberal institution with a focus on social justice. It was there that I began to understand that the liberal agenda was not necessarily socially just.

As a first-year doctoral student in a graduate school of education known for the work of its "progressive" scholars, I was less than encouraged when I discovered that I would be expected to develop and practice a politics of dissemblance in order to make it, in what turned out to be an extremely competitive, cut-throat environment. After the first few weeks of classes, I found myself being lectured by a number of scholars (most of them scholars of color) about how to "play the game" and be more "strategic" with regard to expressing my views in class. At the same time, my relationships with other students of color in the department began to disintegrate when it became clear that I was a rebel rouser with an annoyingly "critical" disposition. A number of faculty and students were using the word "critical" as though it was a dirty word. "Oh, you're one of those *critical* students right?" I would often be asked. I was being cast in such a light when I was merely involved in theoretical discussions about the nature of racial oppression in the U.S. I was not confronting faculty or administrators with lists of grievances regarding inadequacies at the institution nor was I making any calls for sweeping changes in the manner of life at this auspicious campus. I simply dared to have an identity that could not be shaped, molded, or sent into hibernation by others with more power and prestige. Moreover, unlike other students of color, instead of complaining constantly to friends about the racist and sexist remarks made by fellow classmates, I openly confronted such views in and out of class.

I noticed that I was not alone. Other students who espoused critical feminist, Marxist, or Nationalist ideologies were also discouraged from engaging in either a critique of the liberal/conservative binary or discussing the way in which race, class, and gender impact the lives of the oppressed. While I knew that I was being associated with this term, I had no idea what the fallout would be. One thing I quickly realized was that even those who were considered "critical" were not ready to engage in conversations that looked beyond Marxist and feminist discourses for explanations of the problem of social inequality. As a result, I was also not a part of the criticalist community. The institution was being guided by a particular philosophical orientation which was in opposition to my own, especially since I was interested in conducting research as a way in which to bring attention to issues of social inequality.

The political binarism of this institution had a decidedly negative impact on many students. Some students of color as well as white students with feminist or Marxist orientations began to completely shut down. They ceased to make comments in class at all. Occasionally, I would see them in the hall and we would chat briefly about the repressiveness of the institution or the unfairness of faculty with selfish agendas. Other students chose to leave their political identities at home while some chose to completely change their identities in order to suit the needs of faculty and students who complained incessantly about troublemakers in their classes. Nevertheless, most of us have remained in the program. We were forced to learn how to make alliances with those who held similar beliefs. I was able to find a faculty advisor, albeit in another department in the school of education, with whom I could work. While my situation improved, the question of what occurred still bothers me a great deal. Not only am I concerned about what damage was done to my colleagues and myself—one woman left the program because of emotional instability after a year, while others disassociated themselves from nearly everyone—I am concerned about how these institutions manage to push their own agendas onto graduate students who, in many instances, are forced to comply. What impact does this have on the communities that serve to benefit from the work of African American, Latino, Marxist, or white feminist scholars concerned about issues of social inequality? If academia is to serve as one of the few places where we can ponder the complex problems that plague our world and find solutions to those problems, then how is society served when scholars are turned into automatons that are willing to sell their souls for a Ph.D. or for tenure? Whose interests are served?

The Graduate School Climate

My experience has taught me that while access to higher education has improved tremendously for African Americans in recent years, the political climate of most colleges and universities has not changed significantly. In some cases, due to the obliteration of Affirmative Action programs and other initiatives aimed at increasing and retaining students from historically underrepresented ethnic and racial groups, the campus climate has worsened for many African American students (Cross & Slater, 1999). The increasingly limited presence of students of color at institutions such as the University of California has created an environment that appears even more inhospitable for students from diverse backgrounds, as some reports would indicate (Cross, 1999). For some students this has led to an even greater degree of isolation. For others, it has not made much difference. In other words, an institution's on-the-surface commitment to maintaining racial and ethnic diversity cannot effectively serve as a barometer for measuring the extent to which there might exist great tensions around the politics of race, class, and gender. It must be acknowledged that since all academic institutions serve the interest of the dominant class, one would be hard-pressed to argue that they can serve as support mechanisms for the majority of oppressed peoples.

While I could tend to the myriad questions around this topic, I am mainly concerned with how the political climate of institutions of higher education can serve to have an even more damaging impact on the self-esteem of students of color. More specifically, I will utilize my own experience as a backdrop for tending to the following questions: How does the political climate of institutions of higher education contribute to the further marginalization of students of color? I would argue that besides the obvious problem of alienation and isolation that minority students on white campuses are inevitably forced to contend with, students of color attempting to integrate into openly hostile academic environments must also grapple with, perhaps, an even greater problem: the ever-present fear of retaliation from an administration and student body that does not want them in the first place. As I have observed on the campus of my institution—which is currently in its post-Affirmative Action phase—students of color are far more prone to remain silent in the face of blatant and undeniable injustices for fear that their I-got-in-on-my-own-merits membership card could be revoked by an angry mob of disenfranchised bureaucrats awaiting the next opportunity to rid the institution of its remaining students of color.

In light of this, I am led to ask several more questions: (1) How does a black graduate student maintain a politics of opposition in the academic plantations we call institutions of higher education when other students of color are far less apt to be openly concerned about politics at all for fear that they might ruin their academic careers? (2) What are the costs? And (3) in what ways do institutions of higher education thwart or enhance the development of oppositional identities among African American students, graduate students in particular?

Academicians and graduate students of color, inarguably a limited presence in the academy, are forced to find myriad ways in which to contend with the constraints placed upon them by the academy. Not only are they forced to accept conditions as they exist in such institutions, but they also find themselves supporting time-honored practices and traditions that are, by their very nature, exclusionary. One explanation is found in Gramsci's theory of hegemonic control which offers us an analysis of the dialectical nature of oppression (Crenshaw, 1995; Hoffman, 1970). This theory puts forth the notion that the dominant culture—through the threat of physical force and "mentacide" (Wright, 1993), the deadening and controlling of the mind— convinces the oppressed that they should collude in their own social, economic, and political disenfranchisement and subsequently participate in and approve of oppressive structures of domination. In this way, racist, classist, and sexist social structures are made legitimate. Moreover, hegemonically derived discursive practices are not questioned but are supported by oppressor and oppressed alike. In this sense, graduate students and faculty of color have no other choice but to submit to the will of the academic elite who are responsible for creating the standards by which they are to be judged.

The dialectal relationship between scholars of color and the elites leads the oppressed (folks of color in academe) to develop a dual consciousness. DuBois (1982) has referred to it as a double consciousness, i.e., blacks' ability to see the world from both black and white perspectives simultaneously. According to the author, this dual consciousness exists in all segments of black civil society, regardless of class or economic standing. Others, however, argue that black consciousness and identity development is greatly impacted by class, Gay, 2000; Hill Collins, etc.; Haymes, 1995; Kelly, 1997; Marable, 1996). Because of their relatively greater degree of integration and participation in white middle class culture, black scholars are more likely to hold themselves and others up to a white middle class standard. Members of the black poor and working classes are also forced to contend with racist and classist social standards. However, because their contact with whites is less frequent, the impact is not as great (Haymes, 1995). In other words, black scholars who, for the most part, exist in a world where there are few blacks have to take on an oppressor consciousness in order to survive in the world of academia. Chicana feminist scholars refer to this as the impostor phenomenon (Cordova, 1998). Scholars of color soon become the oppressors within—identifying more strongly with the dominant class than with other people of color (Cordova, 1998). This duplicity or false consciousness is one of the chief manifestations of the psychosocial pressures placed on scholars of color. Not only are they expected to perform as well or better than their privileged counterparts, but they are also expected to conform to certain behavioral and attitudinal standards. These standards have always existed for blacks within the wider social realm.

Within the plantation system of the Old South, for instance, whites caricatured their African captives in very distinct ways in order to allay their fears about the inevitability of slavery's demise (Blassingame, 1972; White, 1987). While it should be pointed out that caricatures are well-developed myths about the supposedly static and one-dimensional nature of the African personality, it is important to recognize that those enslaved had a variety of ways of resisting their dehumanization, including taking and owning the caricatures as they were created by whites. In this sense, caricatures that formerly held completely negative connotations can be perceived as multidimensional and dynamic. Caricatures of the African personality differed for men and for women. In his widely read book on slave culture in the south, John Blassingame argued that three prototypical personality types or caricatures existed (and still exist) for African male slaves: the Nat or the ravenous revolutionary capable of tearing down the slave system if left unchecked; the Jack or the generally mild-mannered, dependable worker capable of harboring resentment toward slave owners; and the Sambo, whom they deemed completely incapable of exercising any real agency (Blassingame, 1972; Genovese, 1974). In this sense, it is important to understand that while the African personality was far more layered and multidimensional than the caricatures allow for, the majority of slaves were seen as fitting into one category or another. Over time, as slaves began to master the art of dissemblance, they sometimes willfully conformed to these stereotypes in the presence of whites as a way to ensure the livelihood of their families (Blassingame, 1972). Similar kinds of expectations existed for female slaves.

The chief caricatures of female slave were that of the Jezebel and the Mammy (White, 1987). According to Southern slave-owner mythology, black women who exercised any degree of agency with regard to their bodies and/or the sexual advances of their masters were considered Jezebels who were unruly and could not be trusted. In some way, this could be likened to the Nat caricature, for she was considered to be capable of disobedience as well. The Mammy, on the other hand, was much more like the Sambo, devoted to her Master and his family. More importantly, she and the Sambo were often depended upon to warn their masters about impending rebellions being planned by more recalcitrant slaves. Although whites feared that all slaves were, in some way, capable of committing dastardly acts in order to obtain their freedom, they trusted slaves whom they considered to be Mammies and Sambos a great deal. According to Genovese (1974), slaves who exhibited these stereotypical characteristics were also rather handsomely rewarded by being given preferential treatment over others. Slaves considered to be troublemakers suffered severe physical abuse and were forced to toil longer and harder than those who could curry favor with their masters. This might also characterize the distinction whites made between field slaves and house slaves. Such distinctions took on critical significance in the black community as they were often made according to skin color: darker slaves were generally given more difficult tasks and lighter-skinned slaves were generally required to toil less. Although this was not always the case, it created a divide between blacks with more direct European ancestry and those who, for the most part, appeared to have no white ancestry. These distinctions were only part of the complex fabric of African American interethnic social relations. In addition to this, African Americans emerged out of the slavery era with a variety of political orientations—many of which were often at odds with each other (Watkins, 1994).

Academic Slavery

Because institutions exist in a largely racist, sexist, and capitalist context, they are part and parcel of the hegemonic social structure. Moreover, those who attempt to work within the walls of institutions such as the academy are positioned in ways that force them to practice forms of self-annihilation. In an exploratory study I conducted with urban school teachers of color in the New York City metropolitan area, I found that teachers of color could be self-annihilating in two ways: First, by remaining silent on nearly every social justice issue at work, they were left with a low sense of self-efficacy and regarded their teaching as ineffectual. Second, by openly addressing **all** questions and issues with social justice relevancy, they ignited a firestorm of resistance from colleagues and administrators and were eventually forced to leave schools where they contributed greatly to the well-being of African American children and their families. In both cases, African American teachers do not emerge victorious. In the first case, they lost their soul. In the second case, their soul remained intact, but they lost their job and, as a result, their ability to have direct influence over the lives of those whom they cared so deeply about.

While universities claim to provide their "workers" with more intellectual autonomy, scholars of color often meet similar fates. Academicians of color are expected to conform to certain codes of behavior within academe. For fear that they could be on the "academic path to pariah status" scholars of color have been reduced to workers on this plantation called academia (Schneider, 1999, p. A12). Most have been forced to act either as overseers or house slaves who attempt to control and maintain the intellectual labor of less conformist workers, would-be fugitive workers, or field slaves seeking various ways to subvert the dominant research paradigms. To an extent, this explains the behavior of professors of color who attempted to get me to change my political orientation in graduate school. They saw it as their responsibility to chide and control those with whom they shared common characteristics—lest the whole lot be damned.

Contrary to what one might think, the plantation makes room for most of its workers, even those who attempt to question its very underpinnings. Workers are forced to decide, early on, whether or not they are going to directly challenge the hegemony of the plantation, work within its confines to make slow and incremental changes, or take on the identity of an "impostor" (Cordova, 1998), someone who trades in his or her integrity for a credential or for tenure. In this regard, it would seem that workers or intellectuals of color fit within three broad categories: the critical researcher (viewed by the hegemon as either a Nat or a Jezebel), who works within the system but challenges it at every turn; the plantation scholar (viewed as a Jack); and the hegemonic scholar (viewed as the intellectual Sambo or Mammy).

Figure 1

Relationship of Researcher Typology to Slave Caricature

Research orientation	Slave caricature
Critical researcher	Nat, Jezebel
Plantation researcher	Jack
Hegemonic researcher	Sambo, Mammy

Plantation researchers seek to do work that does not challenge the existing social order. Their work is of a non-threatening nature and fits neatly within existing dominant research paradigms. In general, plantation research is atheoretical and seeks mainly to understand, define, and analyze microlevel phenomena without any real concern for how macrosociological phenomena impact and construct the microsociopolitical sphere. Researchers in this category may be guided by a sense of altruism or duty to inform the world about a particular group, its culture, its activities, and such, but it is, in many ways, uncritical. This would not include culture-centered work that seeks to transform existing notions about the culture of Africans or Mexicans, for instance. This would, however, include anthropological interpretations of those communities done by outsiders with little or no understanding of the realities of the people whom they are studying. In sum, plantation research works, most often unknowingly, to sustain and strengthen existing structures of domination by legitimating the ways in which knowledge is produced and disseminated within and outside of the academy.

Hegemonic researchers, often funded by large conservative think tanks, seek to do work that has the explicit goal of maintaining and strengthening the existing social order. This research, which many might also consider positivist, relies heavily on mathematics and quantitative methodology for understanding and defining the human condition. This does not include the work of scholars seeking to quantify various forms of oppression through the use of such methods. The hegemonic researcher, like the authors of *The Bell Curve* (Herrnstein & Murray, 1994) for example, utilize deficit or culture of poverty theories to explain the failure of schools to properly educate students of color (Valencia, 1997). Researchers operating under this paradigm might be considered conservative (Aronowitz & Giroux, 1985; Solorzano & Solorzano, 1997).

Students and faculty of color who espouse a plantation or hegemonic intellectual or research orientation are provided with greater opportunities to work as graduate student researchers on large projects with well-known faculty. They are also provided with more financial support than those of us who tend to want to question everything. In a sense, because they have mastered the art of doing what it takes to get what they want, their graduate school experiences are richer. This is not to suggest that some of these students and faculty do not actually agree with the liberal agenda. I believe that a number of them do. However, I believe that the majority of them live two different lives: a public and a private one. In their view, they have no choice. What if they did have a choice? What if graduate schools like this one sought to encourage students and faculty to have a critical disposition toward the social order for the purposes of transforming it? What kind of research would be encouraged? More importantly, what kind of researchers would be borne out of such a system?

Such institutions might give way to the development of more critical researchers who seek to do research that has the goal of liberating the oppressed or changing existing social relations in some fundamental way. This work, usually with a strong theoretical foundation, would seek to understand and explain how social structures impact and shape people's lives. The interdisciplinary work of such scholars would draw from a wide range of theoretical and methodological traditions. Critical researchers would also seek to utilize their research as an opportunity to reflect on their own experiences with domination and subjugation. They would seek also to highlight and draw attention to their subject position within the body of their work as well. While working marginally within several existing paradigms, critical researchers would look for ways in which to form new epistemologies about the nature of oppression. Work guided by Black Feminist, LatCrit, and Critical Race paradigms are examples of this type of work. Work in this field is led by a sense of urgency to end all forms of oppression. Researchers working within this tradition most often emanate from oppressed communities and maintain close contact with those communities about whom they write and research.

In many respects, critical researchers would also attempt to "decrease the distance between what they say and what they do" (Freire, 1993, p. 28). They would not, for example, write about the necessity for revolution and then refuse to participate in revolutionary struggle. They would support the work of other scholars attempting to work in this tradition as well. They would also work to stay abreast of popular social and political issues and be prepared to act when necessary. Critical researchers teaching or attending school at the University of California, for example, would be actively engaged in struggles with the administration over anti-affirmative action legislation recently passed. In this sense, critical researchers would also be activist in every sense of the word. While their scholarship would often be led by activist intentions, they would also commit themselves to being involved in other overt actions aimed at eliminating existing inequalities. Finally, while the critical researcher would express concern about the nature of oppression for all groups, he or she would also express a degree of solidarity with others who identify with groups that have been historically marginalized (i.e., African Americans, Native Americans, Chicanos, and Puerto Ricans). To that extent, he or she would seek to maintain relationships with members of various underrepresented communities and provide support to them whenever necessary.

Conclusion

In this chapter, I have attempted to find theoretical explanations to help bring some understanding to the plight of graduate students and faculty of color in academe. In doing so, I have highlighted my own personal experience as a way in which to bring greater attention to the issues at hand. As I have attempted to show, the academy is fraught with inconsistencies and problems that negatively impact the lives of those who are at the mercy of those who hold power. While this is certainly a truism, it goes without saying that for a number of people, including members of oppressed groups like myself, the academy still offers the possibility of supporting liberatory work. While I can think of numerous examples of persons who have been depotentiated and ideologically incarcerated in their pursuit of their academic dreams, there are just as many examples of people who have been able to utilize the resources provided by academia as a way in which to highlight existing social inequalities and not self-annihilate. Some of them, many of whom are scholars of note, managed to do it without selling their souls. As a young academician, I look to those examples for inspiration and insight as I continue to struggle to do work that has the effect of illuminating inequalities and improving the lives of African Americans.

References

Aronowitz, A., & Giroux, H. (1985). *Education under siege: The conservative, liberal and radical debate over schooling.* South Hadley, MA: Bergin & Garvey.

Blassingame, J. W. (1972). *The slave community: Plantation life in the antebellum South.* New York: Oxford University Press.

Cordova, T. (1998). Colonialism in the academy. In C. Trujillo (Ed.), *Living Chicana theory.* Berkeley, CA: Third Woman Press.

Crenshaw, K. (1995). Race, reform and retrenchment: Transformation and legitmation in anti-discrimination law. In K. Crenshaw, N. Gotanda, G. Peller, & K. Thomas (Eds.), *Critical race theory: The key writings that formed the movement.* New York: The New Press.

Cross, T., & Slater, R. B. (Eds.). (1999). Why the '4 percent solution' won't restore racial diversity at selective California campuses. *The Journal of Blacks in Higher Education, 24.*

Cross, T. (1999). African American opportunities in higher education: What are the racial goals of the center for individual rights? In T. Cross & R. B. Slater (Eds.), *The Journal of Blacks in Higher Education, 23.*

DuBois, W. E. B. (1903/1982). *The souls of black folk.* New York: Penguin Books. (Original work published in 1903).

Freire, P. (1993). *Pedagogy of the oppressed.* New York: Continuum.

Genovese, E. D. (1976). *Roll, jordan, roll: The world the slaves made.* New York: Vintage Books.

Haymes, S. N. (1995). *Race, culture and the city: A pedagogy for Black urban struggle.* Albany, NY: SUNY Press.

Herrnstein, R. J., & Murray, C. (1994). *The bell curve: Intelligence and class structure in American life.* New York: Free Press.

Hoffman, J. (1984). *The Gramscian challenge: Coercion and consent in Marxist political theory.* Oxford: Basil Blackwell.

Kelley, R. G. (1996). *Race rebels: Culture, politics and the black working class.* New York: The Free Press.

Marable, M. (1996). *Speaking truth to power: Essays on race, resistance, and radicalism.* Boulder, CO: Westview Press.

Schneider, A. (1999). The academic path to pariah status. In C. Gwaltney (Ed.), *The Chronicle of Higher Education.* July 2, 1999.

Solorzano, D. G., & Solorzano, R. W. (1995). The Chicano educational experience: A framework for schools in Chicano communities. *Educational Policy, 9* (3).

Valencia, R. R. (Ed.). (1997). *The evolution of deficit thinking: Educational thought and practice.* London: Falmer Press.

White, D. G. (1985). *Ar'n't I a woman?* New York: Norton.

Wright, B. E. (1994). *The psychopathic racial personality and other essays.* (Rev. ed.) Chicago: Third World Press.

# Racialized Technology: Computers, Commodification, and "Cyber-race"

Jamel K. Donnor

One of the great tragedies of modern education is that most people are not taught to think critically. The majority of the world's people, those of the West included, are taught to believe rather than to think.
—Haki Madhubuti (1999)

When Beverly Gordon remarked that the twenty-first century would be marked by a "battle for control over who would educate minorities within Western societies and the nature of that education" (1990, p. 88), I do not think she or anyone else could have imagined what would be the role of information technologies in this fight. The U.S. Department of Education in 1999 hosted a forum entitled "The Future of Technology in Education: Envisioning the Future." The proceedings of the forum resulted in the identification of "emerging priorities" (p. 1). These priorities include: (1) All students will be technologically literate and responsible "cybercitizens," and (2) Education will drive the "E-learning economy." More recently, the International Society for Technology in Education, in collaboration with the Milken Exchange on Education Technology, published the "National Educational Technology Standards for Students" (1998). In it they postulate that "our educational system must produce technology capable kids."

With such "emerging priorities" in education come new pedagogical concerns and assumptions about how best to pursue this endeavor. For example, in what ways are information technologies ideologically and epistemologically biased? In discussions specifically addressing computers within the context of education, cultural theorists of technology (Bowers, 2000; Bigum, 1998; Bromley, 1998) assert that computers and computer-related discourse are firmly rooted within a Western discourse, which has no room for "others." Bromley sums it up best by stating, "Far from being neutral instruments, computers, like other technologies, are involved in many ways in the construction and use of power: in the way they are designed and built, in how they are sold and to whom, and in how they are used...They partake in an epistemology that promotes certain visions of knowledge and notions of who counts as a knowing subject" (1998, p. 2). Computers and the courseware they operate are not objective instruments; instead, they are involved in the construction and use of power in terms what counts as knowledge, and how knowledge gets constructed.

Race not only plays a significant role in the design of information technologies such as computers and computer-assisted courseware, but it is also essential to the understanding of the ways in which such "pedagogical devices"[i] are used in the education of African Americans. Technologies—such as those discussed here—that are created within Western societies are designed for sole purpose of maintaining the present status quo in education (Carter, 1998). The overarching goal of this essay is to articulate a re-conceptualization of information technologies within education by examining the dominant uses of computers in the education of African American children. This objective will be met in part through the use of the theoretical framework known as critical race theory (CRT).

Second, I argue that the concept of racialized property is a way to speak of information technologies themselves. I will support my argument (1) by drawing on examples that discuss the pedagogical uses of computers in education, and (2) by discussing the social relationships that are formed because of property. Regarding (2), property is more than a material object owned for private benefit. "Property," as it is employed here, is not only meant to refer to a way in which social relationships are shaped and determined through the use of information technologies. Property has more to do with information technologies being mechanisms that solidify the educational status quo.

Lastly, I will argue that one strategy for disrupting the ideological and epistemological biases of technology is to engage in what Ladson-Billings (1995) calls "culturally relevant pedagogy" (CRP). CRP's thorough examination of the computer-based education of African American students shows that there is nothing revolutionary about the methods employed in this education. Instead, the current ways in which computers are used in educational settings that are predominantly African American prepare the students to be consumers of information, rather than producers of it.

Critical Race Theory

Critical race theory (CRT) is a contemporary theoretical framework that criticizes white hegemonic discourse and power, analyzes the social disparities between races, and challenges popular notions of the construction and employment of race, racism, and racial power in American society. CRT is based on (1) incorporating the "absolute centrality of history and context" (Crenshaw, Gotanda, Peller, & Thomas, 1995); (2) rejecting notions of objectivity and neutrality; (3) recognizing that racism is endemic in U.S. Society (Bell, 1995); (4) employing a variety of theoretical traditions including Feminism, Marxism, post-structuralism, and critical legal studies to provide a more complete analysis of raced people (Tate, 1997); (5) incorporating one's "experiential knowledge" which posits "reality" is situational and socially constructed (Ladson-Billings, 1998, p. 11); and (6) working toward the elimination of racial oppression with the goal of ending all forms of oppression (Crenshaw, Delgado, Lawrence, & Matsuda, 1993).

CRT in this discussion serves to (1) historicize and contextualize these technologies, and (2) reject the dominant notion of neutrality and objectivity that proponents of these devices promulgate.

CRT in Education

Currently, there is a cadre of education scholars that have started the daunting task of applying CRT as a cutting-edge research paradigm for understanding and informing how race, racism, and racial power within education occurs and is structured. Ladson-Billings (1998) has cogently articulated how CRT explains the way race, racism, and racial power affect:(1) the educational experiences of African American students (i.e., instruction); (2) the educational outcomes of African Americans (i.e., assessment); (3) the allocation of resources (i.e., funding); (4) the content of the official school curriculum, thus making it a "culturally specific artifact designed to maintain a White supremacist master script"; and (5) school desegregation (pp.18–21). In addition, Ladson-Billings and Tate (1995) argue for a CRT perspective in education based on the following propositions: (1) race continues to be significant in the U.S.; (2) American society is premised on "property rights rather than human rights"; and (3) "the intersection of race and property creates an analytical tool for understanding inequity" (p. 45).

I will use CRT to argue that the pedagogical use of technology presents problems of actual use, as opposed to access. Such an understanding runs counter to the popular assumption that information technologies will improve the education of African Americans.

Racialized Property

Borrowing from Ladson-Billings and Tate's (1995) thesis of the "intersectionality of race and property" I submit that the way in which technology is used in the education of African Americans is such that the students should be viewed as *racialized property* (p. 48). I contend that in order to fully comprehend the race—both its formation and effects on material outcomes—in the U.S. one must understand the construction of property within this setting, and vice versa. In other words, race and property in America are intertwined concepts. According to Harris (1995) "the origin of property rights in the United States is rooted in racial domination" (p. 277). For example, she asserts that it was the "racialization of identity and the racial subordination of [B]lacks and Native Americans [that] provided the ideological basis for slavery and conquest...undergirding both was a racialized conception of property implemented by force and ratified by law" (p. 277). Chattel slavery relied first on the identification of people based on physical traits and lines of descent in order to determine who would be "free" and who would be enslaved (e.g., Africans). Second, it required the creation of a system to regulate the relationships of those who were "free" and those who were branded as slaves (e.g., slave codes). For instance, Watson (1989) writes that English slave law in America shaped the lives of the early African Americans in a manner in which "one might almost say that a slave belonged to every citizen—at least he was subordinate to every white" (p. 66). The slave codes enabled whites to purchase Africans for the purpose of labor, as well as dictate how whites were to control their property.

Therefore, the concept of racialization aids in the historicizing and contextualizing of computers. The concept also rejects the neutrality of these devices and their use, contending that their design and content are rooted in a Western epistemological system. More importantly, these devices also perpetuate that system via behavioral objectives and assessments imposed on the learner; they determine what counts as knowledge and how it is constructed.

"Property," for the purposes of this argument, does not refer to the private ownership or use of a tangible object or commodity (e.g., automobiles, land, homes) for personal or economic benefit per se. Although this tends to be the dominant way of understanding property, that understanding will be used as a platform upon which to put forth a more critical and expansive articulation of the concept. Property is not only a human construction designed to exclude and manipulate those who do not possess it; it is also an institution that legitimates these unequal relationships under the guise of being a natural phenomenon. According to Macpherson (1978) "the meaning of property is not static. The actual institution, and the way people see it, and hence the meaning they give to the word, all change over time...The changes are related to changes in the purposes which society or the dominant classes in society expect the institution of property to serve" (p. 1).

Pedagogical Use of Computers in the Education of Urban African Americans

Of the various educational uses of computer-assisted instruction, drill and practice is by far the most dominant approach (Harper, 1987; Kosakowski, 1998; Streibel, 1998). Within educational settings where the student body is predominantly African American, drill and practice is the primary mode of computer use (Carver, 1999). Becker and Ravitz (1998) suggest that in working class schools there tends to be an emphasis on "punctuality, neatness, obedience, and structure because these are the attributes conducive to subordinate labor" (p. 2). By contrast, they indicate that creativity, independence, and higher-level thinking skills are taught to students from middle-class and elite schools in order to prepare the students to maintain their socioeconomic status. As a pedagogical method, drill and practice employs the principle of trial and error (DeVaney, 1998). This principle is premised on two assumptions: (1) "students usually learn more, and learn more rapidly" (Kosakowski, 1998, p. 1); and (2) students can "master" the class material when allotted sufficient time (Streibel, 1998). The learner within this pedagogical paradigm is constructed as a consumer, and the learning process is rationally managed.

Drill and practice programs are based on behaviorist theories of learning, which emphasizes "stimulus, response, and reward" (Healy, 1998). Learning is framed within very individualistic terms and presumes the following: (1) the student has received previous instruction in the subject; (2) instruction is to follow a controlled, step-by-step linear sequence of sub-skills according to an algorithm embedded in the computer program (rote skill building, and pattern skill building; Streibel, 1998); (3) there is a right-wrong answer binary that exists within the logic of the context; (4) instructional interaction occurs in the form of a question-answer format; (5) immediate feedback on each student's response is considered positive; and (6) this approach "frees" the instructor from the more routine aspects of teaching (e.g., grading papers and recording student progress; Cuban, 1986). As a result, the students are not active participants in the learning process. Instead, they are told by the machine that their answer does not "compute." More importantly, this consumer relationship ensures the students' dependency on the machine because it knows more than they do. Thus the "relationship" between the student and the computer is grounded in consumption, because the students' abilities are judged against a set of predetermined expectations and outcomes.

The drill and practice approach in computer-assisted instruction is meant to supplement the teacher and the curriculum. The educational goal of drill and practice courseware is to provide practice for the basic skills the student has already learned. It is designed to put forth a query and elicit a response from the student. If the student does acquire new skills or learning, it is the result of trial and error instead of directed learning (Gagné, Wager, & Rojas, 1981).

Culturally Relevant Pedagogy

Culturally relevant pedagogy (CRP) in essence is a pedagogy that is diametrically opposed to the dominant methods used in the instruction of students of color. CRP not only contrasts with the mainstream teaching pedagogy of drill and practice, but is specifically committed to collective, not merely individual, empowerment" (Ladson-Billings, 1995b, p. 160). This pedagogical discourse is premised on the following three tenets: (1) "students must experience academic success"; (2) "students must develop and/or maintain cultural competence"; and (3) "students must develop a critical consciousness through which they challenge the status quo of the current social order" (p. 160). What begins to stand out immediately is that the learner within this discourse is a "producer" of knowledge rather than a passive consumer.

CRP discourse and knowledge is viewed as being in flux: It is shared, recycled, and constructed. Furthermore, teachers must be passionate about knowledge; they must scaffold or build bridges to facilitate learning. Finally, assessment must be multifaceted, incorporating multiple forms of excellence. This approach contrasts to drill and practice, where knowledge is not only fixed but also disconnected from the learner experientially (Ladson-Billings, 1995c, p. 481). The learner within the CRP paradigm is not merely a producer for the sake of producing, but also in order to meet the criteria of academic success, cultural competence, and critical consciousness (Ladson-Billings, 1995, p. 480). For example, this form of liberating education provides the student with heuristic tools and skills to critique ideas, by problematizing common-sense understandings (Gordon, 1994, p. 65). Again, such an approach runs counter to the superficial knowledge that gets produced through activities such as rote memorization, imparting "facts," and trial and error.

Woodson (1993/1990) had called pedagogical approaches such as drill and practice into question during the early part of the twentieth century. He not only questioned their relevancy to African Americans, but also noted that the methods were of little use to their survival. Moreover, pedagogies such as drill and practice were a means of controlling African Americans. According to Woodson (1990):

> ...[T] he educational system as it has developed both in Europe and America [is] an antiquated process which does not hit the mark...The so-called modern education, with all its defects, however, does others so much more good than it does the Negro, because it has been worked out in conformity to the needs of those who have enslaved and oppressed weaker peoples. (p. xii)

Furthermore, the computer education that is predominantly used in urban African American settings develops a procedural knowledge base. For example, mathematical problems are solved not as a result of trying to solve community problems, but rather by following memorized rules (Tate, 1995).

Perhaps the best example of the merging of the principles of CRP with information technology is "science, technology, and society education (STS)" (Waks, 1991, p. 195). STS has two general guidelines: (1) relevant concerns must be infused across the secondary curriculum, and (2) issues must be first seen as relevant by the students, and be "likely to require ongoing attention in students' adult lives" (Waks, 1991, p. 199). I believe the principles that ground this educational approach are a possible first step in making computer learning a culturally relevant enterprise since the approach takes the student and his or her community as a starting point.

Information technologies as they are used in the education of African American students in urban settings are nothing more than a fragmented projection of a white supremacist psyche. The history of African Americans' experience with technology has been one that has "proved perhaps irremediably devastating to their hopes, dreams, and possibilities" (Walton, 1999, p. 3). Walton also notes that it was Western technology that was responsible for the transatlantic slave trade. Europeans, Arabs, and eventually Americans exchanged Africans for "Western technological wizardry (e.g., firearms and metals), and those same slavers used guns, vastly superior to African weapons of the time" (p. 5).

One could argue that this is the case with information technologies because such devices break cultural boundaries (Willhelm, 1970). To speak of a cultural break is to refer to the increased role these machines have in shaping education, rather than the other way around. Therefore, it would be wrong to continue to place all of our "eggs in the access basket" without understanding what it is that we are getting access to. CRP is required in order to enable urban African American students to understand technology and in turn become producers in a postindustrial society. As DuBois (1973/2001) observed, the increased economic reliance on machines impacted the education of the African American. He writes, "ours is the double and dynamic function of tuning in with a machine in action so as neither to wreck the machine nor be crushed or maimed by it" (p. 104). What is being called to our attention is that education for African Americans first requires training as it relates to their position within society, and then a "technical" training of sorts to function within society (DuBois, 1973/2001).

References

Aptheker, H. (Ed.). (2001). *The education of black people: Ten critiques, 1906–1960 W. E. B. DuBois*. New York: Monthly Review Press.

Becker, H. J., & Ravitz, J. L. (1998). The equity threat of promising innovations: Pioneering Internet-connected schools. *Journal of Educational Computing Research, 19* (1), 1–26.

Bell, Jr., D. A. (1995). Racial realism. In K. Crenshaw, N. Gotanda, G. Peller, & K. Thomas (Eds.), *Critical race theory: The key writings that formed the movement* (pp. 302–309). New York: The New Press.

Bigum, C. (1998). Solutions in search of educational problems: Speaking for computers in schools. *Educational Policy, 12* (5), 586–601.

Bowers, C. A. (2000). *Let them eat data: How computers affect education, cultural diversity, and the prospects of ecological stability.* Athens, GA: University of Georgia Press.

Bromley, H. (1998). Introduction: Data-driven democracy? Social assessment of educational computing. In H. Bromley & M. W. Apple (Eds.), *Education/technology/power: Educational computing as a social practice* (pp. 1–28). Albany, NY: SUNY Press.

Carter, V. K. (1998). Computer-assisted racism: Toward an understanding of "cyberwhiteness." In J. L. Kincheloe, S. R. Steinberg, N. M. Rodriguez, & R. E. Chennault (Eds.), *White reign: Deploying whiteness in America* (pp. 269–284). New York: St. Martin's Griffin.

Carver, B. A. (1999). The information rage: Computers and young African American males. In V. C. Polite & J. E. Davis (Eds.), *African American males in schools and society: Practice and policies for effective education* (pp. 20–33). New York: Teachers College.

Crenshaw, K., Gotanda, N., Peller, G., & Thomas, K. (Eds.). (1995). *Critical race theory: The key writings that formed the movement.* New York: The New Press.

Cuban, L. (1986). *Teachers and machines: The classroom use of technology since 1920.* New York: Teachers College.

DeVaney, A. (1998). Can and need educational technology become a postmodern enterprise? *Theory into Practice, 37* (1), 72–80.

Gagné, R. M., Wager, W., & Rojas, A. (1981). Planning and authoring computer-assisted lessons. *Educational Technology, 21* (9), 17–26.

Gordon, B. M. (1990). The necessity of African American epistemology for educational theory and practice. *Journal of Education, 172* (3), 88–106.

Gordon, B. M. (1994). African American cultural knowledge and liberatory education: Dilemmas, problems, and potentials in a post-modern American society. In M. J. Shujaa (Ed.), *Too much schooling, too little education: A paradox of Black life in White societies.* Trenton, NJ: Africa World Press.

Harper, D. O. (1987). The creation and development of educational computer technology. In R. M. Thomas & V. N. Kobayashi (Eds.), *Educational technology: Its creation, development and cross-cultural transfer* (pp. 35–63). Oxford: Pergamon.

Harris, C. J. (1995). Whiteness as property. In K. Crenshaw, N. Gotanda, G. Peller & K. Thomas (Eds.), *Critical race theory: The key writings that formed the movement* (pp. 276–302). New York: The New Press.

Healy, J. M. (1998). *Failure to connect: How computers affect our children's minds—and what we can do about it.* New York: Touchstone.

International Society for Technology in Education & The Milken Exchange on Education Technology. (1998, June). *National educational technology standards for students.* Eugene, OR: Author.

Kosakowski, J. (1998). *The benefits of information technology* (ERIC Digest). Syracuse, NY: ERIC Clearinghouse on Information and Technology. (ERIC Identifier No. ED 420302).

Ladson-Billings, G. (1995a). Toward a theory of culturally relevant pedagogy. *American Educational Research Journal, 32* (3), 466–491.

Ladson-Billings, G. (1995b). But that's just good teaching! The case for culturally relevant pedagogy. *Theory into Practice, 43* (3), 159–165.

Ladson-Billings, G. (1995). Toward a theory of culturally relevant pedagogy. *American Educational Research Journal, 32* (3), 465–491.

Ladson-Billings, G., & Tate IV, W. F. (1995). Toward a critical race theory of education. *Teachers College Record, 97* (1), 47–68.

Madhubuti, H. (1999). As serious as first love: Building black independent institutions. In W. Mosley, M. Diawara, C. Taylor & R. Austin (Eds.), *Black genius: African American solutions to African American problems,* 51–86. New York, NY: Norton.

Matsuda, M., Lawrence, C. R. III, Delgado, R., & Crenshaw, K. W. (1995). *Words that wound: Critical race theory, assaultive speech, and the first amendment.* Boulder, CO: Westview Press.

Muffoletto, R. (1993). The expert teaching machine: Unpacking the mask. In R. Muffoletto & N. Knupfer (Eds.), *Computers in education: Social, political, and historical perspectives,* (pp. 91–103). Cresskill, NJ: Hampton Press.

Streibel, M. J. (1998). A critical analysis of three approaches to the use of computers in education. In L. E. Beyer & M. W. Apple (Eds.), *The curriculum: Problems, politics, and possibilities* (pp. 284–313). Albany, NY: SUNY Press.

Tate, W. F., IV. (1997). Critical race theory and education: History, theory, and implications. *Review of Research in Education, 22*, 195–243.

Tate, W. F., IV. (1995). Returning to the root: A culturally relevant approach to mathematics pedagogy. *Theory into Practice, 35* (3), 166–174.

U.S. Department of Education. (1999). *Proceedings of the Forum on Technology in Education: Envisioning the future.* Washington, DC: U.S. Government Printing Office.

Waks, L. J. (1991). Science, technology, and society education for urban schools. *Journal of Negro Education, 60* (2), 195–202.

Walton, A. (1999, January). Technology versus African Americans. *The Atlantic Monthly* [On-line]. Available: http://www.theatlantic.com/issues/99jan/aftech.htm.

Watson, A. (1989). *Slave law in the Americas.* Athens, GA: The University of Georgia Press.

Willhelm, S. M. (1970). *Who needs the Negro?* Cambridge, MA: Schenkman Publishing.

Woodson, C. G. (1990). *The mis-education of the Negro.* (6th ed.). Trenton, NJ: Africa World Press. (Original work published 1933)

---

[i] For a complete definition of this term read Bernstein's chapter on the social construction of pedagogic discourse.

PART TWO

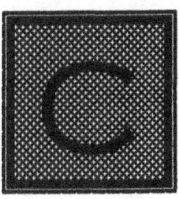

Curricular Hegemony: The Politics of Education and Schooling

ounded (Soul)diers in the Classroom: Qualifying the Black Teacher's Experience

Roderic R. Land

This paper is designed to give voice to African American teaching assistants that teach in a predominantly white institution. Using critical race theory as the theoretical framework, this study examines the dynamics of race and the racialized implications of power, voice, and authority in the classroom. Utilizing critical race methodology, this case study was conducted at a Midwestern university where data collection was done by in-depth phenomenological focus groups along with various other (in)formal discussions with the participants. Traditional scholarship involving teacher training and diversity in the classroom usually involves preparing white teachers to teach or "deal with" students of color while very little attention has been given to the African American teachers' encounters in the majority white class settings. Inasmuch as this essay unveils the experiences of African American instructors in predominantly white classrooms, it will prove to be useful and of increasing importance to the recruitment and retention of professors of color as we continue the struggle to shade the ivory tower.

Warfare is the greatest affair of state, the basis of life and death, the way to survival or extinction. It must be thoroughly pondered and analyzed.
—Sun-tzu

The aforementioned quote seems to be quite appropriate as African Americans appear to be in a state of warfare with the mission of gaining voice, power, and respect in academia and the greater society. For generations African Americans have been systematically marginalized and silenced while their white counterparts have gained and maintained strength, power, authority, and control. The parallel to warfare is proffered to both problematize and illuminate the critical nature of the African American condition and experience in academia. Additionally, much like warfare, education is "the basis of life and death" and "the way to survival or extinction."

Throughout the years, African Americans have suffered many casualties of this "war": the dropouts, push-outs, the racially tracked, the psychologically oppressed, the voiceless, etc. While these conditions are oftentimes linked to students, it is important to critically assess the condition of African American instructors in predominantly white institutions because the vitality of these instructors is important to the survival of the African American academic community.

The under-representation of African American faculty members is a pervasive and persistent problem in higher education. Recent data indicates that African Americans comprise only 4 percent of professors and associate professors in higher education compared to their white counterparts, who comprise 87 percent of tenured faculty members. African Americans represent a slightly larger piece of the instructor and lecturer pool at 7 percent, but this is bleak in comparison to their white peers, who comprise 82 percent of the pool (*The Chronicle of Higher Education*, 2000). If African Americans are consistently being maimed and wounded in the pipeline, this problem will not be alleviated and will only escalate to a point that threatens the very existence of the African American professorate.

As indicated by Allen and Epps (2000), higher education institutions are greatly influenced by the larger social, historical, and cultural context, which in turn creates barriers faced by African American instructors that frequently shape their relations with whites in general. Pervasive racist attitudes, systemic racism, as well differential access and power continue to limit positive experiences and educational opportunities for African Americans. This case study examines the experience of African American teacher assistants in a predominantly white, Midwestern, upper-tier institution. More specifically, drawing on critical race theory (CRT) as my theoretical framework, the essay examines the dynamics of race and the racialized implications of power, voice, and authority in the classroom. The primary goal is to bring forth the experiences and the war-like conditions in the classroom that these African American teaching assistants encounter.

CRT and the Primacy of Voice

According to Delgado (1990), people of color in our society speak with experiential knowledge that is framed by racism. This framework gives their stories a common structure, warranting the term "voice." Because African Americans, through discriminatory policies and practices, were made virtually invisible, their voices were relegated to a "culture of silence." This "culture of silence" served to create the impression of a seemingly common culture and deny the existence of cultural difference (Macedo, 1994). Moreover, there is a structured silence around the issue of how power, history, and culture are organized to secure the authority and interests of specific groups (Giroux, 1992). What is being promoted in the dominant language of culture is a hierarchical and undemocratic approach to social authority, and a politically regressive move to reassert American life with its historic spirit of Euro-centrism, racism, and patriarchy.

Voice is something that is not readily relinquished by those in positions of power. It is a pedagogical concept that alerts others to the fact that all discourse is situated historically and mediated culturally, and derives part of its meaning from interaction with others (McLaren, 1998). Accordingly, voice requires struggle and the understanding of both its possibilities and limitations. It should be understood that this term refers to the cultural grammar and background knowledge that individuals use to interpret and articulate experience. The most educators can do is create structures that would enable submerged voices to surface. A growing body of literature incorporates voice to highlight the "minority" experience in academia (e.g., Bell, 1989, 1992; Delgado, 1989, 1990; Crenshaw, 1995). These scholars, often referred to as critical race theorists, use parables, chronicles, narratives, counter-narratives, fiction, poetry, and revisionist history to illustrate the contradictions within certain policies and practices. Narratives provide the necessary background for understanding, feeling, and interpretation. Most of the scholarship on CRT focuses on the role of "voice" in bringing additional power to racial justice (Delgado, 1989). CRT links form and substance in scholarship through the use of voice or "defining one's own reality."

CRT situates race at the center of study and depends heavily on personal narratives and counter-narratives. CRT allows for the usually objective component of researching the experiences of people of color to be subjective. CRT starts with the understanding that racism is normal and saturates the fabric of American society. Because it is so entrenched in the fabric of our social order, it appears to be both normal and natural to the constituents of this culture (Ladson-Billings, 1998). The epistemological challenge that is being waged by some scholars of color is not solely about the functions, values, and ideas of racism; it is also about the nature of truth and reality. "Critical race theorist[s]…integrate their experiential knowledge, drawn from a shared history as 'other,' with their ongoing struggles to transform a world deteriorating under the albatross of racial hegemony" (Barnes, 1990). Thus the experience of oppression such as racism furthers the development of a CRT perspective (Ladson-Billings, 1994).

There are three key factors essential to CRT that Delgado (1989) lists for interjecting the viewpoints of people of color: (1) reality is socially constructed; (2) stories provide members of outgroups a method for mental self-preservation; and (3) the discussion between teller and listener can aid in overcoming ethnocentrism and the dysconscious way that many people view the world. The point of working in these racialized discourses and ethnic epistemologies is not simply to "color" the scholarship, but to challenge the hegemonic structures that maintain and perpetuate injustice and inequity (Ladson-Billings, 1994).

A reason that voice scholarship is necessary, as stated before, is to aid in a healthy mental preservation of marginalized groups. Members of subordinate groups may internalize the stereotypes that various segments of society have perpetuated to maintain their position of power (Crenshaw, 1988). Delgado (1989) contends that people of color have used stories throughout time to heal wounds caused by racial oppression. The testimony of one's situation allows for better understanding of how one came to be oppressed. This in turn makes it possible for the oppressed not to internalize their oppression.

Yet another reason for involving voice scholarship is for the potential influence it may have on the oppressor. It is often argued that most oppression does not register as oppression to the oppressor (Lawrence, 1987). The dominant group of society justifies its position of power with stock stories (Tate, 1994). These stories construct reality in a way that legitimizes power and privilege. The testimonies by people of color are used to counter the claims of the oppressor.

Theoretically, to effect change Foucault (1980) contends that analyses of power should begin at the local level where it is exercised at its point of application in and through the social relations that produce subjectivity. By analyzing these practices at the local level, it is possible to map out those larger discourses and social practices that are embedded in the mechanisms of power in these local contexts (Duesterberg, 1999). In this way, it becomes possible to create counter-discourses that legitimize and validate the views of those who are oppressed.

CRT has primarily been used as a tool to critically analyze questions of law. Until recently, it has maneuvered its way into different areas of study, more specifically, the discipline of education. CRT in education begins with the premise that race and racism are endemic and permanent. It challenges the traditional claims the educational system and its institutions make toward objectivity, meritocracy, color-blindness, race neutrality, and equal opportunity (Solorzano, 2001). As noted by Calmore (1992) critical race theorists view these claims as a camouflage for the self-interest, power, and privilege of dominant groups. Furthermore, the utility of CRT in education lies in its recognition that the experiential knowledge of students, faculty, and staff of color is critical to understanding, analyzing, and teaching about racial subordination in the field of education (Solorzano, 2001). Solorzano further contends that CRT in education uses a multidisciplinary knowledge base ranging from ethnic studies, women's studies, sociology, history, law, and other fields to better understand racism, sexism, and classism in education. Drawing on a myriad of disciplines, epistemologies, and research approaches, CRT provides the opportunity for an in-depth analysis of racialized oppression.

Critical Race Methodology

The approach to critical race methodology begins with an examination, conceptualization, operationalization, and analysis of a set of concepts, ideas, and experiences (Solorzano, 2001). In order to unpack, develop, and give meaning to these concepts, ideas, and experiences one must explore various avenues. The way one defines and interprets different concepts and experiences depends on the experiences of the researchers themselves. Drawing on the work of Strauss and Corbin (1990) and Bernal (1998), Solorzano (2001) borrows two concepts: theoretical sensitivity and cultural intuition. Strauss and Corbin define theoretical sensitivity as:

> ...the personal qualities of the researcher. It indicates an awareness of the subtleties of meaning of data. Theoretical sensitivity refers to the attribute of having insight, the ability to give meaning to the data, the capacity to understand, and capability to separate the pertinent from that which isn't. (1990, pp. 41–42)

Delgado Bernal's notion of "cultural intuition" differs slightly from theoretical sensitivity in that it "extends one's personal experience to include collective experience and community memory, and points to the importance of participants engaging in the analysis of data" (pp. 563–564). Thus, cultural intuition is "a complex process that is experiential, intuitive, historical, personal, collective, and dynamic" (pp. 567–568).

Relying on my own theoretical sensitivity and Bernal's (1998) concept of cultural intuition, and incorporating the tenets of CRT, I began to develop and qualify the African American teachers' experience from four different sources[i]: the data gathered from the interviewing process itself; any existing literature on the topic of study; my own professional experiences as an African American teaching assistant; and my personal experience as an African American teaching assistant. I searched through the data looking for patterns, themes, and examples of concepts to highlight.

I began my inquiry by analyzing my own experiences and interactions with white students in my class. I started asking myself critical questions: How do I deal with racial topics in a classroom that is approximately 85 percent white, and how do I think my white students will receive the information that is presented and discussed? Will they challenge my authority as an instructor because I am what they would consider "the other" or will they challenge me because of my status as a teaching assistant? Then I began to wonder what other African American teaching assistants who were teaching a class that was predominantly white were experiencing. I began to do a library search to find out what literature was out there to aid me to further conceptualize this issue before I began my quest to inquire about other teaching assistants' experiences. However, I found very little information on the subject. There was extensive research done on student teacher interaction, pre-service programs dealing with white teachers teaching and/or "dealing with" students of color, recommendations for successfully teaching African American students, and the African American professorate's experience of being junior faculty and dealing with the politics of getting tenure—all which are important topics that need to be discussed. However, I was quite disturbed that, given the statistics on African Americans on faculty, there was no research done on the experiences of African American teaching assistants.

An area of the literature that is worth noting is the dialogue centered on the notion of difference. The way difference is constructed in this body of literature is primarily focused on social difference (Bloom, Davis, & Hess, 1965; Bettleheim, 1965; Davis, 1948; Ornstein & Vairo, 1968). More specifically, social difference implies various themes such as race (Goldberg, 1993; Gould, 1984; Omi & Winant, 1994; Smedley, 1993), class (Marx & Engels, 1888; Moynihan, 1969; Myrdal, 1962; Parsons, 1947; Wilson, 1987), and gender (De Beauvoir, 1952; Epstein, 1988; Gayle, 1975; Hubbard, 1990). As noted by Ladson-Billings (1998), the construction of difference is a key discursive practice for justifying the need to "prepare teachers for student diversity." Within the context of her chapter, Ladson-Billings quotes Allison Davis, an African American social psychologist:

> In order to help the child learn, the teacher himself must discover the reference points from which the child starts...In every so-called "lesson," the pupil always has something important to tell the teacher; he may tell her what he has already learned that either aids or obstructs the new learning the teacher seeks to instigate. (pp. 1–2)

This passage is worthy of note because of the possible implications it has for the way students themselves construct difference in their interactions with teachers, instructors, and professors. Although Davis defined difference as a social class construct, racial differences and how we come to know or formulate, internalize, and give meaning to these differences cannot go unmentioned.

According to Omi and Winant (1994) race is a concept that signifies and symbolizes social conflicts and interests by referring to different types of human beings. It is a socio-historical process by which these categories are created, transformed, and destroyed. Furthermore, the categories denote differences in skin color, or other racially coded characteristics, to explain social differences.

Thus, I began holding extensive conversations with other African American teaching assistants who, like myself, taught a predominantly or all white class, and conversed with various faculty of color whose class demographics are similar. Just as I expected, common themes began to emerge. Some of the comments offered by respondents were: "I think some students find it difficult to accept my authority"; "There are times when it is difficult for me to go back into the classroom and teach knowing how they view or feel about me"; "It's very frustrating for me when they just don't want to accept the facts and then think that I am a racist."

After extensive conversations both formal and informal, I established a time to conduct a tape-recorded, in-depth phenomenological focus group. This focus group was used to collect the narratives of three African American female teaching assistants and one African American male teaching assistant at an upper-tier institution. I also conducted five phone interviews and distributed eleven online survey questionnaires with open-ended questions. All respondents were African American, fifteen were female, and five were male. The analysis of the testimonies suggests that each person's experience is unique; however, there are some commonalities. Most participants feel that their race does play a major role in their interactions with students. They identify gender as having an influence as well. Although I feel that gender is a major issue, this paper does not make the attempt to examine this variable, which is a limitation of this analysis.

The Initial Estimations: Setting the Stage

Being at a predominantly white, Midwestern, upper-tier, research-one university can prove to be quite challenging and intimidating when most of the students who attend are from a white, suburban, middle-class background and you hail from an urban or rural, black or minority, lower or middle-class background. In this setting, different ideologies, values, and philosophies meet head on and are often in conflict with each other. In assessing the makeup of their classes, respondents reported that most of their students are conservative in their thinking and usually open up and share their conservative ideas more voluntarily after the first couple of weeks. Some also reported that most of their students had little to no interaction with African Americans prior to attending college. Lastly, most of the respondents want to be future educators. Given the description of the classrooms, they have the possibility of co-opting the discussion of race and/or setting the stage for a good dialogue. Furthermore, in light of the demographics given, one must question where the students are getting their perceptions about race, how these perceptions are formed, and whether racial stereotypes will become a major factor in the experiences of the African American teaching assistants.

As Essed (1997) stated, those who are the targets of racist stereotypes usually face a range of experiences where they are constructed as "other," excluded, and made to feel inferior. Teachers that are seen as "others" by their students are more likely to encounter these various obstacles in the classroom (Vargas, 1999). Not only is this social construction of the "other" problematic, but teachers of color oftentimes find that students who buy into the colorblind ideology can be equally problematic and sometimes worse. Saying that one does not see color or that one is not conscious of color has served as a mechanism for the justification of white privilege and power. It indicates one buys into a theory of meritocracy. Furthermore, it implies that one is not color conscious, when in fact one has to be color conscious to prevent stereotypes associated with different race and ethnic groups from flooding their psyche in the initial contact.

One respondent remarked that dealing with a student who claims not to see color[ii] "can be quite frustrating. I'm not saying that color is everything or the only thing that matters, but when you fail to see the color of my skin, you fail to see me and you fail to see or acknowledge the struggles of my people." Another respondent offered the following:

> I've had that same question posed to me and a student said that they don't see race and I responded by saying that you may not have to see race. It hasn't been

structured for you that way in society because you are of the dominant race. And you are reaping the benefits of society. You are not challenged in a lot of aspects of your life as it relates to your racial background. When you are apart of the dominant society, you are viewing things from that dominant lens and you don't see other perspectives. And not even to call them wrong. That's just the background that they grew up with, it's more so ignorance.

Students have this attitude of it's not me, it's them. I'm not the racist one. It's those other folks that we are seeing in the videos or reading about. It's not me it's them. That's the perception that they have of themselves. They don't see themselves as being racist. Not even saying that they are racist, but sometimes through the experiences, they do not realize that the things that they are saying, their thought process, and their actions have racist implications.

Combating a colorblind ideology and teaching in a predominantly white class can make it challenging to discuss issues of race. Those students who claim not to see color run the risk of imposing Euro-centric, white culture on others. Tatum (1992) outlines three reasons why students are resistant to discussing and learning about race and racism:

1. Race is considered to be a taboo topic, especially in diverse settings.
2. Many students, regardless of race, have been socialized to think of the U.S. as a just society.
3. Many students, more specifically white students, initially deny personal prejudice; they may recognize the impact of racism on other people's lives, but fail to acknowledge its impact on their own and how they benefit from it.

Tatum's work reveals that some students are resistant to developing a knowledge base and/or strategies to deal with racism.

Research in cross-cultural communication has shown that those receiving commands or information are more receptive to a speaker perceived by them as relatively similar and sharing a similar language or mode of communication (Delpit, 1995; Irvine, 1990; McCarthy, 1993). The more students perceive that the teacher's attitudes and values are similar to theirs, the greater probability the teacher will have of influencing the students' attitudes, values, and ultimately behavior. Interesting enough, this phenomenon works both ways. The following quotes shed light how teachers who feel their views are different from those of their students deal with issues surrounding race:

> Carefully, very carefully. Be honest, and tread carefully. It's kind of difficult for me because my students don't want to hear the truth. It's like what Jack Nicholson said, "You can't handle the truth!" They don't want to hear it...They don't say right off that they're disbelieving or that they feel uncomfortable—they just kind of sit and nod and listen and every now and then I'll get that idealistic person that says, "Why can't we all just get along?" I don't know; it's difficult to get the point across to help them to understand this is how it is and I'm not just making it up. And they usually don't want to talk about issues of race. I don't know how they plan to be future educators and want to avoid that topic.

Another respondent had this to offer:

> Even though some of my students can be categorized as "liberal" or "conservative," I challenge them both the same, because both arguments have their own set of politics. So I try to...I don't necessarily know how successful I am because I have my own set of biases, but I try to challenge both sides and try to get them to understand the different dynamics within each setting. So I try to present both arguments and potential arguments from both sides. I think that arguing race issues becomes a matter of critically analyzing from various points of view so that they get that understanding that it's not a simplified answer.

The teacher's voice normally carries an authoritative power and reflects the values, ideologies, and structuring principles that teachers use to understand and mediate the histories, cultures, and subjectivities of their students (McLaren, 1998). As aforementioned, the teacher's voice takes on an authoritative quality that may sometimes silence the students' voice. As an instructor, more specifically an African American instructor, it is important to remain objective in discussing issues of race with white students.

> ...[A]s an instructor I try to remain objective with the question especially when I try to challenge both sides. Because once your view is strongly out there as an instructor it's going to close off some of your students to talk about certain issues because they think that the instructor may look down on them because they disagree with what I'm saying and I want it to be an open dialogue, even if it's one that I don't agree with, so that everyone can see their own perspectives. And I continue to try to get them to think outside their own box.

The oppressive power of a teacher's authoritative voice can be seen in instances of what Bourdieu (1977) refers to as symbolic violence. Symbolic violence is exercised when a teacher presents his or her values and/or views so as to challenge and disconfirm the experiences and beliefs of his or her students. To make this concept race-specific, Kailin (1999) contends that most white teachers operate from an impaired consciousness about racism. Furthermore, Kailin argues that a majority of white teachers "blamed the victim," citing blacks as the cause of racism.

Drawing on my own experience, I can remember at times it seemed as if I had my hands tied behind my back. Even when I presented compelling information about the conditions of African Americans and how some of these conditions came to be, some students still held on to the same views. After I challenged both sides of the issue while keeping my position neutral, some students still maintained their original position, despite witnessing that the position I favor is clearly more logical and compelling. At that point I truly believe that it is just a matter of comfort for them.

Waging War

Values, attitudes, and ideologies greatly influence the experience of African Americans in academic environments. As stated before, when teachers are in the position of the "other," they are more likely to face barriers in the classroom. They are confronted with different challenges that make it difficult to simply do their job. When these challenges become an everyday struggle, their motivation, their desire, and their willingness begins to falter and their soul becomes weary. To illuminate this discomfort, frustration, and weariness I draw on a dialogue that took place during the in-depth phenomenological focus discussion[iii]:

Jamila: The most challenging thing is to go into the classroom, and get revved up and excited or try to get excited about teaching this information to future educators who quite frankly don't want to be there, don't care what I have to say, and if this class wasn't required wouldn't take it. So it's challenging for me to go in there and try to get them to open their minds and be willing to accept this information and try to use it to improve them as individuals and as future educators. You know they get the information and all they do is spit it back up on a page later on for an exam just to show that I've read or I came to lecture or discussion. It's challenging for me...sometimes I just want to shake them and say, look, this is reality. This is not something that Walt Disney made up or something. This is reality and you need to be able to deal with this and understand these situations and understand the students that you will be coming in contact with. You are going to be doing more harm than good—you're going to just add more fuel to the fire. We don't need you! Go away! But I can't do that. They're in the program and they want to be there, so that's the most challenging thing to try to get them to actually care about what they're learning and have an open mind and get them to realize that it's important that they learn this information.

Safiya: I think one of my most challenging things has been based on what I said earlier: trying to get them to understand that African Americans didn't just exist in this society post civil rights. Reading and writing was going on prior to 1619, the founding of Jamestown and so forth. Once again, I think my biggest challenge is trying to get my students to understand that African Americans have made significant contributions to this country. Unfortunately they have not been recognized. It's important to them to understand it.

Zakiya: My biggest challenge about teaching at the collegiate level is the way the students viewed me. They always challenged my views or always gave me stern looks throughout the class during discussion. And what would really make it uncomfortable for me is when I got feedback, anonymous feedback from the students to see what they were saying about me. My biggest challenge was going back to teach these same group of students knowing how they felt about me, and how they felt about me as an instructor: to be up there hypocritically almost and try to still get them to talk about these issues and knowing where they stood on these issues and how they viewed me as an instructor.

Jamila: As far as the stern looks and being challenged, maybe I'm used to the stern looks because I taught at another university before and they were worse. So maybe I'm used to the looks, but the challenging part of going back, I had to deal with this summer and this semester. During the spring I had two sections to teach. The students, I wouldn't call them deceitful, but in the classroom everything seemed to be going OK. They didn't agree with everything I said—well most of what I said, but they never came across as just being resentful of having to be there, and then I get that anonymous feedback on the evaluations. And you know suddenly I'm this racist person and I blame them and all other white people in the world for racism. You know it was just all this stuff that had never been said. I was just presenting them the information that had to be presented over the duration of the course. It was challenging for me to have to think that I have to go back to this. Even though it was a new group of students, I couldn't help but to wonder if they all were going to come in with this same mindset of "I don't want to hear this, and if you are telling me this, it is something wrong with you, not society, not me." And the resistance that I meet is unbelievable. This was challenging for me.

Zakiya: I would say that "resistance" is a key word about what you are talking about. They're very resistant. We were talking in class about how Columbus is taught in schools and some of them were learning for the very first time—not that he didn't discover America I thinks that's pretty much mainstream now—but how much of a mercenary he was throughout the films we watched. They were really resistant in receiving that information. And if they were that resistant in receiving that information then I know they wouldn't in turn teach that information to their students. We teach social studies in our class as a social justice type of framework and more of an inquiry approach, where the students ask the questions, and they are not used to that framework at all. They ask how you do it. They just don't get it.

Regardless of the nature of the challenge encountered, if it is persistent and becomes a burden, the end result will inevitably be the same. The respondents in the dialogue clearly unveil their burdens of being challenged and begin to exhibit the wounds inflicted upon them by their experiences in the classroom. Furthermore, the resistance and challenges the respondents meet in these types of classroom settings appear to have deleterious effects on the number of graduate students in the pipeline to become faculty members at the type of universities in which they graduate from. While CRT provides the avenue for these narratives to surface, it may also lay the foundation to effect change.

Military Combat: Fighting for the Class

There are several important feelings that enter into the dialogue of racism. Drawing on the work of Blumer (1958), I would like to limit myself to three basic types of feelings that seem to be persistent within the context of this study. They are (1) a feeling of superiority; (2) the feeling that people of color are inherently different and alien; and (3) a feeling of ownership to certain areas of privilege and advantage[iv] (Blumer, 1958). The narratives of the African American teaching assistants, as evinced in the prior section and later in this section, are replete with these themes.

Compounding these feelings are racial microaggressions, or unconscious and subtle forms of racism. Although they are pervasive, racial microaggressions are seldom investigated. Little is known about microaggressions, and yet these subtle forms of racism have a major impact on the lives of African Americans. Racial microaggressions have consequences that oftentimes leave African Americans struggling with feelings of frustration, self-doubt, and isolation (Solorzano, 2000). Jamila mentions, "…[F]or me I go between frustrated, helpless, and hopeless to just really I just don't give a damn. I go between those because the frustration is on so many different levels." Usually, these acts are so subtle they go unnoticed by the perpetrator or oppressor.

What appears to be a major issue that the respondents have to deal with is the student playing out the role of the oppressor. Although there is—in theory—a hierarchy where the instructor has the authority, at times that authority is revoked. "I think that students in their mind," as noted by one respondent,

> see us as just little nobody peons and we don't know anything and they don't have to respect us or our authority. It's our class! We're grading the papers; we're assigning the grade. We're the one who know you and see you the most. And yet, they have no problem with going over our heads—before talking to us about something—and going to the instructor to bitch and moan about nothing.

After reviewing the data, I found this theme to be similar to one of Jamila's experiences. Jamila offered, "Sometimes I feel as if it's literally their class. They are running the class and what we think as educators trying to teach them our feelings about how they should be graded is not valued and it's very hard to deal with.

"I've had a situation where I had some students who—I'm trying to help them out mind you. I gave them an exam and there was a question on there that I thought was too difficult for them. It wasn't worded in a way that couldn't be readily understood especially for freshmen, sophomores, and maybe even a junior in undergrad. I wasn't trying to minimize their ability but I just thought that it might be a little challenging for them. So, I told them, 'If you don't want to deal with the question, don't. As a matter of fact you can pretend like it's not even there and deal with the other one.' And I asked them who was looking at this question and they were like nobody—nobody raised their hands. And so I said OK fine, cool, whatever.

"A week and a half later, I get an e-mail from the instructor saying that 'some of the students came to me complaining saying that you told them that they couldn't answer that question and that you wouldn't grade it and they felt very upset because they wanted to answer the question.' I was sitting up there thinking, OK; I'm trying to help you out. As it is I've already seen their writing. I'm trying to help you to get a good grade on this exam. And I felt that they undermined all my authority and I really resented that. And I went back to class next week and said, 'Look, when you have a problem with me you bring it to me. Do not go over my head! There is such a thing as chain of command!' I was quite heated to say the least and I have had that happen a couple of times. I'm the teacher—you're interacting with me once a week as far as discussion; I'm the one who does the grading. Come talk to me about it. Don't go over my head."

Surrendering Arms: Teachers (De)Tracked

In the final section I highlight the dialogue that transpired in the interview. The testimonies of the respondents speak for themselves better than any theory can theorize. This discussion reinforces the notion of the student as the oppressor, which is the main catalyst for pushing these instructors out of the professorate track. In analyzing this dialogue, one cannot help but to take note of the wounds that are created that eventually lead the respondents with a displeasing perception of teaching at the collegiate level.

Power, voice, and authority, the components an instructor—in theory—possesses over their class, are systematically deconstructed, devalued, and de-legitimized. The use of CRT creates the platform to analyze an instructor's marginalized feelings and allows the voices of these wounded (soul)diers to speak for themselves.

At this juncture of the interview, an inquiry about the respondents' overall experience led to the following dialogue. They had this to say:

Safiya: I can't classify my experiences as being good or bad. I would have to classify it as a learning experience. It's one that has taught me a lot. First I would definitely agree with Jamila that it has caused me to shake my head in terms of knowing the types of educators we are going to have in the future. And the types are not necessarily "bad" educators—bad meaning unable to teach—but educators whose views are very narrow in perspective. That's what frightens me. So in that regard, I'm very saddened by that notion, but I guess it takes different types to make the world go round. Secondly, it has caused me to know that my own skills in communication have to be of such quality to somehow convince the most narrow-minded person to reconsider things, because if the goal is to change or recreate and so forth I have to be responsible for my own set of skills, so the issues and the needs don't go unmet. So it becomes my responsibility, my very endowed and unique responsibility, to again make conscious efforts to remove myself from it and allow the rational and logical perspective to take over because if I don't, then the message is lost.

Zakiya: I would have to say that it has been an awakening experience, and I'm glad that I've had the experience. There are a few individuals in the class that have expressed growth and gratitude from the information they're receiving.

I would have to say that I was ignorant when I first started because I thought that all this information is so good; it's a lot of information that I didn't get before I started teaching and part of my personal goals was to eventually teach at the collegiate level, to teach students who are going or wanting to be teachers and bring policy into that. And so I was glad that I was able to meet that goal, but I didn't expect the students not to be receptive of the information. Part of the reason—my advisor and I were just talking about this today—this is part of the reason why I don't want to teach. I don't want to be a professor, particularly at a white college. I said if I ever do teach at a collegiate level again, it's going to be at a HBCU, and it will be for folks who are in the teacher education program.

Even today he (my advisor) knows how passionate I am about not wanting to teach on a collegiate level. And when I was in his office today, he said, "Zakiya!" And he starts shaking his head and I was like, "What? What?" He starts telling me I got so many job offers right now, please consider being a professor. He knows that I'm doing the admin and policy track where there are a lot of jobs opening up in that field and he literally showed me about fifteen different postings that I could apply for. He told me folks are calling him asking for females or African Americans to go into the program. And he tells them that he has one but she doesn't want to be a professor. And he told me that he has said that over and over to folks and I couldn't believe him but he doesn't know part of the reason why I don't want to do it, but this is the reason why: not only from the pressures you get in academia of the research and all that stuff, for the minimum amount of money, but also the lack of gratitude you get from your students and the lack of respect you get from your students and just how I might as well be a TA if I'm a professor—they look at me the same way. I think that that reception would be different at a black college teaching all black students and that's my love, that's what I want to do anyway eventually, after I do this policy stuff. I want to have a hand in creating tomorrow's teachers that are African American. I know that they will appreciate all the experiences that I have had in the different facets of the educational field and walk away like, OK...yeah.

Jamila: Just to piggyback off of what they are saying, definitely to agree with Safiya and Zakiya: It was a learning experience and a growing experience in the fact that it did help to show me what I am not cut out for. And for that I have to say thank God. Better to learn this now than to get out with my degree and go in some job that I signed a contract and I hate it, and I'm dealing with the same experiences. And I agree with Zakiya that this has solidified for me that I am not meant to be a professor; I am not meant to be in a classroom. Particularly at a white institution that is research intensive. That's not for me because I feel like for me to fully make use of this degree, and whatever gifts and/or talents God has bestowed upon me, I need to be some place where I'm going to be effective and I can make not a whole lot of difference, but some difference—a place where I can help and give back to my community. And just seeing these future educators we have coming out—I'm not suggesting—as Safiya said—that they're bad but limited in some regards as far as the way they are thinking or what have you. I am more than certain that I want to establish my own school where I can hand pick my teachers, curriculum, everything. This experience has definitely shown me that I am not cut out for this. It has kind of shown me a path that I have never seen before.

Zakiya: Can I ask a question dealing with what Jamila is saying?
RL: Yeah!
Zakiya: OK now think of what Jamila and I are saying as far as we don't think that we don't want to teach these future teachers that are all white because of the reception that we are getting—not just because of that but that's one reason. But, if we don't, if it's not us who's teaching them, then who else? So how is that going to help as far as like, at least now they are getting exposed to that information whether they chose to accept it or not. Maybe they will later on down the line say like, "Oh, I see what they were saying and I see it playing out in everyday life now." But if we're not doing it, then who's going to do it?

Jamila: I don't know. I guess like I said we're not all cut out for it, but Safiya just said this is helping her as far as her approaching things. And maybe you know she'll deal with her approach and get across to more. My approach ain't working. And the way it's looking now, it's not going to change. I am what I am and it's just not working and I can work so much better with students who I can be real with. I feel that my Upward Bound students can appreciate it. I have thought about that though; if I leave and everyone else feels the same way that I do, then what's going to happen? Not to get all spiritual and everything, but I feel that God calls people to do different things. He don't want Jamila to do this. He just don't. He might call you back later. But Jamila? Nah!

Conclusion

In light of the experiences conveyed in this article, the condition and the number of African American faculty at the collegiate level will continue to be less than promising. Fortunately or unfortunately, there isn't a standing "teacher education" program for college professors or any assigned space for African American teachers to articulate their experiences of teaching in predominantly white classroom settings. It is often said that being black in America comes with three different experiences: Knowing what it means to be black, knowing what it means to be white, and knowing what it means not to be white. But these experiences do not safeguard African American teachers, instructors, and professors from the attacks they receive from their white students in a hostile environment. Although the experiences may better prepare the African American instructor for "dealing with" and/or teaching white students, the instructor is still susceptible to the adverse affects of working in such environments.

If we are to effect change, we cannot continue to allow these voices to be relegated to a culture of silence. M. L. King, Jr. stated, "When people are mired in oppression, they realize deliverance only when they have accumulated the power to enforce change" (King, 1967). CRT has created the platform for marginalized voices to be heard, and we must mobilize around counter-narratives to foster change. CRT theorists attempt to insert the viewpoints of people of color, derived from a shared history of oppression, into their efforts to reconstruct a society that is falling under the burden of systemic racism and racial hegemony. We must continue the struggle to have these experiences and narratives represented in academic discourse. They provide the window for society to view the conditions of African Americans from an African American perspective. These stories paint an ugly picture of the racial crisis in America in general and in academia specifically, one that white Americans refuse to see and acknowledge. Not only do we need to talk about voice and narratives in terms of CRT, but we also have to listen and then act on the voices that are speaking through narrative.

References

Allen, W., & Epps, E. (2000). The Black academic faculty status among African Americans in U.S. higher education. *Journal of Negro Education, 69* (1/2).

Barnes, R. (1990). Race consciousness: The thematic content of racial distinctiveness in critical race legal scholarship. *Harvard Law Review, 103,* 1864–1871.

Bell, D. (1989). The final report: Harvard's affirmative action allegory. *Michigan Law Review, 87,* 2382–2410.

Bell, D. (1992). *Faces at the bottom of the well: The permanence of racism.* New York: Basic Books.

Blumer, H. (1958). Race prejudice as a sense of group position. *Pacific SociologicalReview, 1* (1), 3–7.

Bourdieu, P. (1977). Symbolic Power. *Critique of Anthropology, 13,* 77–85.

Calmore, J. (1992). Critical race theory, Archie Shepp, and fire music: Securing an authentic intellectual life in a multicultural world. *Southern California Law Review, 65,* 2129.

The Chronicle of Higher Education (2000). The nation: Faculty and staff. (2000–2001 Almanac).

Crenshaw, K. (Ed.). (1995). *Critical race theory: The key writings that formed the movement.* New York: The New Press.

De Beauvoir, S. (1952). *The second sex.* New York: Knopf.

Delgado, R. (1989). Storytelling for oppositionists and others: A plea for narrative. *Michigan Law Review, 87,* 2411–2441.

Delgado, R. (1990). When a story is just a story: Does voice really matter? *Virginia Law Review, 76,* 95–111.

Delgado Bernal, D. (1998). Using a Chicana feminist epistemology in educational research. *Harvard Educational Review, 68,* 555–582.

Delpit, L. (1995). *Other people's children: Cultural conflict in the classroom.* New York: The New Press.

Duesterberg, L. (1999). Theorizing race in the context of learning to teach. *Teachers College Record, 100* (4), 751–775.

Epstein, C. (1988). *Deceptive distinctions: Sex, gender, and the social order.* New York: The Russell Sage Foundation.

Essed, P. (1997). Racial intimidation: Sociopolitical implications of the usage of racist slurs. In S. H. Riggins (Ed.), *The language and politics of exclusion: Others in discourse*. Thousand Oaks, CA: Sage.

Foucault, M. (1980). *Power/Knowledge: Selected interviews and other writings, 1972–1977*. New York: Pantheon Books.

Gayle, R. (1975). The traffic in women. In R. Reiter (Ed.), *Towards an anthropology of women*. New York: Monthly Review Press.

Giroux, H. (1992). *Border crossings: Cultural workers and the politics of education*. New York: Routledge.

Gould, S. (1984). *The mismeasure of man*. New York: Norton.

Hollins, E. (1994). The burden of acting White revisited: Planning school success rather than explaining school failure. Paper presented at the American Education Research Association, New Orleans, LA.

Hubbard, R. (1990). *The politics of women's biology*. New Brunswick, NJ: Rutgers University Press.

Irvine, J. (1990). *Black students and school failure*. Westport, CT: Greenwood.

Kailin, J. (1999). How White teachers perceive the problem of racism in their schools: A case study in "liberal" Lakeview. *Teachers College Record, 100* (4), 724–750.

King, M. L. (1967). *Where do we go from here: Chaos or community?* New York: Harper & Row.

Ladson-Billings, G. (1994). Racialized discourses and ethnic epistemologies. In Denzin, N., & Lincoln, Y. (Eds.), *Handbook of qualitative research*. Philadelphia: Temple University Press.

Ladson-Billings, G. (1999). Preparing teachers for diverse student populations: A critical race theory perspective. *Review of Research in Education, 24*, 211–247.

Lawrence, C. (1987). The id, the ego, and equal protection: Reckoning with unconscious racism. *Stanford Law Review, 39*, 317–388.

Marx, K., & Engels, F. (1888). Manifesto of the Communist Party. In R. C. Tucker (Ed.), *The Marx-Engels Reader*. New York: Norton.

Macedo, D. (1994). *Literacies of power*. Boulder, CO: Westview Press.

McCarthy, C., & Crichlow, W. (Eds.). (1993). *Race identity and representation in education*. New York: Routledge.

McLaren, P. (1998). *Life in schools: An introduction to critical pedagogy in the foundations of education.* New York: Longman.

Moynihan. (1969). *On understanding poverty.* New York: Basic.

Myrdal, G. (1962). *The challenge to affluence.* New York: Pantheon.

Omi, M., & Winant, H. (1994). *Racial formations in the United States.* New York: Routledge.

Weber, M. (1947). *The theory of social and economic organization.* New York: Free Press.

Sawyer, R. (1994). *The art of war.* New York: Barnes & Noble.

Smith, D. (1987). *The everyday world as problematic: A feminist sociology.* Boston: Northeastern Press

Solorzano, D. (2000). Critical race theory, racial microaggressions, and campus racial climate: The experiences of African American college students. *Journal of Negro Education, 69* (1/2), 60–73.

Solorzano, D., & Yosso, T. (2001). Critical race and LatCrit theory and method: Counter-storytelling. *Qualitative Studies in Education, 14* (4), 471–495.

Tatum, B. (1992). Talking about race, learning about racism: The application of racial identity development in the classroom. *Harvard Educational Review, 62* (1), 1–24.

Vargas. (1999). When the "other" is the teacher: Implications of teacher diversity in higher education. *The Urban Review, 31* (4), 359–383.

Wilson, W. (1987). *The truly disadvantaged: The inner city, the underclass, and public policy.* Chicago: University of Chicago Press.

---

[i] Adopted from Solorzano's (2001) article.

[ii] I posed the following question in all the interviews: What if a student comes to you and says, 'I don't see race/color?' How would or do you deal with students who hold on to this colorblind ideology? A couple responses were: "I've never come into contact with the notion of the colorblind society in raised in class"; and "None of my students have come to me and said that they don't see color or that race isn't an issue." This second response will prove to be a factor later on in the paper.

[iii] During the interview I asked the respondents, "What has been the most challenging experience in your classroom?" The following text is a transcription of their responses. Also, the names used are pseudonyms to protect the privacy of the respondents.

[iv] Blumer (1958) outlines four feelings. The fourth one he lists is the fear of suspicion that the subordinate race dominant race.

8

EAVING A WOMANIST DISCOURSE TO UNRAVEL WHITE MALE PRIVILEGE IN THE CLASSROOM

Dianne Smith

I write my thoughts in a journal in order to journey into a space of deep, spiritual reflection. For example, I write about my life with my aunts, Miss, Polly, and Liza. I have other aunts, but for some reason these three are such wild wisdom women that they have made a significant impact on my identity formation, particularly as I think about being a womanist. Their acid tongues could spew venom four times that of a rattlesnake. Each in her own way decided how she would live her life, even though tremendous struggle was a daily adventure. I remember, as a girl-child and an adult woman, watching Miss weave blankets and quilt quilts. It was such tedious work, but she enjoyed giving them to us for winter warmth. However, life for Miss was not a bowl of cherries. For I also remember the time that she was beaten and pushed out of a moving car.

So, writing down my thoughts and feelings helps me to understand the contradictions, struggles, and good times; and it gives me a sense of renewal, or revival—rather like when we blacks go to "Revival Services" to shed the old and put on the new. I will share a journal entry that I wrote on January 20, 1998, because it will help me to begin the process of weaving my womanist discourse as a means of unraveling white male privilege in the classroom.

The Politics of Curricular Change

> I was insane with the spirits of Essie, Tenar, Libby, Elizabeth, Beatrice, Polly, Sylvia, Jennifer, and the list goes on and on and on. It was Martin Luther King Day. I was trying to be a community advocate for young women. The tears are still very much present. I said some hot-tongued stuff to [---]. I am tired of her white girl privilege...me me me me. Chris calls it those closet racists. I really don't see her as such, but she hasn't visited her class stuff enough. I was a medium for all of the black women who have wanted to say, vent, rage, be temporarily insane with a white woman. Sorta like Mrs. Henderson, Maya Angelou's grandmother, who stood and sang a hymn while a white girl mooned her. Keep it to yourself. I couldn't. I spoke with them in spirit. I couldn't stop. I rambled, fast, coherent, incoherent because sometimes I didn't recognize my voice. Whose voice was it anyway? I have tried to make me feel remorseful. It doesn't come. I have tried to beat myself up—emotionally—about such a demented outburst. It doesn't happen. What am I willing to lose—[-]'s friendship? Yes!! I found my voice for my mother's. I volcanically erupted centuries of oppression. Was I correct? I don't know and at this point, I am not concerned with that. Eliza would come home from Cindy's, after working for little pay, caring for her children and talk about her tribulations. Mama would talk about washing Jess Fowler's pajamas that were laced with boogers and snot; she hated it. Evelyn's bloody drawers lying around for mama to pick up and wash. Rage. Beautiful rage. Not killing. Not violence. Not not not. Being tired. (p. 98)

I use this rather lengthy journal entry quote to illustrate how I will be using the term "womanist" in this essay. It shares threads with Alice Walker's definition of "womanist." Walker (1983) writes that a womanist is "a black feminist or feminist of color. Usually referring to outrageous, audacious, courageous or willful behavior" (p. xi). She continues explaining her concept of womanist: "Committed to survival and wholeness of entire people, male and female. Not a separatist, except periodically, for health" (pp. xi–xii). Walker includes the notion that a womanist is "Responsible. In charge. *Serious.* Womanist is to feminist as purple is to lavender" (pp. xi–xii).

In addition, my "outrageous" or "willful" behavior, evident in my journal entry, is tied to bell hooks's (1989) voice related to black women who must talk back. bell hooks intimates that "it is that act of speech, of 'talking back,' that is no mere gesture of empty words, that it is the expression of our movement from object to subject—the liberated voice" (1989, p. 9). This is what I experienced with my white female "class privileged" friend. My words are not empty and I refuse to be objectified. That is, I demand that my voice be heard and attended to, as bell hooks suggests. Maria Lugones and Elizabeth Spelman write that the demand that the woman's voice be heard and attended to has been made for a variety of reasons: not just so as to greatly increase the chances that true accounts of women's lives will be given, but also because the articulation of experience (in myriad ways) is among the hallmarks of a self-determining individual or community. There are just not epistemological, but moral and political reasons for demanding that the woman's voice be heard after centuries of androcentric din. (1983, p. 574)

The weaving frame that I seek to establish is that while black women struggle with white women and their privilege on a daily basis, for me, these struggles become even more cumbersome when dealing with white men. I am an associate professor of education at a predominately white urban university and my ideas and experiences resonate with Nellie McKay (1997). She tells her reader that "No one could have explained what it really meant to be a black woman professor in a white college or university for the long haul. The following incident illustrates this point" (p. 14). She writes:

In my office, I was engaged in conversation with a black woman colleague in the Afro-American Studies Department. She was standing just inside my door. A white male professor from another department stopped at the door and, without apology, pushed his way past my colleague. Before either she or I realized what had happened, he preempted her presence in our space to make a request of me. I had scarcely grasped the politics of the situation before it was over—he was gone and my female colleague had retreated to her office across the hall. It was another everyday incident, in our days of such incidents, when white colleagues, without even trying, asserted the privilege of whiteness, especially male whiteness, over those they perceived to be unequal to themselves by the authority of race and/or sex. (p. 14)

McKay (1997) continues with her spirit of audaciousness by noting, "Unfortunately, white male professors and administrators are not the only group that offend black women by their racist [and I add, sexist] verbal expressions" (p. 14). I agree with her assertion in that white male students can be just as offensive to black women in the academy.

For example, I am primarily responsible for teaching graduate curriculum theory courses; however, six years ago I revived an undergraduate foundations course—Cultural Diversity and American Education. This course has become a requirement for all undergraduate teacher education students. Since it is a required component of their program, the school of education offers this course in the fall, winter, and summer. I teach it during the summer session. I willfully include scholarship on women and men of color and white women because "for centuries, women and men of color, as well as White women, have concentrated on the culture of White males as a central point of discourse," as Ruth Farmer conceives (1993, p. 196). The white male students either drop the course or contest (overtly or covertly) my notion that history, knowledge, values, and educational systems romanticize and glorify white male dominance. Farmer proposes that,

> Integration of the curriculum is opposed by those who believe it threatens educational excellence. 'Excellence,' in their minds, is a euphemism for a preponderance of White values, perspectives, and ideals, that is, White supremacy. The mainstream is based on the necrophilia philosophies of patriarchy and White supremacy, both of which require worship of dead White men, the marginalization of scholarship that threatens the fantasy that White men are greater than anyone else, and the killing of creativity by forcing these ideals as normative. (1993, p. 197)

It is my experience that, as Brenda Hoke (1997, p. 296) acknowledges, "many men believe that their 'whiteness' is a privilege that gives them a right to dominate"—not only me as the professor but other women who are classroom participants. For example, after three weeks of reading and hearing stories that disrupt white male dominance, Herbert (name changed), a white male student in this class, uses his "big male voice" to say: "I hate women; when I see blacks on television news I immediately think they did a crime; I am homophobic, I think it's a sin." Fortunately, the students and I engage him in a critical debate about his assumptions. What this means for me is that Herbert's white maleness was threatened and he sought to re-center his privilege in the classroom.

Hence, each day that I prepare for battle in the classroom against white male student privilege I read a passage written by, about, and for black women. And I remember my grandma Tenar's stories about getting up before dawn to pick a bale of cotton in some white man's cotton field. For these women's thoughts and stories are my armor and shield. I ride their backs and I sit in their laps for comfort and spiritual power. As I write these thoughts, I am reminded of my mama who uses daily prayer to ground and strengthen herself. Sometimes, I walk into her bedroom "telling" her something and I find her on her knees, praying. Thus, in this essay I will present some of these black women warriors who have and continue to plow paths of empowerment and joy in struggle. My intent is not to offer curricular suggestions for "unraveling" (or de-centering) white male privilege in a classroom environment.

As Patricia Hill Collins (1990) postulates, "Oppressed groups are frequently placed in the situation of being listened to only if we frame our ideas in the language that is familiar to and comfortable for a dominant group. This requirement often changes the meaning of our ideas and works to elevate the ideas of dominant groups" (p. xiii). What this means for me is that I claim this essay as a project that "centers" black women's thoughts, theories, ways of knowing, and transformation through written discourse. "Traditional scholarship" requires that I create a recipe for countering white male privilege and that I provide this recipe in a language that is abstract and relegated for the ears of an elite few (Collins, 1990; hooks, 1994; Benjamin, 1997; and Smith, 1996). Therefore, I accept the charge that hooks (1989), Walker (1983), and Collins (1990) bring forth, that is, to write so that black women (and other women and men) who are not in the academy desire to read our work. To do this, I dance in and out of my home talk and my school talk because I claim both as part of my multiple identities. And, hopefully, this will satisfy my friend, Marilyn, who asks me why I never let her read my work.

In essence, this essay (our writings) becomes a form of pedagogy that grounds and strengthens us as we seek to change white male privilege and dominance, not only in classrooms but also throughout society. Remember, my reader, this is not a "how-to" piece but it is "food for thought" and sorta like my mama going into her prayer room, in order to make it through the day. Thus, what follows next are written discourses by black women and I will weave our voices around a discourse of resistance as a ligature for self-recognition and self-emancipation. I will show how we have used autobiography, novel, poetry, and political essays as womanist theory to resist domination. Since there is a plethora of writings by black women, I will focus on several who have become my bridge and lap, and know that there are many more whom I cherish as path plowers and wisdom women.

Womanist Women as Givers of Wisdom Through Words

Joy James (1993) writes the following:

> Ours is a spiritual tradition. So, I want to begin class with meditation....
>
> We must continue to thank our ancestors, our spirits for the ground upon which we stand, for their struggles enabled us to survive genocidal wars, enslavement, and dehumanizing oppression.
>
> First, I thank our ancestors, elders, and those who prepared the space for us, then I tell my story.... Ours is an oral tradition.
>
> We tell stories to illuminate the paths we travel to share humor, courage, and wisdom in this liberation struggle. Our storytelling is our theorizing. And so an "introduction" to theory is an introduction to spiritual, political struggles for peace and freedom.
>
> I consciously began "theorizing," as Barbara Christian calls it, when I was nine and my father, returning from Vietnam, brought the war home with him. (pp. 31–32)

James is appropriate in that we do tell stories to share humor, courage, and wisdom as we struggle to live; and the oral tradition of storytelling continues to permeate black communities. However, there are black women such as Harriet Adams Wilson (1859/1983) and Elizabeth Keckley (1868/1988) who "write" story. For example, Wilson's work shows that enslaved women not only raised the issue of hatred and maltreatment by the white male slaveholder, but she also includes in her story the hatred and maltreatment by white women (wives of the men). A prime example of such acts is etched in her book *Our Nig*, 1859. The primary character is a young girl named Alfredo. Wilson weaves a tragic tale of social, racial, and abject economic abuse. This work shows a different side of the institution of slavery; that is, the north was not as "sympathetic" to ending slavery as is theorized. Additionally, "it exposes white women who were committing the sins of the patriarchs, as well as those of southern mistresses, in their relationships with black women" (Shockley, 1983, p. 86).

In addition to naming their personal violent experience of oppression in stories, these women used narrative as an instrument to channel their feelings of pain and outrage during the separation of their families. The slave system was notorious for the disintegration of the black family in the states. Children were sold from their mothers' crying arms; fathers were placed on the selling block for inspection, as were women (Davis, 1981; Braxton, 1989; Shockley, 1983; and Fox-Genovese, 1988). Keckley pursues the theme of family disintegration as she describes the sale and departure of her "thought-to-be father" (her mother's white owner was her biological father):

> My mother's name was Agnes, and my father delighted to call me 'Little Lizze.' While yet my mother and father were speaking hopefully, joyfully of the future, Mr. Burwell came to the cabin, with a letter in his hand. He was a kind master in some things, and as gently as possible informed my parents that they must part; for in two hours my father must join his master at Dinwiddie, and go with him to the West, where he had determined to make his future home. The announcement fell upon the little circle in that rude log cabin like a thunderbolt. I can remember the scene as it were but yesterday; how my father cried out against the cruel separation; his last kiss; his wild straining of mother to his bosom; the solemn prayer to Heaven; the tears and sobs—the fearful anguish of broken hearts. The last kiss, the last goodbye; and he, my father, was gone, gone forever. (1868, p. 53)

The wet tears and thunderous sobs of Keckley's parents are felt by the reader; therefore, in narrating or naming this horrible act, she changes from acquiescence to opposition. And she confronts the white ideology of the family with her lived experience of slavery and oppression. I ask, how can they (white people) assume the slave mother, spouse, and keeper of the family was so "nonhuman" that she could watch as her family disintegrates before her eyes without a care? For an animal will wail, cry, and fight to save its family. The pain, anger, and outrage felt by the enslaved woman because of her race, sex, and family were buttressed with strong spiritual beliefs. These women believed in the "god-head" as the savior and protector from all wrongs and evils. The belief that one day "we'll enter the pearly gates and we'll walk the streets made of gold and we won't have to cry no mo" was a mechanism for hope and faith. Or, we'll "steal away, steal away to Jesus, I ain't got long to stay here" (Smith, 1990).

Then, here comes Zora Neale Hurston, who writes against the stereotypes of the day and gives us new categories of perceptions (women's images) and new ways to consider the stuff of our lives, according to Toni Cade Bambara (1984). Ralph Story (1989) notes that Hurston's work foreshadowed the issues of black women which came to prominence in the early 1970s, specifically the plight of black women as a subject matter in and of itself deserving of literary scholarly attention. She is a black woman who, through her writings, refused to adhere to the mold chiseled for black women. According to Joanne Braxton (1989), Hurston represents the first generation of black and female autobiographers who did not continually come into contact with former slaves; her works turn away from the restrictions and limitations of the slave narrative and extend the quest for a dignified and self-defining identity to include a search for personal fulfillment.

Not only does her text include reversals, as Elizabeth Fox-Genovese (1988) maintains, but Hurston's text also created a stir among critics and scholars because she chose to conceal certain factual accounts of her life (the date of her birth, the names of men in her life, and the number of times that she was married). In addition, Mary Helen Washington (1979) suggests that her "point of view on race, true to her personality, was unpredictable, ambivalent, sometimes contradictory, but certainly never conventional" (p. 8). I use Hurston as an entree to black women thinkers of the 1970s and 1980s because her work invited future black women to aspire to be unconventional in our ways of writing and "truth-telling." For example, Daniel Moynihan's scathing report, *The Negro Family* (1965), which concludes that there was "pathological" behavior in our communities traceable to "female-headed households," possessed black women to raise a level of consciousness to "challenge this ideological assault on us" (Angela Davis, 1990, p. 94).

As Davis intimates, 1970 was the year, and the decade, of black woman consciousness raising: It was at that time that we became thinking, knowing, speaking subjects. Kay Lindsey (1970) furthers this position by adding that,

What we truly are as women or as Black women or human beings or groups is an unknown quantity insofar as we have not determined our own destiny. We have an obligation as Black women to project ourselves into the revolution to destroy these institutions which not only oppress Blacks but women as well. (p. 89)

In this spirit black women became revolutionaries to destroy the institutions of white male privilege and domination that bring about racism, sexism, and economic oppression.

In 1970 Toni Cade engaged the assistance of a group of black women and entered the literary world with fire and outrage. They authenticated their existence with *The Black Woman's Anthology*, writings by and about black women (Foster, 1973).

According to Foster, this anthology records women's efforts to discover and to redefine themselves through their discourse, which is indicative of their realities and experiences. For example, Abbey Lincoln (1970) writes that "A good job has been done on the Black people in this country, as far as convincing them of their inferiority is concerned. The general white community told us in a million different ways and in no uncertain terms that 'God' and 'nature' made a mistake when it came to the fashioning of us and ours" (p. 81). She continues with the idea that:

> The fact that white people readily and proudly call themselves 'white,' glorify all that is white, and white-wash all that is glorified, becomes unnatural and bigoted in its intent only when these same whites deny persons of African heritage who are Black the natural and inalienable right to readily and proudly call themselves 'black,' glorify all that is black, and black-wash all that is glorified. (pp. 81–82)

Kay Lindsey echoes Lincoln's discourse on black female oppression. Her essay is a liberating piece that projects her outrage, as my journal entry portrays:

> Black women who spend their working lives not only as mothers but also as domestics are yet another instance of Black women penalized on two counts and forced into roles which are extensions of those of white women. Where the white woman is the wife, the Black woman is the mother on welfare and the bearer of future workers for the State; where the white woman is the call girl or mistress, the Black woman is the street prostitute; where the white woman is married to a man who can afford it, a Black woman takes over the care of the home and children for her. In short, to be a Black woman is to operate almost totally as a physical body without the inducements offered her white counterpart. While white females are sexual objects, Black women are sexual laborers, White females are the tokens among women in this society, in that they have titles, but not the power, while Black women have neither—although Black women are frequently described by the white agency in terms that suggest power, such as "strong," "domineering," and "emasculating." (pp. 88–89)

Kay Lindsey's fiery disquisition suggests that "when we are defined by those other than ourselves, the qualities ascribed to us are not in our interests, but rather reflect the nature of the roles which we are intended to play" (p. 89). Her discourse is evident in Toni Morrison's work.

One of Morrison's (1970) main female protagonists, Pauline Breedlove, addresses the theme of black female oppression and racism as she becomes employed as a domestic in a white well-to-do home. The nature of the roles ascribed to us is revealed as Morrison describes the environment of Breedlove's employment:

> Power, praise, and luxury were hers in this household. They even gave her what she never had—a nickname—Polly. It was her pleasure to stand in her kitchen at the end of a day and survey her handiwork. Hearing, 'We'll never let her go. We could never find anybody like Polly. She will not leave the kitchen until everything is in order. Really, she is the ideal servant.' (pp. 100–101)

While Lincoln, Lindsey, and Morrison speak out against black woman oppression in the 1970s, in the 1980s there is a widening discourse of naming and speaking. A weaving of a discourse of resistance becomes evident in the writings of black lesbians.

Subsequently, Barbara Smith (1982) intimates that by writing from a black lesbian's perspective she realized it was something unprecedented and dangerous. She courts this idea: "A community which has not confronted sexism, because a widespread Black feminist movement has not required it to, has likewise not been challenged to examine heterosexism. Even at this moment I am not convinced that one can write explicitly as a Black lesbian and live to tell about it" (p. 172). Smith (1980) lives to "illuminate the existence of Black lesbian writers and to show how homophobia insured that we were even more likely to be ignored or attacked than Black women writers generally" (p. 213).

As many black lesbian writers were focused on naming heterosexism and homophobia, Mane Bogus (1988), a black lesbian, pursues a theme of celebrating her existence in this universe. She writes,

> Because dyke hands are the sexual organs of lesbian love, they can be as shocking to view as the penis through an open fly, or as bold (delicious) to behold as the breast of a woman suddenly uncovered. And because of this, dyke hands ought to be given the covered respect they deserve.
>
> The hands that stroke my hair, caress my flesh, that grip my thighs, press my love button, that slide between the satin readiness of my labia, ought not be seen by the

daily populace. They belong in gloves, or mittens, and perhaps as a nation of womyn identified lesbians, white, black, or brown leather gloves can be made the symbol of our private sexuality, and between us at least the idea that we are lovers of womyn can be acknowledged by us all...I wish for the lesbian nation a consciousness of our sexuality for our strength lies in it. (pp. 64–65)

While most womanists did not challenge the sexism that imbues homophobia, Walker (1982) pursues the theme of oppression by resisting sexist, male dominance. Walker announces the love that black women share with each other. For Walker it becomes important to "name the reality that black women do engage in lovemaking and comfort each other" (p. 109). Walker's protagonists, Celie Johnson and Shug Avery, care for each other in a sexual as well as nonsexual manner. In a letter to God, Johnson talks about their first sexual encounter: "Nobody ever love me, I say. She say, I love you, Miss Celie. And then she haul off and kiss me on the mouth. Um, she say, like she surprise. I kiss her back, say, um, too" (p. 120). What this means for me is that Walker insists that the black woman's responsibility is to herself and to other women, and she aligns herself with women who acknowledge male dominance in the world. Moreover, Walker claims her freedom in exploring issues of sexism and racism in our society.

Lorraine Bethel (1982) indicates that black women have consistently rejected the suppression and falsification of our black female experience. Black woman identification is most simply the idea of black women seeking our own identity and defining ourselves through bonding on various levels: psychic, intellectual, and emotional, as well as physical, with other black women. According to Bethel, "Choosing Black lesbianism, feminism, or woman-identification is the political process and struggle of choosing a hated identity: choosing to be a Black woman, not only in body, but in spirit as well" (pp. 176–188). In other words, it is dangerous for a black woman to consciously take a womanist stance for liberation and peace. It is dangerous for us to name our multiple identities but it is more dangerous to be silent. For Audre Lorde (1983) sermonizes that "You're never a whole person if you remain silent, because there is always that one little piece inside you that wants to be spoken out, and if you keep ignoring it, it gets madder and madder and hotter and hotter, and if you don't speak it out one day it will just up and punch you in the mouth from the inside" (p. 42).

I now understand why my mama would say, "I can't hold this any longer 'cause I gotta speak my mind! They done pushed me too far, now!"

Elizabeth Smith's theory is connected to Lorde's in that these two women (among others) realize that it ain't healthy to be silent when something needs to be said. Mama would say that if she didn't speak her mind, then she couldn't sleep at night. And then she would go into her prayer room. So, on this note I end this section with a statement made in an earlier publication:

> I am a womanist! I am a womanist! I am one of Maya Angelou's "strong black birds of promise who defy the odds and gods and sing their songs" (1970, p. 211). Contrary to regulations, I use praise song because I am happy. I sing because I am free. I sing because the stories by black women, as Maxine Greene (1988) notes, "shed many kinds of light on the meanings of freedom and the search for freedom...in such writings we find a dialectical relation to what surrounds us, a conscious pursuit of freedom as an existential project, a central life task." (Smith, 1996, pp. 180–181)

Conclusion

bell hooks (1995) writes that to speak as an act of resistance is quite different from ordinary talk; it is quite different from the personal confessional that has no relation to coming into political awareness, to developing critical consciousness. The idea of finding a voice risks being trivialized or romanticized in rhetoric; but the struggle to move from object to subject is expressed in the effort to establish a transformed voice. Throughout this essay I have intertwined my voice with the voices of others; and I have used our voices to disorganize the existing knowledge about black women thinkers, living and non-living. Hopefully, I have created a shift in the ways that we talk about and act upon white male privilege in the classroom (and society as a whole). However, I do caution my reader that "not being monolithic, we women vary in our approaches and connections" (James & Farmer, 1993) to writing discourses of resistance and change. Some of us talk about racism, white male patriarchy, black male patriarchy, black lesbianism, family life, black middle class life, and the list continues. Many of us own or deny our historical or cultural baggage. What I mean is that while we have profound similarities, we also have grave differences.

For example, I am a black southern working middle-class intellectual-heterosexual who can code switch when I want to (and there are other parts of me not named). I add this because I do not want to appear to romanticize our work, for I would be practicing that which I preach against. But bell hooks (1994), when criticized for using Paulo Freire's "patriarchal" liberation theory, provides a metaphor that is so telling: I walk in the woods on a hot day and I become real thirsty and dry. I happen upon a running brook that looks delicious. And I bend down and cup my hands together and scoop up some of that cool refreshing water. As I ready my dry mouth to be quenched, I notice that there are specks of dirt settled at the bottom. Do I not drink the water because of the specks of dirt? I drink the water because it nourishes me; it gives me what my body needs to continue my journey.

This is what I invite you to do with this essay and the works of other black women: consume that which is useful for you. Use our work as a foundation to support your commitment to liberation struggle. Know that I dance in and out of contradictions of fear and courage; I dance in and out of subversiveness and subservience; and I dance in and out of talking back and silence (Smith, 1996). In conclusion, always remember that male domination can never be the primary focus of the womanist/feminist movement and that the revolutionary womanist/feminist movement is not anti-male (hooks, 1995).

References

Angelou, M. (1970). *I know why the caged bird sings.* New York: Random House.
Bambara, T. C. (1984). Salvation is the issue. In M. Evans (Ed.), *Black women writers 1950–1980: A critical evaluation* (pp. 41–47). New York: Anchor Books.
Bethel, L. (1982). This infinity of conscious pain: Zora Neale Hurston and the black female literary tradition. In G. T. Hull, P. B. Scott, & B. Smith (Eds.), *All the women are white, all the blacks are men, but some of us are brave* (pp. 176–188). New York: The Feminist Press.
Bogus, S. D. (1988). *Dyke hands and sutras erotic and lyric: Poems and essays.* San Francisco: WIM Publications.
Braxton, J. (1989). *Black women writing autobiography.* Philadelphia: Temple University Press.
Cade, T. (Ed.). (1970). *The black woman: An anthology.* New York: Mentor Books.

Collins, P. A. (1990). *Black feminist thought.* Boston: Unwin Hyman.
Davis, A. Y. (1981). Rape, racism, and the capitalist setting. *The Black Scholar, 12,* 39–45.
Davis, A. Y. (1990). Woman talk. *Essence Magazine, 21,* 93–94.
Farmer, R. (1993). Place but not importance. In J. James & R. Farmer (Eds.), *Spirit, space, and survival: African American women in (white) academe* (pp. 196–217). New York: Routledge.
Foster, F. (1973). Changing concepts of the black woman. *Journal of Black Studies, 3,* 433–454.
Fox-Genovese, E. (1988). My statue, my self: Autobiographical writings of AfroAmerican women. In S. Bernstock (Ed.), *The private self: Theory and practice of women's autobiography* (pp. 63–89). Chapel Hill, NC: The University of North Carolina-Chapel Hill Press.
Greene, M. (1988). *The dialectic of freedom.* New York: Teachers College Press.
Hoke, B. (1997). Women's colleges: The intersection of race, class, and gender. In L. Benjamin (Ed.), *Black women in the academy* (pp. 291–301). Gainesville, FL: University Press of Florida.
hooks, b. (1989). *Talking back.* Boston: South End Press.
hooks, b. (1994). *Teaching to transgress.* New York: Routledge
hooks, b. (1995). *Killing rage, ending racism.* New York: Owl Books.
James, J. (1993). African philosophy, "theory," and living thinkers. In J. James & R. Farmer (Eds.), *Spirit, space, and survival: African American women in (white) academe* (pp. 31–46). New York: Routledge.
James, J., & Farmer, R. (Eds.). (1993). *Spirit, space, and survival: African American women in (white) academe.* New York: Routledge.
Keckley, E. (1988). *Behind the scenes: Or thirty years a slave and four years in the White House.* New York: G. W. Carlton. (Original work published 1868). London: Oxford University Press.
Lincoln, A. (1970). Who will revere the black woman? In T. Cade (Ed.), *The black woman: An anthology.* New York: Mentor Books.
Lindsey, K. (1970). The black woman as a woman. In T. Cade (Ed.), *The black woman: An anthology.* New York: Mentor Books.
Lorde, A. (1984). *Sister outsider.* Freedom, CA: Crossing Press.

Lugones, M., & Spelman, E. (1983). Have we got a theory for you! Feminist theory, cultural imperialism and the demand for the woman's voice. *Women's International Studies Forum, 6,* 573–581.

McKay, N. Y. (1997). A troubled peace: Black women in the halls of the white academy. In L. Benjamin (Ed.), *Black women in the academy* (pp. 11–22). Gainesville, FL: University Press of Florida.

Morrison, T. (1970). *The bluest eye.* New York: Washington Square Press.

Moynihan, D. (1965). *The Negro family: The case for national action.* Washington, DC: U.S. Department of Labor, Office of Planning and Research.

Shockley, A. A. (1988). *Afro-American women writers 1746-1933: An anthology and critical guide.* New York: Meridian Books.

Smith, B. (1982). Toward a black feminist criticism. In G. T. Hull, P. B. Scott, & B. Smith (Eds.), *All the women are white, all the blacks are men, but some of us are brave* (pp. 157–175). New York: The Feminist Press.

Smith, D. (1990). *A social and political construction of child abuse.* Unpublished doctoral dissertation, Miami University, Oxford, OH.

Smith, D. (1996). Womanism and me: An (un)caged black bird sings for freedom. *The High School Journal, 79,* 176-182.

Story, R. (1989). Gender and ambition: Zora Neale Hurston in the Harlem Renaissance. *The Black Scholar, 20,* 25–31.

Walker, A. (1982). *The color purple.* New York: Washington Square Press.

Walker, A. (1983). *In search of our mothers' gardens: Womanist prose.* San Diego, CA: Harcourt.

Washington, M. H. (1979). Zora Neale Hurston: A woman half in shadow. In A. Walker (Ed.), *I love myself when I am laughing: A Zora Neale Hurston reader* (pp. 724). New York: The Feminist Press.

Wilson, H. A. (1985). *Our Nig: Or, sketches from the life of a free black.* Boston: George Rand and Avery. New York: Random House. (Original work published 1859).

racticing Multicultural Education: Answering Recurring Questions About What It Is (Not)

André J. Branch

Questions and misconceptions about multicultural education persist for many reasons, not the least of which is that when implemented successfully, multicultural education addresses controversial issues of race, hegemony, and power. Pre-service teachers in my Introduction to Multicultural Education class (and some of my colleagues in various faculty-committee meetings) pose many questions about these and other controversial issues in their quest to better understand multicultural education. Although their individual questions are different, they consistently point to one of six thematic questions: What is the importance of multicultural education? For whom is multicultural education designed? Will the focus on differences and issues of racism divide our nation against itself? What is the curricular composition of multicultural education? How is multicultural education relevant to the "hard sciences," e.g., mathematics? Who can accomplish multicultural education?

In this chapter, I will answer these six questions and show researchers, policymakers, and administrators how teachers can be empowered to practice multicultural education. As questions are answered and examples are offered, I hope the reader will come to an understanding of what multicultural education is and what it is not. Before answering these questions, some academic and cultural positioning is in order. My academic preparation in curriculum and instruction, as well as in multicultural education, will form the basis of my answers to these important questions. My experience as an African American male assistant professor and teacher of the required course, "Introduction to Multicultural Education," informs my responses to these questions and my conceptualization of multicultural education. Multicultural education is a discipline that is practiced by professional educators. Educators are professionals in the sense that doctors, engineers, and lawyers, for examples, are professionals. Multicultural education has a theoretical base, a lexicon and literature, tools, and practices that are driven by one's theoretical or philosophical base. I practice multicultural education; and, in the way that medical interns are prepared for the practice of medicine, I prepare pre-service teachers for the practice of multicultural education.

Synopsis of Previous Thought on Multicultural Education

First, let us review some of the previous thought on multicultural education. Critical readers of the multicultural education corpus will be hard pressed to find consensus among its writers, researchers, and theorists about the nature, purpose, and process questions that surround this discipline. There is a diversity of conceptualizations of the discipline, as in all disciplines. In 1987, Sleeter and Grant provided the first comprehensive analysis of the literature and practices of multicultural education. These writers did not find consistency of thought about what is called "multicultural education," but they were able to codify five broad "approaches to multicultural education which emerge from the literature" (p. 422).

The five broad approaches identified by Sleeter and Grant are: "Teaching the Culturally Different," "Human Relations," "Single Group Studies," "Multicultural Education," and "Education that is Multicultural and Social Reconstructionist" (1987, p. 422). As the names of the approaches suggest, the nature and purpose of multicultural education differs according to the approach taken. One example of the significant differences between them is immediately evident as one compares the first two approaches and tries to answer the question, "Who is multicultural education for?" Those who "Teach the Culturally Different" understand multicultural education to be the use of a special pedagogy for teaching *students of color*, i.e., those outside the white middle-class mainstream. Those using a "Human Relations" lens in multicultural education endeavor to help **all** students, regardless of their race and ethnicity, and focus on commonalties in the human condition while living, working, and playing harmoniously. For a full discussion of their analysis of multicultural education, see the seminal work by Sleeter and Grant (1987).

The theoretical framework that I will use to answer the questions of this chapter is that formulated by Banks (1997). He writes that multicultural education is a concept, a school reform movement, and an ongoing process. Multicultural education, writes Banks, is "a reform movement that is trying to change the schools and other educational institutions so that students from all social class, gender, racial, and cultural groups will have an equal opportunity to learn" (Banks, 1997, p. 4). Today's teachers are required to do more than teach human relations concepts, or teach those who are culturally different. They are required to do much more than impart knowledge about individual ethnic groups. To be an effective school reform movement, multicultural education must also help students to understand their role in improving their world (social reconstruction). I include all of these components in the practice of multicultural education, for which I prepare my students, and that I will explain here.

What Is the Importance of Multicultural Education?

One of the early questions my students ask is "Why do I have to be a multicultural educator?" Variations on this question are: "Why can't I just be a good teacher?" and "Why do I have to concern myself with all this cultural difference BS?" Many of the questioners appropriately associate multicultural education with the negative experiences they have had with the related issues of race and ethnicity. In the U.S., where we are in a racial crisis, it is likely that these students have experienced deep emotional hurts as regards race and do not want to be reminded of these hurts. Other students resent that this class is required in our teacher education program, and what they perceive to be the suggestion that they might need the class to help them unearth and resolve some unresolved prejudices. Still other students (and some of my colleagues on the faculty) are convinced that they can be good teachers, helping students to excel academically, without attention to cultural differences.

Given that our country is in a racial crisis, it is reasonable that some would rather let the proverbial "sleeping dogs lie" ("all this cultural difference BS"), and "just be good teachers." The fact that there is some real good teaching happening in various schools all over the U.S. led Gloria Ladson-Billings (1995) to ask "why so little of it seems to be occurring in the classrooms populated by African American students" (p. 159). Banks (1997) has written that in contrast to the parity in achievement between students of color and white students at lower grades, "the longer these students of color remain in school, the more their achievement lags behind that of White mainstream students" (p. 4). In my own city of San Diego, standardized test scores in the previous two years have increased in the San Diego Unified School District. The increases, however, have been in those schools where white students are in the majority. In fact, the "focus schools," those with the lowest scores, are consistently those schools in which students of color are the majority (Spielvogel, 2001).

In the twenty-first century, those who want to be good teachers, who are effective with all students, have a thorough understanding of the theory, methods, materials, and practice of multicultural education. These good teachers understand that multicultural education is a school reform movement (Banks, 1997) that uses the cultures that children bring to school as powerful tools for teaching subject matter content. Multicultural education provides methods for attending to culture (Pewewardy, 1993; Au & Jordan, 1981; Vasquez, 1990; Garcia, 2001; Gay, 2000; Irvine & Armento, 2001) to insure the academic success of all students. Educators who understand the benefits of multicultural education for all students are eager to consider seriously the diverse sociocultural contexts from which students come as they design lessons and activities for the teaching/learning process.

For Whom Is Multicultural Education Designed?

Another question students ask in varied and subtle ways is: "Why do I need to practice multicultural education if there are no students of color in my class?" Most of my students will teach in the San Diego Unified School District, California's second largest school district. As 72 percent of the students in that district are students of color, it would be curious to have no students of color in a class, and this diversity is the trend in most cities in the

U.S. At least three assumptions seem to be imbedded in the question. The first and obvious assumption the questioner makes is that multicultural education is *only* for students of color. Banks (1999) characterizes the misconception that multicultural education is only for ethnic groups of color and the disenfranchised as "one of the most pernicious and damaging misconceptions with which the movement has to cope" (p. 5). Banks (1999) writes, "...the image of multicultural education as an entitlement program for the 'others' remains strong and vivid in the public imagination as well as in the hearts and minds of many teachers and administrators" (p. 6). Contrary to the notion that multicultural education is for the culturally and politically marginalized "others," multicultural education has the potential for providing *all* students with a high-quality educational experience and an accurate understanding of the roles that many different cultural groups have played—and continue to play—in the life, structure, and institutions of our country.

What multicultural education specialists have said for years bears repeating: All students benefit from, and are motivated by, seeing themselves in the curriculum. All students benefit from the practice of multicultural education that attends to both curricula and pedagogy. Irvine and York (1995) found that all students benefit from the use of various instructional strategies and methods of teaching. At the heart of multicultural education is ensuring the academic success of *all students*, but especially those students who, historically and traditionally, have not been reached by mono-cultural curricula and pedagogy.

The second and less obvious assumption embedded in this question is that multicultural education is only content integration, the infusion of ethnic content knowledge into subject matter content. Trivializing multicultural education, this second assumption goes to the implementation of multicultural education—that is, what would multicultural education look like if one walked into a classroom where it was being practiced? The assumption here is that multicultural education concerns only curriculum, or what Banks (1997) has called the "content integration" dimension of multicultural education. Infusing ethnic content knowledge into one's lesson designs is but one way to practice multicultural education. Using content integration to practice multicultural education means using examples from many different cultural perspectives (Banks, 1997) to teach the subject matter called for by district and state content and performance standards. By using content integration, teachers will transform the curriculum and lead students to take action in their world based on what they learn.

But content integration is only one way to practice multicultural education. There are at least four other dimensions of multicultural education, or four other ways to practice multicultural education that do not necessarily call for including historical information about ethnic groups in lesson designs. Educators who practice multicultural education have the option of designing lesson plans that reflect students' different learning styles, values, and belief systems. Multiculturalists call this the "equity pedagogy" dimension of multicultural education (Banks, 1997) or culturally relevant pedagogy (Gay, 2000; Ladson-Billings, 1995). Teachers who use an equity pedagogy may also facilitate students' ethnic identity development through curriculum and pedagogy (Branch, 1999). When teachers demonstrate for students that all knowledge is socially constructed, and teach their students to investigate the bias that exists in all disciplines, they are reflecting the "knowledge construction" dimension in their practice of multicultural education (Banks, 1997). Teachers who smartly reject the erroneous notion that all students come to school loving everybody, and therefore use strategies that teach students democratic values, are practicing multicultural education using the "prejudice reduction" dimension of this discipline (Banks, 1997). When entire schools embark upon a comprehensive multicultural education program, those schools are said to be developing an "empowering school culture and social structure," the fifth dimension of multicultural education (Banks, 1997). For a full explanation of the dimensions of multicultural education, see Banks, 1995 and 1997.

A third assumption related to the demographics driving the practice of multicultural education is that only students of color need, or would be interested in, ethnic content knowledge or culturally relevant pedagogy. Quite the contrary: Students tell us by the classes in which they enroll that they are eager to learn about the different cultural groups in the multicultural society in which they live. A Southern California institutional example is perhaps representative of other colleges and universities across the nation. Six professors in the Africana Studies Department at San Diego State University teach three Africana studies classes each semester. These classes are consistently filled to capacity, with the majority of those enrolled being white and Latino students. One of these professors recently moved from the

University of Maryland at College Park where he reports that each quarter his Introduction to Africana Studies class was consistently filled to capacity at three hundred students—all white. If students at these markedly different universities, in opposite regions of the country, are representative of students nationally regarding their desire for ethnic content knowledge, this generation of students is clearly interested in learning about racial, ethnic, and cultural groups different from their own.

At least as important as the students' demonstrated desires for ethnic content knowledge is the teachers' professional need of ethnic content knowledge. Teachers who live and teach in the U.S.'s multiracial, multi-ethnic society need knowledge of the history, values, and beliefs of the various racial and ethnic groups in the society in order to teach children effectively. Teachers cannot use examples from different ethnic groups to teach key concepts in subject matter content if they have no knowledge of the ethnic groups represented in their classrooms. Similarly, they cannot develop culturally relevant pedagogies if they have no knowledge of the values, beliefs, preferences, and cognitive styles associated with different racial, ethnic, and cultural groups. Teaching can be student-centered only when teachers know their students—including their cultures.

Knowledge of cultural differences on the part of teachers and students is invaluable to the teaching and learning process and to peaceful living, loving, and learning in our culturally diverse schools and the larger society. The physical attacks on innocent Muslims, Arabs, and other Middle Easterners following the World Trade Center and the Pentagon attacks provide ample evidence of the importance of learning to appreciate and value the differences encountered in race, ethnicity, language, dress, religion, behavior, and decision-making. These lessons are invaluable insofar as they reduce suspicions and doubt about those who are different, which often lead to hysteria, false accusations, and violence. In addition to students' desire for knowledge of cultural differences, there is a historical precedent for this practice and its success in reducing racial tensions and promoting interracial harmony. Of historical significance here is the work of the Inter-group Education Movement of the 1940s and 1950s. The leaders of this movement believed that providing students with an understanding of differences among diverse racial, national, and religious groups would promote interracial harmony and positive human relations (Banks, 1995).

Will the Focus on Differences and Issues of Racism Divide Our Nation Against Itself and Destroy the Western Way of Life?

It is not uncommon for students in the Introduction to Multicultural Education course to voice their concern that "focusing on our differences, and talking about things like racism and prejudice will only divide us." They believe that "forgetting the past and moving forward" should be the priority for all concerned parties, especially teachers. First, it is fair to say that multicultural education does not focus on differences, but encourages the recognition and use of cultural differences to enhance the educational process. The misconception that multicultural education will divide the nation grows out of a difference of opinion about the nature of unity and how unity may be achieved in the school context and in larger societal contexts. Multiculturalists believe that unity within diversity is possible. That is, within the celebration of our cultural and ethnic diversity, there can be unity.

That individuals or groups recognize and celebrate their individual ethnic cultures does not preclude them from affirming and celebrating the common culture shared by those born and reared in the U.S. Daily, U.S. citizens from different racial and ethnic groups unite to work on projects, to protest policies and procedures to which they object, to organize programs in which they believe, and to affirm their good will and hope in humanity. Attesting to this reality, millions of U.S. citizens—from countless racial and ethnic groups—united in mourning the loss of life from the tragedies at the World Trade Center, the Pentagon, Columbine High School, and Oklahoma City. Racial and ethnic differences alone do not divide people and groups in the U.S. The issues and controversies that do have this power are far beyond the scope and intention of this chapter. Within the scope of this chapter is the reality that racial, ethnic, and cultural differences can be used effectively to engage students in academic achievement. When teachers use examples from different cultures in their teaching, students are likely to feel a greater sense of allegiance to the U.S. because of the important connections that will have been made between their culture and their educational experience.

The idea that multicultural education is likely to destroy the North American way of life because it is against the West and against Western civilization is not new (Ravitch, 1990; Schlesinger, 1991). Rather than being against the West, multicultural education seeks to advance and realize some of the most significant Western ideals, like "freedom" and justice (Banks, 1999). Writes Banks,

> Although multicultural education is not against the West, its theorists do demand that the truth about the West be told, that its debt to people of color and women be recognized and included in the curriculum, and that the discrepancies between the ideals of freedom and equality, and the realities of racism and sexism, be taught to students. (1999, p. 6)

What Is the Curricular Composition of Multicultural Education?

One of my students recently lamented to me: "Dr. Branch, in my classroom, I have Chinese, African American, Hmong, Chaldean, Russian, Mexican American, European American, and American Indian students. After I get finished teaching the cultures of all these students, when will I teach the math, science, English/language arts, and social studies that I am supposed to be teaching?" This student is not alone in her misunderstanding of multicultural education. The teacher educator Diane Ravitch makes a similar query. She writes, "By the time every culture gets its due, there may be no time left to teach he subject itself" (1990, p. 47). The demographics to which the student refers are now prevalent in major cities across the U.S. Perhaps these demographics, accompanied by a misconception of multicultural education, lead some to think that teachers who practice multicultural education allow the teaching of culture to preempt the teaching of subject matter content. Multicultural education neither requires nor suggests that teachers trade the teaching of subject matter content for the teaching of culture. Classroom teachers are hired and required to teach the subject matter content appropriate to their discipline, and none of the theorists, researchers, and practitioners specializing in multicultural education advocate the abandonment of one's job—teaching students the subject matter content. Because culture has the power to facilitate learning, what we do recommend is that teachers use the culture that students bring to the classroom to teach subject matter content.

Using Culture to Teach Subject Matter Content: An Example

To demonstrate how students' cultures can be used to transform the curriculum in the practice of multicultural education, I will describe a lesson that I teach each semester in my Introduction to Multicultural Education course. Using English/Language Arts Standards for high school, I show preservice teachers how they can implement content-integration strategies to transform the curriculum. At the beginning of this session, I ask the class to generate a list of concepts they remember learning in high school English/Language Arts. Typically, the list includes concepts or genres such as "poetry," "the novel," "short story," "play," and "mystery." After this list of concepts is generated, I then ask the class to list examples of each of these concepts used by their high school teachers to teach these concepts. Students must also identify the names of the authors of these works. Each semester, upon the completion of this task, this list of examples consistently includes the work of individuals such as Clemens, Dickinson, Fitzgerald, Frost, Milton, Poe, Shakespeare, Shelley, Thoreau, and Whitman.

As these teacher education students review the lists that they have generated which reflect the concepts and people they have studied in high school, what startles them is how overwhelmingly white and male are these lists. My task now is to demonstrate for them how they can transform the curriculum. First, it is important that they understand that it is the concepts ("novel," "poetry," etc.) that are the focus of instruction, not the examples and their authors ("Milton," "Poe," "Shakespeare," etc.). Once they understand this critical point, I ask them to provide examples of the concepts from different cultural perspectives. Their list of additional examples typically includes the following authors of color: Cisneros, *La Casa en Mango Street*; Langston Hughes, "Freedom Train"; Linda Logan, *Mean Spirit*; Toni Morrison, *Beloved*; Nabokov, *Native American Testimony*; Amy Tan, *Joy Luck Club*; and Villaseñor, *Rain of Gold*.

At the completion of this lesson, students understand that using examples from various ethnic groups to teach these English/language arts concepts transforms the curriculum in two ways. First, the original concepts are viewed from different cultural and ethnic perspectives. Second, new concepts, topics, and constructs are added to the curriculum by the diverse perspectives of the different authors of color. The poetry of Langston Hughes, for example, will bring very different themes and topics to the curriculum than will works by Poe or Dickinson because of Hughes's different race and socioeconomic class. After participating in this lesson, teacher education students also understand that using examples from different cultural perspectives to teach one, two, or a few lessons each year or semester will not be sufficient to transform the English/language arts curriculum. Transforming the curriculum will mean using examples from different cultural perspectives to teach every lesson in the English/language arts curriculum. Every culture need not be present in every lesson; but every lesson should include examples from different cultural perspectives.

Political Challenges to Curricular Transformation

Recently, I conducted a workshop for university professors representing various academic disciplines. One of the challenges to the aforementioned technique of transforming the curriculum[i] came from a European American Rhetoric and Writing professor, and sounded like this: "I don't like the idea of telling students when the authors in the curriculum are minorities. I include minority authors in my curriculum because they provide examples of good writing, not because they are minorities." This response represents a widespread pernicious resistance to multicultural education, as well as a resistance to the recognition and celebration of racial and ethnic differences. To avoid identification of the race and ethnicity of authors of color is to sabotage the purposes of their inclusion in the curriculum: facilitating the academic achievement of students of color by insuring that they see themselves in the curriculum. The race and ethnicity of writers often provide important clues to the writer's perspective—a perspective that might be shared by students in one's class. In *White Teacher*, Vivian Paley (1989) discusses her own development as a teacher in this area of talking about differences:

> In the beginning it was more comfortable to pretend the black child was white. Having perceived this, I then saw it was my inclination to avoid talking about other differences as well. Stuttering, obesity, shyness, divorced parents—the list was long...As I watched and reacted to black children, I came to see a common need in every child. Anything a child feels is different about himself which cannot be referred to spontaneously, casually, naturally, and uncritically by the teacher can become a cause for anxiety and an obstacle to learning. (xv)

Karen Evans, a white third-grade teacher, visits my Introduction to Multicultural Education class each semester to show my students some of the multicultural education lessons she designs and teaches in her third-grade class. She regularly shocks my college students when she tells them that her third graders want to talk about race and ethnicity, while it is her colleagues and other adults who have concerns about her teaching lessons and doing projects that call attention to race in the school setting. Evans's third graders take their cues from her; she is comfortable discussing these concepts and related issues, so her students do not know they should be uncomfortable. This is reasonable because adults are more likely than third graders to have painful memories related to issues of race and ethnicity. It is the adults who remember the awkwardness, confusion, and sadness associated with race-related experiences. They do not want to feel this pain, so they avoid any discussion of race and any distinctions related to race—within or without the curriculum. They would rather be colorblind.

This avoidance of discussion of racial and ethnic differences prevents students from seeing themselves in the curriculum, and possibly presents obstacles to learning. Schofield (1997) identifies an additional negative consequence of the colorblind perspective: the assumption that the only individuals and groups whose accomplishments and contributions are worthy of academic study are white. Schofield and her colleagues studied peer relations between blacks and whites at a middle school in which the administrators had outlawed all references to race or ethnicity by all school personnel and students. Whether in the execution of lesson plans, the resolution of conflicts between students, or casual conversations in the halls, offices, or cafeterias, no mention of race was to be made in spite of the awkwardness that this sometime created (1997).

In her summary of the consequences of this perspective in public schools, Schofield writes,

> The colorblind perspective and its corollaries not only made it more likely that individual faculty members would ignore the challenge of presenting students with materials which related in motivating ways to their own experience, but actually led to a constriction of the education provided to students. (1997, p. 266)

In her conclusion, Schofield cites a teacher at the school she studied who specifically did not mention the race of individuals on a list of great Americans whom students could choose for further study. The list included one African American. Of the decision not to mention race in such a context, Schofield writes:

> In the best of all worlds, there would be no need to make such mention, because children would have no preconceptions that famous people are generally White. However, in a school where one White child was surprised to learn from a member of our research team that Martin Luther King was Black, not White, it would seem reasonable to argue that highlighting the accomplishments of Black Americans and making sure that students do not assume famous figures are White is a reasonable practice. (1997, p. 266)

How Is Multicultural Education Relevant to the "Hard Sciences," e.g. Mathematics?

This next thematic question usually has a prelude that sounds a little like this, "All this touchy feely crap (interpreted, "instructional strategies") sounds fine for the English/language arts and social studies, but I teach mathematics." And then come the questions, "How is multicultural education relevant to the hard sciences, like math?" Or, "I teach math; what am I supposed to do?" Some aspiring math teachers have been even more pointed: "all that loosey goosey stuff might work in social studies, but two plus two is four no matter what color you are." The pedagogical process for engaging students so that they may be able to compute and understand the relative Arabic reality of "two plus two equaling four" is central to practicing multicultural education.

Tate (1995) describes how a middle-school teacher he studied practiced multicultural education using a culturally relevant pedagogy. Sandra Mason (the pseudonym the researcher gave to the teacher who taught mathematics in a predominantly African American middle school) did not use examples of concepts from different ethnic groups to teach subject matter (content integration), which is common in the teaching of social studies and English/language arts. Mason modified her teaching to be consistent with her students' life experiences in order to facilitate their academic success (equity pedagogy) in mathematics. To ensure that instruction would be relevant to students' lived experiences, Mason required students to identify problems that touch their lives to which they would apply the mathematics concepts.

In the year that Tate studied Mason's pedagogy, one of the problems identified by Mason's students was the overabundance of liquor stores in their school neighborhood. Students perceived the liquor stores and the drunks who patronized them as immediate threats to their safety, and a detriment to their quality of life. Implementing a problem/project-based approach to learning, Mason required students to investigate the problem further. After using their knowledge of mathematical concepts and skills (addition, subtraction, decimals, percents, estimation, fractions) to analyze informational resources at the local and state level, these middle-school students created a system to protect their school from the liquor stores. The system they created altered the tax advantages and other fiscal inducements that brought liquor stores to their school community. This work required students to count stores, measure distances between stores and the school, and compare these data with those found in local laws and codes. Tate writes:

> This required the students to think about mathematics as a way to model their reality. Real situations in the students' lives were transformed into mathematical representations. Percentages, decimals, and fractions became more than isolated numbers as the students tried to mathematically manipulate these different, yet related, symbol systems and to link them to real problem solving and decision making. (1995, p. 170)

In addition to maintaining the integrity of the subject matter (mathematics), and reflecting cultural relevance to the lived experiences of these African American students, two other aspects of this pedagogy make it exemplary: It was interdisciplinary and it contained a social-action dimension. The students worked with a local newspaper organization to prepare written and oral presentations (competencies from the English/Language Arts Standards) to be made before local and state governing bodies, including their state senate—and they won national acclaim for their work. The researcher reports that "police have issued over 200 citations to liquor store owners,"..."two of the 13 liquor stores were closed down,"...and "the city council adopted a resolution that liquor not be consumed within 600 feet of the school..." (1995, p. 171).

Tate warns that "Failing to provide African American students with a mathematics curriculum, instruction, and assessment centered on their experiences, culture, and traditions is a major obstacle to achieving equity in mathematics education" (1995, p. 168). I have provided Tate's example of Mason's pedagogy because her pedagogy facilitates equity in mathematics education. The project described in the preceding paragraphs included aspects of African American students' preferred learning styles. According to learning-style specialists, African American learners tend to focus on people rather than things, prefer group work, oral communication, and kinesthetic/active instructional activities (Irvine & York, 1995). What cannot be overemphasized about this teacher's pedagogy is that it located students' experiences and realities in the center of the educational process—and did so without compromising the mathematics subject matter content.

Who Can Accomplish Multicultural Education?

Many of the students in the teacher education program in which I teach are enthused about the prospects of becoming teachers. Even after the myths about multicultural education have been dispelled for them, they consistently ask questions like, "But can *I* really be a multicultural educator? How can one person do all this? How can I know the profession, know my subject matter, know all this cultural content, know all the national, state, and school district standards, and put it all together for teaching every day?"

As a university professor, I have learned the habit of hearing "the questions behind the question." Behind the question, "Can I really be a multicultural educator?" I hear two very quiet questions from the heart of the questioner. If you listen closely, you can hear them too: "Am I adequate?" and "Am I good enough to do this?" Because my teacher education students, like a preponderance of the students entering the teaching profession across the nation, are primarily white women, I hear another question behind the question: "Can a white person really be effective teaching students of color?" These questions about adequacy come from the heart and seem to be void of the cockiness and arrogance that is likely to result in frustration, anger, and mediocrity in the teaching profession. The research of individuals (some of whom are white) who have been successful multicultural educators (Branch, 1999; Ladson-Billings, 1994, 1995; McAllister & Irvine, 2000; Paley, 1989;

Tate, 1995) reveals that: (1) they knew their students—including the students' culture; (2) they knew their subject matter content thoroughly; and (3) they knew their professional roles and responsibilities.

These individuals were effective multicultural educators because they possessed and demonstrated compassion in their work, the courage to take risks, and a commitment to stay the course when the work becomes uncomfortable. The question asked by aspiring teachers, "Am I adequate?" can be answered in the affirmative, if these aspiring teachers can be courageous, compassionate, and committed to children in the practice of multicultural education. Being courageous means being willing to take risks to succeed in the teaching profession. One also needs courage to be introspective. Courageous introspection in the teaching profession means taking the risk to look inside oneself and admit what one does not know and what one needs to learn to be an effective multicultural educator. Courage is necessary to do the emotional work of resolving uncomfortable race-related issues that may prevent one from being effective with children from different race and ethnic groups.

Taking risks to be an effective multicultural educator will mean exercising compassion and patience with oneself, one's colleagues, and one's students as together you try new methods and materials in multicultural education. New and seasoned multicultural educators allow themselves to make mistakes because they know that making mistakes is a part of the human condition. New methods, materials, and processes may be difficult and uncomfortable at first, but they can be perfected over time with liberal amounts of compassion and patience extended to students, colleagues, and oneself.

Finally, a commitment to being the best, and staying the course, will accompany the courage and compassion characteristic of effective multicultural educators. Our children deserve nothing less than the highest quality teachers. Commitment, then, means making the effort, and succeeding at being the best teacher one can be for all of the children in one's care. Commitment also means continuing to do one's best for all of the children in one's care even in the hard times. Hard times may be characterized by insufficient amounts of support from administration, colleagues, or parents; insufficient resources for doing the best job; or momentary feelings of inadequacy because of mistakes made. Commitment, in these hard times, will mean extending all of one's own support, resources, and energy to ensure the academic success of the students in one's care. If you can be courageous, compassionate, and committed, you can be an effective multicultural educator.

References

Au, K. H. & Jordan, C. (1981). Teaching reading to Hawaiian children: Finding a culturally appropriate solution. In H. Trueba, G. P. Guthrie, & K. H. Au (Eds.), *Culture and the bilingual classroom* (pp. 139–152). Rowley, MA: Newbury House.

Banks, J. A. (1997). Multicultural education: Characteristics and goals. In J. A. Banks & C. A. M. Banks (Eds.), *Multicultural education: Issues and perspectives.* (3rd ed.). (pp. 3–31). Boston: Allyn & Bacon.

Banks, C. A. M. (1999). *An Introduction to multicultural education.* (2nd ed.). Needham, MA: Allyn & bacon.

Banks, J. A. (1995). Multicultural education: Historical development, dimensions, and practice. In J. A. Banks & C. A. M. Banks (Eds.). (1995), *Handbook of research on multicultural education.* (pp. 3–24). New York: Macmillan.

Banks, J. A., & Banks, C. A. M. (1995). *Handbook of research on multicultural education.* New York: Macmillan.

Branch, A. J. (1999). *Teachers' conceptions of their role in the facilitation of students' ethnic identity development.* Unpublished doctoral dissertation, University of Washington, Seattle.

Cisneros, S. (1994). *La casa en mango street.* New York: Vintage.

Garcia, E. E. (2001). *Hispanic education in the United States: Raíces y alas.* Lanham, MD: Rowman & Littlefield.

Gay, G. (2000). *Culturally responsive teaching: Theory, research & practice.* New York: Teachers College Press.

Hughes, L. (1987). Freedom train. In L. Hughes (Ed.), *Selected poems of Langston Hughes.* (pp. 276–278). New York: Vintage Books.

Irvine, J. J., & Armento, B. J. (2001). *Culturally responsive teaching: Lesson planning for elementary and middle grades.* Boston: McGraw-Hill.

Irvine, J. J., & York, D. E. (1995). Learning styles and culturally diverse students: A literature review. In J. A. Banks & C. A. M. Banks

(Eds.), *Handbook of research on multicultural education.* (pp. 484–497). New York: Macmillan.

Ladson-Billings, G. (1995). But that's just good teaching! The case for culturally relevant pedagogy. *Theory Into Practice, 34* (3), 159–165.

Logan, L. (1990). *Mean spirit.* New York: Ivy Books.

McAllister, G., & Irvine, J. J. (2000). Cross cultural competency and multicultural teacher education. *Review of Educational Research, 70* (1), 3–24.

Morrison, T. (1987). *Beloved.* New York: Knopf.

Nabokov, P. (1999). *Native American testimony.* New York: Penguin.

Paley, V. G. (1989). *White teacher.* Cambridge, MA: Harvard University Press.

Pewewardy, C. (1993). Culturally responsible pedagogy in action: An American Indian magnet school. In E. Hollins, J. King, & W. Hayman (Eds.), *Teaching diverse populations: Formulating a knowledge base* (pp. 77–92). Albany, NY: SUNY Press.

Ravitch, D. (1990). Diversity and democracy: Multicultural education in America. *American Educator, 14,* 16–20, 46–48.

Schlesinger, A. (1991). *The disuniting of America: Reflections on a multicultural society.* Knoxville, TN: Whittle Direct Books.

Schofield, J. W. (1997). Causes and consequences of the colorblind perspective. In J. A. Banks & C. A. M. Banks (Eds.), *Multicultural education: Issues and perspectives* (3rd ed.). (pp. 251–271). Boston: Allyn & bacon.

Sleeter, C. E., & Grant, C. A. (1987). An analysis of multicultural education in the United States. *Harvard Educational Review, 57* (4), 421–443.

Spielvogel, J. (2001, August 16). Scores on writing exam 'sobering,' here and statewide. *The San Diego Union-Tribune.* pp. B1, B8–9.

Spielvogel, J., & Magee, M. (2001, August 16). County students merely hold their own on basic skills test. *The San Diego Union-Tribune.* pp. B1, B8–9.

Tan, A. (1991). *Joy luck club.* New York: Vintage.

Tate, W. F. (1995). Returning to the root: A culturally relevant approach to mathematics pedagogy. *Theory into Practice, 34* (3), 166–173.

Vasquez, J. A. (1990). Teaching to the distinctive traits of minority students. *The Clearing House, 63,* 299–304.

Villaseñor, V. (1991). *Rain of gold.* Houston, TX: Arte Publica.

[i] Transformation is the third level or approach to Content Integration (Banks, 1997). The first two levels, Contributions and Additive, are not effective for transforming the structure and goals of the curriculum so that it effectively engages students from culturally diverse backgrounds and helps to increase their academic achievement. Beyond Transformation is the Social Action level of Content Integration. This level includes characteristics of the transformation level, and it encourages students to take action in their world as a result of what they have learned.

 African American Students in the Desegregated P–16 Pipeline: Opportunities, Outcomes, and Value - Based Ideologies[1]

M. Christopher Brown II
RoSusan D. Bartee

Education must be redefined and revamped in order to accommodate diverse student populations. The policies and practices implemented in P–16 education have substantial impact on the quality and quantity of African American students who complete high school, college, and/or enter the global workforce (Hodgkinson, 1985). The "flow" within the academic pipeline of elementary and secondary education is critical to the students' lifelong outcomes, including their opportunity for higher education. For African American students in particular, the academic pipeline leading to higher education has the greatest importance (see Brown & Davis, *Black Sons to Mothers: Complements, Critiques, and Challenges for Cultural Workers in Education*).

The K–12 "pipes" of P–16 education are riddled with clogs, leaks, and eroded sealant. According to the Michael Nettles (1997), African American students overall are not performing at a satisfactory level within desegregated systems of elementary, secondary, and higher education across the nation. He further argues that this persistent level of underachievement impacts their opportunity for social mobility and economic stability. The statistics below highlight the state and place of many African American students within the educational pipeline:

1. African Americans only represented 12.5 percent of those students receiving regular high school diplomas in 1993–1994 (Nettles, 1997, p. 7).

2. Despite desegregation, many private (36 percent) and public (20.3 percent) elementary and secondary schools have virtually no African American students enrolled. African Americans cluster in schools that are often (but not always) academically inadequate, focused on vocational-technical (25.6 percent) and special education (16.8 percent), and/or are participants in alternative school models (14.3 percent) rather than regular schools (8.6 percent) (Nettles, 1997, p. 8).

3. After forty-six years of desegregation, public schools with no African American students exhibit near perfect on-time graduation rates compared with baseline averages for public high schools in which African Americans students were in the majority. Similar trends exist as it relates to college application, acceptance, and attendance (Nettles, 1997, p. 10).

4. The disparities between African American and Caucasian college student graduation rates and percentages suggest a potential paucity of qualified African American applicants for positions that require college degrees (Nettles, 1997, p. 2).

The above research findings related to the academic performance of African American students in public education highlight the problems endemic to the current pipeline. In the pages that follow we will explore the role of value-based ideologies in P–16 education. We will focus on the affective and civic aspects of education in order to address some of the pipeline issues concerning African American youth. Additionally, certain values will be discussed as a means of academic (and potentially psychosocial) empowerment for African American students who are currently encumbered by the conditions of desegregated public education.

Rethinking the Import and Impact of Desegregation

As the watershed ruling regarding segregated public education, *Brown v. Board of Education* (1954) establishes the judicial and social standard for open access within school settings. More specifically, *Brown* had two primary planks: (1) a formal rebuke and condemnation of the American system of apartheid in public education, and (2) the issuance of a clarion call for the provision of educational opportunities for African American students (Carter, 1996; Lagemann & Miller, 1996; Wolters, 1984). Policymakers hailed these two planks as the remedy for all of America's social ills. Policymakers believed that 300 years of social, civic, and educational disparity could be resolved via a new initiative—school desegregation. However, despite evidence of "good faith," the formal structures of school desegregation did not eradicate the racial hierarchalization that was now wedded to the national social structure, nor the damage to the collective and individual consciousness of the citizenry (Brown, 1999). Leon Higginbotham (1996) elaborates on this point. Higginbotham posits that the

> *Brown v. Board of Education*...decision merely struck down state-enforced segregation in public schools. It did not, however, convince a great many white parents in either the North or the South to send their children to school with black children...Eventually the precept of black inferiority and white superiority worked itself into the fabric of the American legal process. The social and color ladder became a legal one as well. Looking for evidence of the precept of inferiority in the American legal process, however, is very much like looking for evidence of slavery in the United States Constitution as originally ratified...Similarly the legal process institutionalized the premise of black inferiority without ever specifically delineating in any one case or statute the entire rationale for the precept of black inferiority...But the legal process as a whole was more subtle in assimilating and perpetuating an ideology in which whiteness was the nimbus of superiority, and blackness the stigma of inferiority. (p. 15–16)

The *Brown* ruling was first applied to higher education when the *Florida ex rel. Hawkins v. Board of Control of Florida* suit (350 U.S. 413 [1956]) reached the Supreme Court. The case involved Virgil Hawkins and three other African American students who were denied admission to the University of Florida's law school. The ruling highlighted the potential impotence of the *Brown* ruling in relation to American education. In fact, in order "to free itself from the constraints of the *Brown* implementation decree, the [National Association for the Advancement of Colored People] cited the whole roster of pre-*Brown* higher education cases to support Hawkins's claim for immediate relief" (Preer, 1982, p. 141). Hawkins was never admitted to the University of Florida's law school, and many speculated that "had it not been for the advent of *Brown*...Hawkins* would have been decided differently (T. Jenkins, 1958, p. 200). Beyond the myriad faults, flaws, and failures of the school and collegiate desegregation cases, the general criticism remains: legal precedent is ineffectual in resolving the issue of African American student achievement in the P–16 pipeline, much less the prevailing psychological shackles of racial inferiority on America's public logic (Brown, 1999; Stefkovich & Leas, 1994).

> One of the primary failings of P–16 desegregation has been the focus on colorblindness. According to Preer, The decade after *Brown* saw the fullest definition in terms of color blindness...Generally, in the 1950s, color blindness meant [African American] students entering white school, measuring up to white standard, and [black] institutions merging into white...Academic color blindness not only opened the way for [African American] students to compete for places with whites. In theory, it forced [black] colleges to compete with white colleges. (1982, pp. 148–149)

Even with the nationwide good-faith (and on a rare occasion felicitous) efforts for colorblindness in public education, "the races remained 'separate' and their education 'unequal'" (M. C. Brown, 1995a, p. 34). In fact, the continuing inequality is supported by national statistics (see Frederick D. Patterson Research Institute of the College Fund, (1997 a, b, c) volumes I, II, and III). The disparate achievement rates of African American students within desegregated educational systems raises important questions regarding the P–16 pipeline.

In its recent report, the Southern Education Foundation (1995) similarly calls for rethinking the state of P–16 education. In a discussion of the requisites for P–16 educational reform, the report states that

> Meeting these criteria depends not only on vigorous efforts at colleges and universities, it requires continuous interaction between those institutions and elementary and high schools. These interactions must be mandated and systematized by state policies. These policies should enable public school officials to assess what they consider to be the barriers to minority student access and success in college, while at the same time allowing higher education leaders to comment on problems in public school preparation, as they understand them, and to propose remedies. (p. 45)

Consequently, the issue of African American student success in P–16 systems of public education is unlikely to be resolved soon. Educators and policymakers find themselves treading on unfamiliar ground, since public education has historically been provided great latitude in realizing its professed goals. Notwithstanding, more attention must be paid to the role of value-based ideologies in the educational experiences of African American students.

The Value of Equity, Efficiency, and Community

The physical presence of African American students in a school or classroom does not necessarily mean they will be given fair and equitable treatment. While both school and collegiate desegregation in theory promote equal opportunity in education, both concepts fail to provide meaningful guidance for efficient student outcomes. Equity fights to ensure equality irrespective of conflicting political and rational ideologies. Efficiency, however, addresses costs and benefits as well as inputs and outputs. This market of economic and social capital demands high levels of quality assurance, characterized by the least possible deficits and deficiencies in educational outcomes. Similarly, the value of community must also be considered.

The values of equity, efficiency, and community are key components within the P–16 academic pipeline. The first value, equity, regards meritocracy as a fundamental component of its distribution process. The meritocratic classifications of "most qualified" or "best candidate" presuppose complex notions such as talent, motivation, proper socialization, and equal opportunity (Hurn, 1993). While individual talent and motivation are correlated with the level of academic performance, proper socialization is dependent on adequate resources. To be considered "properly socialized" in a heterogeneous society, one must have access to formidable social networks. Likewise, since socialization outcomes have a preordained market value, this same platform can be used to argue legitimate "talent" and "motivation" as reflections of the status quo.

Meritocracy controls the flow of the academic pipeline. Particularly for African Americans, this "invisible hand" creates visible and devastating effects, as demonstrated in previous statistical findings. Thus, meritocracy does not unequivocally measure individual intelligence and/or qualifications. As a contest-based system, meritocracy is defined by the kinds of access and opportunities it simultaneously enables and delimits. If African American students cluster in impoverished, single race, pseudo-desegregated, inner city schools which employ outdated textbooks and laboratory equipment, is it logical to expect them to demonstrate score parity on nationwide standardized examinations and/or other required assessments with students from well-equipped suburban schools? Since the learning conditions are not the same within the schools, the levels of academic performance cannot reasonably be expected to be the same. Wade Boykin (as cited in Neisser, 1986) states:

> What a child does or does not do is essentially the question of academic performance. It is what Black children do not do in school that creates the need for the present volume. The issue of what a child can do, in contrast, is one of cognitive competence. In its strong form, it implies maturational constraints or structural limitations on ability; in a weaker form it refers to what a child cannot do at present but could in the future if conditions were favorable. (p.7)

Although good, hard-work ethics and study skills are greatly needed, access to resources and opportunities significantly impacts the level of academic performance. Consequently, the issue of the P–16 pipeline is not "the black-white test score gap" (Jencks & Phillips, 1998), but rather the nature of the assessment. Research indicates that students in identical situations score similarly on tests regardless of race (Lemann, 1999).

Furthermore, meritocracy fails to consider institutionalized inequalities, discrimination, and racism as contributors to the disparate rank-based distributions of African American student achievement. These racial vices can greatly affect the attrition rate of African American students flowing through the P–16 academic pipeline. Although racism and discrimination are often labeled as "isolated events," these factors can account for the disproportionate numbers of African Americans faring marginally (at best) in America's desegregated school systems.

Unquestionably, racism and discrimination are endemic to the institutionalized practices of America's public schools (Brown and Ratcliff, 1998). In order to counter these vices, a group-based model of distributive equity must be implemented. Edmund Gordon (1995) offers support for notion of group-based distribution. He states that "equity speaks to and references fairness and social justice" (p. 363). Further, Gordon states that equity "requires that the distribution of social resources be sufficient to the condition that is being treated" (p. 364). Stone (1997) too admonishes that greater attention be paid to "group-based equity," particularly for African Americans.

Likewise, the statistical findings of volume two of the Frederick D. Patterson Research Institute of the College Fund's *The African American Education Databook* (1997 a, b, c) reconfirm the need for a racially conscious group-based equity distribution. The databook reads: "53.8 percent of public schools in which African Americans represented more than one-half of enrollments were located in urban areas, 24.0 percent were located in suburban areas, and 22.2 percent in rural areas" (p. 68). Because urban schools tend to be underfunded and under

resourced, group-based equity distribution is warranted to lessen and perhaps alleviate those reigning inequalities which impact the attrition rates of African Americans in the desegregated academic pipeline (Kozol, 1994).

Efficiency is comprised of benefits and costs, inputs and outputs, and imports and exports. These group-based dichotomies involve significant amounts of exchange according to the value of resources. The ability to gage efficient financial choices becomes key to sustaining the market. According to Stone (1997), "efficient choices are ones that result in the largest benefit for the same cost, or the least cost given the benefit" (p. 61). Stone argues that maximizing potentials and minimizing costs are the fundamental needs of the market. In the context of public school and collegiate desegregation, the argument evokes certain questions: Who or what determines the amount of input, benefits, and imports for public schools? What role does efficiency assume in the community? What is considered a valued resource within the market of public schools? By exploring the implications of these "value" questions, the impact that desegregated schools have on the attrition rates of African Americans in secondary education should become clearer.

Stone (1997) identifies the community as an entity sharing collective goals. Given the importance of defining who carries out community concerns, questions such as the following arise: "Who will be the spokesperson?" "What goals should be given priority?" and "Who holds the power and access?" Since those with access to resources are most likely those with power, those individuals will determine the collective goals. Joel Spring (1998) also addresses the issue of local community politics and its effect on the governance of public education. The political economy and prevailing ideologies impact the educational practices and policies, and such relationships form community power structures that perpetuate the status quo.

Institutional governing boards become authority figures on inputs, benefits, and outputs as part of their role as school administrators. Consequently, there is an increased likelihood that self-serving and/or biased goals will be promoted and served. According to the 1997 report of the National School Boards Association (as cited in the spring 1998 report, p. 134), the following characteristics describe the 95,000 school board members in 14,700 school districts:

1. 60 percent are men.
2. 95 percent are white.
3. 40 percent are between 41 and 50 years of age.
4. 54 percent are self-described religious conservatives.
5. 65 percent are self-described political conservatives.
6. Over 40 percent reported annual incomes of $40,000 to $80,000.

Given the above demographics, it is accurate to declare that school boards reflect a homogeneous, status-quo perpetuating interest. Collegiate-level boards of trustees have similar demographics. Meier, Stewart, and England (also cited in Spring 1998) argue that community and political structures within school governance prohibit equal opportunity from emerging in educational policies and practices.

The homogeneous, classist, and conservative cohort of academic administrators identified above perennially fails to enact policies and practices to accommodate the diverse needs of African American students.

Research shows that African American students disproportionately occupy the lower academic tracks and special education programs within public schools (Niesser, 1986; Frederick D. Patterson Research Institute, 1997a, 1997b, 1997c). There is something inherently disconcerting about these findings.

Is it the case that the educational experiences of African American students do not qualify as legitimate concerns? Hernstein and Murray (1994) argue that African Americans are intellectually inferior based on their biological capacities. Thus, there is no benefit to implementing educational policies and practices geared toward academic success for African American students. Or perhaps, it is seemingly "more efficient" to track African American students into less academically challenging groups rather than provide networks of opportunities and access to enhance their academic performance. Tracking African Americans in such curriculums further decreases their likelihood of attending college.

African American college enrollment is a major P–16 pipeline issue. When African American students are disproportionately tracked into lower-level academic programs their chances of college admission and professional career success is greatly limited. Hence, in order to achieve justice, African American students must have equality of educational opportunity and equity in educational outcomes. While equality is based on the importance of sameness, equity uses resource distribution as a method to combat inequalities. The concept of equality, in theory, becomes manifested in the form of equity in practice.

Academic outcomes in primary and secondary education are critical components to future higher education enrollment, completion, and lifelong career success (Slavin, 1994). Although the pursuit of higher education is considered "choice-based," educational credentials acquired in compulsory education affect the types of postsecondary "choices" available to students (Brown, 1999). Examining the implied value system of school and collegiate desegregation provides a context for understanding the P–16 matriculation process of African Americans.

The Need for More Values—Security and Liberty

The values of security and liberty affect the flow within the P–16 academic pipeline. Stone (1997) identifies security as "protecting people's identities as well as their existence" (p. 90). Power and privilege, which have the physical and social rewards of access and opportunity, are needed to sustain people's identities. Although often disregarded, such needs are critical to students' security, and all reasonable student needs must be met. Hence, when examining the levels of student achievement in desegregated schools it is necessary to investigate the issue of student needs. The investigation should determine whether African American students have access to meaningful networks, adequate resources, and enriching opportunities—their most basic academic needs. Meritocracy and selectivity affect the level of security insofar as they impact resource allocation to the classroom, intervention by the administrative body, and reform initiatives for the policy stakeholders.

The second value is liberty, which grants the freedom of choice. Although this idea of liberty seems to support widespread opportunities for African American students, how liberty gets exercised is highly contingent upon the quality of choices provided by the educational officials. In fact, the value of liberty relates to the value of community because the perspectives of the administration become assimilated into homogeneous goals irrespective of community "needs" or priorities. Whether intentionally or incidentally, the community acts as a political mechanism by forging and/or misconstruing heterogeneous ideologies into "unified" objectives. They can do this through their active involvement in the education of their youth or their silent acquiescence to the dominant orthodoxies practiced by academic officials.

The idea behind desegregation was originally to provide better education for African American students (Halpern, 1995; Kluger, 1975). The original logic posited that a desegregated education would grant African American students access to resources, networks, and opportunities currently unavailable in their segregated schools. The original logic, however, did not prescribe any alteration in the culture, climate, or constitution of the instructional setting, which already embodied equity, efficiency, community, security, and liberty. While the segregated school systems provided a uniquely affirming educational environment for African American students within the social era, the logic argued that desegregated schools would provide new intellectual outlets. Further, the contention was that desegregated schools would be catalysts for universal social mobility.

What has gone unexplored in the era of desegregated, compulsory, and collegiate schooling is the significant role of education as a source of empowerment. However, empowerment only occurs when educational settings provide students with a sense of ownership and belonging. African American students do not by-and-large feel a sense of ownership and/or belonging to the desegregated school (see Jawanza Kunjufu's *To Be Popular or Smart*, 1988). As African American students proceed through the P–16 academic pipeline, public schools must seek to accommodate their diverse educational needs. Educational differences must not be treated as educational deficits. Failure to acknowledge the importance of self-affirmation through security and serendipitous learning through liberty creates disempowering, desegregated educational settings which ill-serve African American students.

From another perspective, Lisa Delpit (as cited in Halsey et al, 1997) argues that African American students must be granted participation in the "culture of power." Delpit cites five aspects of this culture of power essential to the matriculation of African American students in P–16 public education. They include the following: (1) issues of power are enacted in classrooms; (2) there are codes or rules for participating in the structures of power; (3) the rules of the culture of power reflect the rules of the culture of those who have the power; (4) if you are not already a participant in the culture of power, being told explicitly the rules of that culture makes acquiring power easier; (5) those with power are frequently the least aware of, or the least willing to acknowledge, its existence, while those with less power are often most aware of its existence (p. 583).

By asserting the importance of knowing the rules of the culture of power, Delpit sets the stage for preparing African American students for the right kinds of access and opportunities. It is not enough that African American students can read, write, and speak English. They must be able to both articulate and communicate effectively. Likewise, the educational needs of African American students must be defined according to the emerging global market demands. Education must meet the demands at the nexus of African American student preparedness and the extant market forces.

In order to be well prepared, African American students require liberty, which entails the power and privilege that stem from access and opportunity. Liberty sets territorial boundaries between parties that, if crossed, risk the possibility of reaction and rebuttal. Liberty grants freedom of choice within an educational setting. Liberty also connotes meritocracy or selectivity. Liberty, in its effects, prioritizes not only position, but also the "kinds" of choices. According to Edgar Epps (1995):

> Although varying in content and purpose across countries, the most universally recognized function of the schools is to impart knowledge and skills that will enable the learner to participate successfully in the society's institutions...The school's success as a socializing agent depends upon its ability to teach students to see themselves as the school and the society defines them. (p. 596)

This argument pinpoints schools as the source of a person's social power. Thus, African American students in desegregated schools seemingly have very little liberty to exercise.

The school is a socializing agent which significantly impacts all processes within the P–16 academic pipeline. From the liberty standpoint, public schools must begin to assume more responsibility for their role within society. Schools and colleges set the standards and objectives for African American students to follow. George Counts (1932) argues that

> Education as a force...must bridge the gap between school and society and play some part in the fashioning of those great common purposes which should bind the two together...If the schools are to be really effective, they must become centers for the building, and not merely for the contemplation of our civilization. (pp. 28, 34)

Educational settings must engage in mutually respectful relationships with their primary constituents—students. For African American students in desegregated schools, this requires educational settings to investigate what is required to provide a quality education. To the extent that this is done, many of the P–16 pipeline issues involving African American students in primary, secondary, and higher education will be addressed.

First on the list of educational issues to be addressed is the composition and distribution of knowledge. Knowledge contains significant power that can be used to perpetuate ideologies stemming from the status quo or evoke radical educational change. The issue of knowledge has been avoided because of the continuing dispute regarding whose voice should be the definer, the developer, and the disseminator of knowledge. Currently, the debate centers on the roles of the traditional canon of literature versus multicultural perspectives, the centrality of evolutionism versus creationism, and the standardization of age-old language versus politically correct forms. For African Americans, the type of course content has a direct effect on their level of learning (Witherspoon, Speight, & Thomas, 1997).

Public schools are settings for ongoing political battles, and this is demonstrated in the way knowledge is disseminated. Despite the perpetuation of homogeneous ideologies in desegregated schools, systemic reform requires that African American students be provided with classroom situations which value both security and liberty. Security and liberty are manifested when the educational policies and practices reflect the needs of all of the students that they serve. The success of African American students in the P–16 educational pipeline will be contingent upon the willingness of the system to respond to their needs and interests.

Conclusion

The progression of African American students through the P–16 academic pipeline is a major educational policy issue. As the value arguments demonstrate, African American students are failing within desegregated educational settings and desegregated educational settings are failing African American students. The African American student attrition rates are deplorable. Likewise, the matriculation rates of African American students in postsecondary institutions are abysmal.

What do we know?

We know that merit-base equity substantially challenges African American students' opportunity to access the final pipes—13 through 16 (baccalaureate education). We also know that meritocracy, in its present form, does not consider group-based needs. We know that the disproportionate representation of African American students in special education and vocational-technical classes demonstrates that the inequalities are being systematically reproduced, thereby limiting access and opportunity. We know that although racial bias may not impact the academic performance of all African American students in identical ways, the institutionalized practices of discrimination inhibit equitable educational outcomes for African American students. We also know that for African Americans in the desegregated P–16 academic pipeline, the limited resource distributions have created limited access to opportunities. Jonathan Kozol (1991) provides a vivid indication of what happens to students who attend inner-city schools that are under-funded and under-resourced. We know that African American students are not completing the P–16 pipeline at the same rates at which they enter.

For all too many African American students in the academic pipeline, security has been wavering. The matriculation between primary, secondary, and higher education has not been successful. Somewhere within the pipeline, the clogs, leaks, and eroded sealants continue to disrupt the successful flow of African American students. Perhaps they were not informed of the "culture of power" as described by Delpit, or maybe they did not have access to the resources detailed by Kozol (1991). Whatever the reasons, African Americans students are not flowing well within the desegregated P–16 academic pipeline.

Radical systemic change is required in order to move from the equality of educational opportunity offered by *Brown v. Board of Education* to the equity of educational outcomes demanded by the global economy. The goal of placing multicolored bodies in classrooms is not sufficient to guarantee lifelong success. Moving from an era focused on opportunity to one focused on outcomes requires the utilization of value-based ideologies. Infusing the values of equity, efficiency, community, security, and liberty within the P–16 educational settings can potentially prevent African American students from unremittingly succumbing to academic failure. African American students must be provided the power and privileges to successfully participate in the P–16 academic pipeline.

As we enter the twenty-first century, African American students and other similarly situated groups must be prepared to meet the challenges of an ever-evolving global society. Acknowledging and embracing education as a P–16 continuum will enable educators to formulate a systemic remedy to the problems which hinder African American student success. Employing value-based ideologies is only the first (although important) step in responding to the crises that many African American students face in desegregated educational settings. P–16 education must provide the broadest range of opportunity and the highest level of outcomes for African American students, if they are to be prepared for participation in the global workforce. If African American students succeed, the world will prosper and we will all be the beneficiaries.

References

Brown, M. C. (1999). *The quest to define collegiate desegregation: Black colleges, title VI compliance, and post-Adams litigation.* Westport, CT: Bergin & Garvey.

Counts, G. S. (1932). *Dare the school build a new social order?* New York: John Day.

Frederick D. Patterson Research Institute of the College Fund. (1997a). *The African American education databook: Volume I.* Fairfax, VA. Author.

Frederick D. Patterson Research Institute of the College Fund. (1997b). *The African American education databook: Volume II.* Fairfax, VA, Author.

Frederick D. Patterson Research Institute of the College Fund. (1997c). *The African American education databook: Volume III.* Fairfax, VA. Author.

Gordon, E. (1995). Toward an equitable system of educational assessment. *Journal of Negro Education, 64* (3), 360–372.

Halpern, S. C. (1995). *On the limits of the law: The ironic legacy of Title VI of the 1964 Civil Rights Act.* Baltimore, MD: The Johns Hopkins University Press.

Halsey, Lauder, Brown, & Wells. (Eds.). (1977). *Education: culture, economy, society.* Oxford: Oxford University Press.

Hernstein, R., & Murray, C. (1994). *The bell curve.* New York: Free Press.

Hodgkinson, H. (1985). *All one system: Demographics of education, kindergarten through graduate school.* Washington, DC: The Institute for Educational Leadership.

Hurn, C. (1993). *The limits and possibilities of schooling: An introduction to the sociology of education.* (3rd ed.). Boston: Allyn & bacon.

Jencks, C., & Phillips, M. (Eds.). (1998). *The black-white test score gap.* Washington, DC: Brookings Institution Press.

Kluger, R. (1976). *Simple justice: The history of* Brown v. Board of Education *and black America's struggle for equality.* New York: Knopf.

Kozol, J. (1991). *Savage inequalities: Children in America's schools.* New York: Crown.

Kunjufu, J. (1988). *To be popular or smart: The black peer group.* Chicago: African American Images.

Lagemann, E., & Miller, L. P. (Eds.). (1996). Brown v. Board of Education: *The challenge for today's schools.* New York: Columbia University Press.

Lemann, N. (1999). *The big test: The secret history of the American meritocracy.* New York: Farrar, Straus, and Giroux.

Neisser, U. (Ed). 1986. *The school achievement of minority children: New perspectives.* Hillsdale, NJ: Lawrence Erlbaum.

Nettles, M. T. (1997). *Executive summary for the African American education databook: Volume II.* Frederick D. Patterson Research Institute of the College Fund.

Orfield, G., Eaton, S., & the Harvard Project on School Desegregation. (1996). *Dismantling desegregation.* New York: The New Press.

Slavin, R., & Karweit, N. L. (1994). *Preventing early school failure: Research, policy, and practice.* Boston: Allyn & bacon.

Spring, J. (1998). *Conflict of interests: The politics of American education.* (3rd ed.). Boston: McGraw-Hill.

Stone, D. (1997). *Policy paradox: The art of political decision making.* New York: W.W. Norton.

Witherspoon, S., & Thomas, A. (1997). Racial identity attitudes, school achievement, and academic self-efficacy among African American high school students. *Journal of Black Psychology, 23* (4), 344–357.

---

[i] Reprinted with permission. Brown, M. C., & Bartee, R. D. (2000). African American students within the desegregated p–16 pipeline: Opportunities, outcomes, and value-based ideologies. *National Alliance of Black School Educators Journal, 4,* 15–25.

School Mathematics and African American Students: The Need to Revisit Opportunity-to-Learn Standards

William F. Tate

The vision of equity in mathematics education challenges a pervasive societal belief in North America that only some students are capable of learning mathematics. This belief, in contrast to the equally pervasive view that all students can and should learn to read and write in English, leads to low expectations for all too many students.
(NCTM, 2000, pp. 12–13)

Math illiteracy is not unique to Blacks the way the denial of the right to vote in Mississippi was. But it affects Blacks and other minorities much, much more intensely, making them the designated serfs of the information age just as the people that we worked with in the 1960s on the plantations were Mississippi's serfs then.
(Moses & Cobb, 2001, p. 11)

These two quotes help to frame and understand the interrelationship between literacy—broadly defined as reading, writing, numeracy, and technological skills—and opportunity in society. In 2000, the National Council of Teachers of Mathematics can claim without much fanfare or opposition that the pervasive view is that all students can learn to read and write. This has not always been the case in the U.S. In fact, literacy has a legacy associated with the limiting of voting opportunities and ultimately political power, in a system that denied access to the "American Dream." To equate the mathematics literacy movement with the voter rights struggles of the Jim

Crow Era is a powerful and accurate portrayal of the influence of the mathematical sciences in the economic and democratic systems of Western society.

Historically, traditional approaches to mathematics education have been closely associated with a Euro-centric philosophy of elitism and social stratification that aimed to build the economic power and leadership of corporate entities (e.g., Anderson, 1990; Apple, 1992; Cohen, 1982; Ernest, 1991; Hilliard, 1991; Jefferson, 1784/1954; Joseph, 1987; Romberg, 1992; Smith, 1937; Van Sertima, 1988). This approach to mathematics education is represented in tracking systems that provide African American students few opportunities to learn higher-level mathematics (Oakes, 1990). The literature on tracking indicates a disproportionate percentage of African American students are using a mathematics curriculum designed for low-ability or non-college-bound students (Oakes, 1985, 1990). The National Assessment of Education Progress (NAEP) revealed that African American children were less likely than white children to take college preparatory mathematics courses (Dossey, Mullis, Lindquist, & Chambers, 1988). Moreover, white children as a group outperform African American children on NAEP and other national assessments of mathematics achievement (Dossey et al. 1988; Secada, 1992; Tate, 1997 a; Welch, Anderson, & Harris, 1982). Results from the NAEP and other national databases suggest a positive relationship between the number of college preparatory mathematics courses completed by a student and mathematics achievement scores (Dossey et al. 1988; Rock & Pollack, 1995).

Thus, tracking in mathematics education is an important equity problem. The practice of tracking is compounded by the inequitable distribution of resources (Educational Testing Service, 1991; Wong, 1994). The Council of Great City Schools (CGCS, 1992) reported that the average per-pupil expenditure in 1990–91 was $5,200 in a large urban school district compared with $6,073 in suburban public school systems. Although urban public schools allocated the same percentage of their budget (62 percent) to classroom instruction as suburban schools, they spent about $506 less per child on instruction. This discrepancy is especially problematic given that the call for new mathematics standards will increase the burden on fiscally stressed systems of urban education (National Council of Teachers of Mathematics [NCTM], 1989, 1991, 1993). Thus, fiscal management is an important equity problem in mathematics education.

Many educators and policymakers have recognized the equity problems in mathematics education, and opportunity-to-learn frameworks and standards emerged as a response (Elmore & Fuhrman, 1993; NCTM, 1993; Porter, 1993; Stevens, 1993a; Winfield, 1993). However, political considerations resulted in the elimination of opportunity-to-learn standards as a serious policy proposal during the Clinton Administration. The purposes of this article are to reexamine the potential impact of opportunity-to-learn standards on the mathematics experiences of African American students in urban cities and to analyze opportunity-to-learn standards as a policy recommendation.[i] In attempting to conduct such an analysis, I found the paradigmatic boundaries of mathematics education somewhat narrow. Traditional research in mathematics education has not usually analyzed public policy and its relation to equity in the field (Apple, 1992; Davis, 1992). The paradigmatic boundaries of most mathematics education research—mathematics and psychology—have constrained the nature and scope of scholarship to the development and testing of new methods and materials (Kilpatrick, 1992). Thus, the scope of recommendations to administrators and policymakers responsible for urban schools has been limited to suggestions that inform decisions on curriculum, student assessment, and teachers' professional development (NCTM, 1989, 1991, 1993).

In view of these past limitations, I have expanded the paradigmatic boundaries of mathematics education and built on scholarship in which African American culture(s) and experiences have been explicated (e.g., Irvine, 1990; King, 1995; Ladson-Billings, 1990, 1995; Ladson-Billings & Tate, 1995; Tate, 19976). This move is similar to what Bell (1987, 1992) and Williams (1991) have done in law; Collins (1991) in black feminist studies; and King and Mitchell (1990) in sociology and literature. All have crossed the epistemological boundaries of their fields to provide a more cogent analysis of important issues facing African Americans.

Crossing traditional boundaries to explore the potential impact of opportunity-to-learn standards as an equity construct, I first review the political context of mathematics reform and the emergence of opportunity-to-learn standards in this effort. Second, I discuss the epistemological foundation of this approach to equity. Third, I examine the adequacy of opportunity-to-learn standards as a model for achieving equity in mathematics education for African American children in urban schools. In this discussion I address four questions for scholars, policymakers, and administrators charged with developing opportunity-to-learn standards and/or creating opportunity to learn in mathematics.

Mathematics Reform and Opportunity-to-Learn Standards

Some scholars and policymakers attribute the language and arguments for "standards-based" reform to the mathematics education community (National Center for Education Standards and Testing, 1992; O'Day & Smith, 1993). In 1980, the National Council of Teachers of Mathematics (NCTM), a professional organization of mathematics teachers, supervisors, and college professors, published *An Agenda for Action,* which described a ten-year reform process. One purpose of *An Agenda for Action* was to change the focus of school mathematics from a basic skills curriculum to a problem-solving conception of mathematics content and pedagogy. Subsequently, but not as a direct result of *An Agenda for Action,* NCTM sponsored the development of the *Curriculum and Evaluation Standards for School Mathematics* (1989), the *Professional Standards for Teaching Mathematics* (1991), the *Assessment Standards for School Mathematics* (1993), and most recently the *Principles and Standards for School Mathematics* (2000). These documents were a product of extensive literature reviews and a series of working papers that outlined important ideas and issues in the field of mathematics education (Massell, 1994; NRC, 2001; Secada, 1991).

The standards developed by NCTM have been embraced by local and state mathematics organizations, state departments of education, and federal policymakers. For example, with the passage of *Goals 2000,* the rhetoric of federal education policy has begun to move away from attention to the education of traditionally underserved students (e.g., Chapter 1, special education, and bilingual education) and toward a call for high standards for all students. Similarly, state policymakers have been receptive of the NCTM mathematics standards, which have been adopted by forty-one states (Massell, 1994). For example, the Texas Education Agency (1989) used the draft version of the *Curriculum and Evaluation Standards for School Mathematics* as a guide to develop their state textbook proclamation and curriculum objectives.[ii] Other states such as New York, Montana, Michigan, and Delaware have developed or drafted mathematics frameworks built on ideas found in the NCTM standards (Massell, 1994). These state frameworks serve as policy statements that can inform and impact other education-related policymaking (O'Day & Smith, 1993). The idea of the standards serving as the center of policymaking was important to the authors of the *Curriculum and Evaluation Standards for School Mathematics*. They offered three reasons for the creation and adoption of new mathematics standards: (1) to ensure quality, (2) to indicate goals for student learning, and (3) to promote change.

Fuhrman (1993) argued that mathematics curriculum standards alone lack the incentive and accountability mechanisms required for systemic reform and change. O'Day and Smith (1993) theorized that systemic change calls for states and local districts to put in place coherent curriculum policies including (1) the adoption of a curriculum framework (e.g., mathematics standards) to guide the reform effort, (2) instructional materials aligned to the frameworks, and (3) staff development to encourage teachers and to provide them with the knowledge and skills needed for implementing the standards. Most important, systemic reform relies on a top-down accountability model focused on assessments aligned to the mathematics standards. Students would be held accountable by linking decisions about grade promotion, high school graduation, and potential employment to performance on the assessments.

Similarly, federal proposals have called for standards-based systemic educational policies that link school with employment via curriculum reform and high-stakes assessment (Secretary's Commission on Achieving Necessary Skills, 1991, 1992; Pullin, 1994; U.S. Department of Education, 1991). More recently, the Bush administration has supported linking student assessment performance to federal fiscal support. Secretary of Education Rod Paige (2001) stated:

> The President also is proposing a system of rewards for success and sanctions for failure at both the state and local levels. States and schools that make significant progress in closing the achievement gap would be honored with awards from a "No Child Left Behind" school bonus fund and an "Achievement in Education" State bonus fund. States that fail to put in place the required standards, assessments, and accountability systems, or that fail to make adequate yearly progress and narrow achievement gaps, would be subject to losing a portion of their Federal administrative funds. (p. 2)

The current condition of mathematics education for African American students, together with new mathematics standards aligned with high-stakes student assessment with fiscal implications, raises concern about equity and fairness (see, e.g., Winfield & Woodard, 1994). In this political context, opportunity-to-learn standards deserve additional discussion as a possible equity policy.

The Theoretical Foundation of Opportunity to Learn

Opportunity to learn as an important construct influencing, and possibly explaining, the impact of instruction was introduced during the 1960s. Carroll (1963) included opportunity to learn as one of five critical constructs in his model of school learning. He defined opportunity to learn as the amount of time allocated to the learner for the learning of a specific task. If, for instance, the task assigned to a student is to understand the concept of division, opportunity to learn is simply the amount of time the student has available to learn what division is.

In Carroll's (1963) model, opportunity to learn is contrasted with the amount of time the student requires to learn a concept. This latter construct is primarily a function of the student's aptitude in a concept domain. Thus, whereas teachers have some control over the time available for student learning, they have little control over the time required for student learning. Carroll also contrasted opportunity to learn with the amount of time the student actually spends engaged in the process of learning. The latter variable, often referred to as time-on-task or engaged time, is thought to be affected by the perseverance of the student, the quality of the pedagogy, and opportunity to learn. In Carroll's model, opportunity to learn represents the maximum value for engaged time.

In contrast to Carroll, Husén (1967) framed opportunity to learn in terms of the relationship between content taught to the learner and content assessed by achievement tests. In Husén's model, opportunity to learn is the overlap of content taught and content tested. Simply stated, the greater the overlap, the greater the opportunity to learn.

Carroll's (1963) and Husén's (1967) opportunity-to-learn frameworks have two important distinctions. First, whereas Carroll's framework describes opportunity to learn as an instructional variable (under the control of teachers), Husén's framework suggests opportunity to learn is a measurement variable. Second, Carroll considers opportunity to learn to be a continuous variable, whereas Husén describes opportunity to learn as a dichotomous variable. The most important concern from Carroll's perspective is how much time the student has to learn a specific concept. The most important concern from Husén's perspective is whether or not a student has been provided with instruction relative to the concepts included on achievement tests.

Scholars, administrators, and government agencies have used various combinations of Carroll's and Husén's frameworks to construct their own interpretation of opportunity to learn (National Governors' Association, 1993; Robitaille & Travers, 1992; Stevens, 1993b; Winfield, 1987, 1993). However, Stevens (1993a) identified four variables related to teacher instructional practice and student learning that consistently emerge in these interpretations:

1. *Content coverage variables* measure whether or not students cover critical subject matter for a specific grade or discipline.
2. *Content exposure variables* measure the amount of time students spend on a topic (time-on-task) and the depth of instruction provided.
3. *Content emphasis variables* affect the selection of topics within the curriculum and the selection of students for basic skills instruction or for higher-order skills instruction.
4. *Quality of instructional delivery variables* reveals how classroom pedagogical strategies affect students' academic achievement.

The purpose of these opportunity-to-learn variables is to determine whether or not students are provided sufficient access to learn the curriculum expected for their grade level and age. According to Stevens (1993b), the opportunity-to-learn variables are "deceptively simple" (p. 234). In general, research in this area examines one variable at a time; however, the opportunity-to-learn conceptual framework developed by Stevens (1993a, 1993b) encourages teachers, administrators, and researchers to examine the interaction of all four variables simultaneously (see Table 1).

Table 1
Opportunity to Learn: A Conceptual Framework Derived from International and National Research Studies to Examine Students' Access to Intended Curriculum

Variable/Related Study	Description
Content coverage (Leinhardt, 1983; Leinhardt & Seewald, 1981; Yoon, Burstein, Gold, Chen, & Kim, 1990; Winfield, 1987, 1993)	Teacher provides all students access to the intended curriculum. Teacher provides all students access to core subject matter topics. Teacher arranges the curriculum content to overlap test content.
Content exposure (Brophy & Good, 1986; Winfield, 1987, 1993)	Teacher arranges class so that there is time-on-task for students. Teacher arranges adequate time for students to learn subject matter and to cover adequately a specific topic.
Content emphasis (Floden, Porter, Schmidt, Freeman, & Schwille, 1981; LeMahieu & Leinhardt, 1985; McDonnell, Burstein, Catterall, Ormseth, & Moody, 1990; Oakes, 1990; Stevens, 1993b; Porter, 1989, 1993; Suter, 2000)	Teacher chooses content from the curriculum to teach. Teacher chooses the dominant level to teach the curriculum (recall, higher-order skills). Teacher chooses which skills to teach and which skills to highlight with different groups of students (ability grouping and tracking).
Quality of instructional delivery (Brophy & Good, 1986; Stevenson & Stigler, 1992; Stevens, 1993b)	Teacher uses different pedagogical strategies to meet the learner's needs. Teacher has understanding of the subject matter.

Stevens (1993b) stated, "When the opportunity-to-learn framework is used to determine whether or not students are provided sufficient access and information to learn the curriculum provided for their age and grade level, it becomes a powerful concept of educational accountability" (p. 234). Stevens

(1993a, 1993b) and others (e.g., National Governors' Association, 1993; Porter, 1993; Winfield, 1993) argued that some form of opportunity-to-learn framework could serve as a heuristic to guide the evaluation of the systemic reform policy (Goals 2000) calling for new mathematics curriculum standards and high-stakes assessment. However, as the Bush administration and other policymakers formulate their policies on mathematics education reform, especially those on equity, opportunity to learn requires closer scrutiny with respect to addressing the realities of African American students in urban schools.

Opportunity to Learn and Equity in Mathematics Education

Would opportunity-to-learn standards built strictly on constructs of content coverage be sufficient to ensure equity for African American student mathematics? The intent of this section is to examine four issues—purposes of mathematics education, knowledge acquisition, fiscal adequacy, and cultural factors—relevant to the opportunity-to-learn standards debate.

Purposes of Mathematics Education

The question, "what is the purpose of learning mathematics?" is a major issue in the opportunity-to-learn debate. Traditionally, the response to this question has been that students learn one level of mathematics in preparation for the next level and ultimately for their "proper" vocation (Ernest, 1991; Romberg, 1992). This response has long been a part of discussions on the role of mathematics education in economic development (Jefferson, 1784/1954; Smith, 1937). However, the philosophies of mathematics education and principles of economic development underlying these discussions have been problematic from an equity perspective (Secada, 1991). More specifically, the principles guiding these discussions have been closely associated with an elitist Euro-centric ideology of mathematics built on the following beliefs about society, knowledge, children, and education (Ernest, 1991).

1. Society is divided into economic classes, reflecting differences in virtue and ability. All individuals have a place in society, which will remain the same, or slightly improve, if they fulfill their social responsibilities and practice "virtuous" living.
2. Knowledge is derived from authority or experts. True knowledge is certain and above question. Mathematical knowledge is a body of true facts, skills, and theories. Social issues (multiculturalism, environmental issues, world studies, and so on) have no place in mathematics, which is completely neutral and objective.
3. The child is a "fallen angel" and slips easily into play unless checked and disciplined. Strict authority is required to guide the child to a "virtuous" lifestyle.
4. The goal of education is dependent on the social location of the child. For the masses, mastery of basic mathematics skills and training in obedience and servitude serves as preparation for a life of work as befits their social station. For the elite, mastery of a more extended range of mathematics content, as well as training in leadership, serves as preparation for economic and civic leadership roles.

The notion that mathematics is taught strictly to enhance the economic status and development of an entity (individual or corporate) fails to capture the role of mathematics. This vision of mathematics education does not reflect the relationship between the rapid growth of mathematics, the implications of this growth for school mathematics, and the increasing role of mathematics in social decision making (NCTM, 1989, 1991, 1993). For instance, healthcare is a major issue in our society. Decisions to place patients on life support systems will be influenced by technology-driven mathematical modeling. One purpose of this kind of mathematical modeling is to provide doctors, hospital administrators, and insurance companies with cost-benefit analyses of different treatment options for patients (Seligmann & Sulavik, 1992). The potential for undetected racial, class, gender, and age discrimination in this kind of work is real. African American students need to leave school empowered to develop and/or challenge the use of these sorts of mathematical models. Those who have created such models have thus far hidden the biased assumptions of their work from the large segment of society who lack the expertise to expose and counter potentially biased mathematical models with their own mathematically based arguments. A disproportionate number of these disempowered people are African Americans, who bear the brunt of such cost-benefit analyses in the allocation of healthcare (Thomas, 1992; Tranquanda & Glassman, 1992).

Until recently, embedding mathematics curriculum and pedagogy within social and political contexts was not a serious consideration; indeed, it was thought of as an almost heretical activity (Ernest, 1991). The act of counting was viewed as a neutral exercise, unrelated to politics and society (Mellin-Olson, 1987). Yet when do we ever count just for the sake of counting? Only in mathematics classrooms do we count without a social purpose of some kind (Keitel, 1991). Outside of school, mathematics is a tool used to advance or block a particular agenda (Frankenstein, 1995). Unfortunately, mathematics curriculum and pedagogy does not always look to prepare African American students to engage in the authentic contexts of their lives and in the democracy. As another example, the ongoing battle over the construction of racial categories for the census is one of the most technically complex and socially relevant debates of our time (Lee, 1993). Yet the process is rarely discussed in mathematics textbooks. Where will African American students have the opportunity to learn about the mathematical underpinnings of such serious social issues?

It is important that African American students have access to curriculum and pedagogy that looks to prepare them to develop, analyze, and critique mathematized situations.[iii] Moreover, they should be prepared to engage in public discussions about the development and implementation of mathematical models used in social decision-making (NRC, 1999). Such preparation is radically different from merely preparing students to add, subtract, multiply, and divide accurately. Instead, modeling requires these skills, and includes constructing (or selecting) a model, exploring the qualities of the model, adjusting the model, and then applying the model to answer a question of interest. The focus of modeling is on forms of mathematics that are typically underrepresented in the standard curriculum, such as spatial visualization and geometry, measurement, data structure, and uncertainty. Our highly technological society requires all students, not just African American students, to be prepared to use mathematics within real settings of the democracy. Topics such as discrete mathematics, probability, statistics, and mathematical modeling demand increased attention in a technology-driven society (NCTM, 2000).

Technological advancements have made computational and graphical power a vital feature of mathematics. The computer and graphing calculator are changing mathematics and, in turn, increasing the importance of mathematical modeling in school mathematics. Teachers must prepare their students to ask and answer very different questions: Is this the best mathematical model? What methods of mathematical analysis will best support our position? What variables should be included in our analysis to strengthen our position? Can mathematical models minimize the appearance of important variables? Will percentages or fractions make a more striking impression? These questions are especially important given the increased role of mathematics in social decision-making.

Thus far, the opportunity-to-learn framework has been applied only in classrooms implementing rudimentary levels of mathematics (see Winfield, 1993). However, the changes in mathematics, the growth of school mathematics applications, and the escalating role of mathematics in social debates raise the question, should an opportunity-to-learn framework support the rapid growth and changes in the mathematics curriculum?

Race and the reality of assessment reform. The opportunity-to-learn framework should support the rapid growth and changes in the mathematics curriculum. However, an opportunity-to-learn framework built strictly on the overlap of content taught and content tested ignores the role mathematics assessment has played in creating low-level curriculum opportunities for African American students in urban schools. Two factors involving assessment illustrate the problem of fit between this type of opportunity-to-learn framework and equity for African American students.

First, in a comparison of teachers with high and low percentages of African American students, those with high percentages reported significantly more often that test scores were "very" or "extremely important" for evaluating student progress, placing students in special services, planning curriculum and instruction, recommending textbooks, and giving students feedback (Madaus, West, Hannon, Lomax, & Viator, 1992; Strickland & Ascher, 1992). They also more often reported using test-oriented pedagogical strategies and being pressured by their administrations to increase test scores. Madaus and colleagues (1992) found that in high-minority classrooms about 60 percent of the teachers focused on teaching test-taking skills, teaching topics known to be on the assessment, emphasizing tested content, and beginning preparation more than a month before the test. These strategies were reported significantly less often in classrooms with few minority students. The problem with these practices is that teachers are forced to rush instruction and many students do not have the time needed to learn more advanced-level mathematical concepts (Madaus et al. 1992). For example, *The Curriculum and Evaluation Standards for School Mathematics* (NCTM, 1989) called for students to engage in active inquiry, problem solving, and inductive reasoning. Teaching within this context will take more time—to plan, to conduct, and to assess—than coverage of content found on traditional measures of achievement (Wiske & Levinson, 1992). Under these conditions, an opportunity-to-learn model built strictly on a textbook coverage approach would create an equity problem rather than solve one.

A second related problem with an opportunity-to-learn model strictly built on the overlap of content taught and content tested is that, historically, mathematics tests have assessed low-level skills (NCTM, 1993; Berlak, 1992). Emphasizing narrowly defined tested content is a serious impediment to the implementation of a high-level mathematics curriculum. Thus, teachers of African American students who focus largely on mathematics test preparation teach mostly rudimentary levels of mathematics (Madaus et al. 1992). It is possible to argue that by raising the mathematics standards for African American students, and building the tests on these standards, teachers will align their pedagogy with the tests (O'Day & Smith, 1993). However, mathematics assessment that measures both high and low levels of understanding has yet to be perfected (Wilson, 1992). Thus, creating an opportunity-to-learn model predicated on the existence of this capability is premature.

Acquisition of Mathematical Knowledge

The question, how does a student come to know and understand mathematics? is a central issue in the opportunity-to-learn debate. Some opportunity-to-learn models appear to be built on the assumption that mathematical knowledge is an accumulation of discrete pieces of information (e.g., addition of whole numbers or multiplication of decimals) presented in sequential order (Stevens, 1993a; Winfield, 1993). Moreover, these models assume the learner is a passive recipient of these discrete pieces of information. This behaviorist perspective calls for a one-way transmission of information from the teacher to the whole class (U.S. Department of Education, 1994). This view of student knowledge acquisition is being challenged.

Scholars in mathematics education are working to clarify the nature of mathematical cognition and describe it in such a way that educators can determine how to teach mathematics for understanding (e.g., Carey, Fennema, Carpenter, & Franke, 1995; Cobb, Yackel, & Wood, 1992; Fennema, Franke, Carpenter, & Carey, 1993; Mack, 1990). One such line of inquiry, cognitively guided instruction (CGI), provides insight into the shift from a behaviorist interpretation of mathematics learning and pedagogy to a cognitive science framework by suggesting that instruction linked to the thinking and experiences of the student is essential to pedagogical success (i.e., student learning).

The CGI studies are built on Carpenter and Moser's (1983) analysis of young children's teaming of addition and subtraction. They developed a conceptual framework of the content domain of addition and subtraction that identified eleven types of addition and subtraction word problems that could be solved by young children. Using individual interviews with children, they found hierarchies of difficulty for specific types of problems and identified the strategies used by young children to solve these problems. As children matured, they could solve more complicated problem types with increasingly sophisticated strategies.

Thus, knowledge of addition and subtraction is an integrated domain that includes conceptual content analysis combined with children's thinking about the various components of the content. The research by Carpenter and Moser (1983) is important because it focused on mathematics content taught in school and provided insight into children's thinking about this content (Fennema & Franke, 1992). Most importantly, this research served as a significant step toward the development of a knowledge base of students' thinking about a mathematics content domain.

Subsequently, studies were conducted which determined that teacher knowledge of children's thinking about addition and subtraction can affect teachers' instructional decision-making and student learning (e.g., Carpenter, Fennema, Peterson, & Carey, 1988; Carpenter, Fennema, Peterson, Chiang, & Loef, 1989; Fennema et al. 1993). Evidence from the CGI studies indicates that teachers can develop pedagogical strategies for each student when they have organized knowledge of the content domain that includes students' thinking within the domain.

Thus, the CGI studies support the idea that knowledge of students' thinking, when it is integrated, robust, and a part of the established curriculum, can affect the teaching and learning of mathematics (Fennema & Franke, 1992). It is important to point out that most content areas within school mathematics lack this integrated set of knowledge. However, the general consensus in the mathematics education research community is that learning is dependent on the knowledge the learner brings to the experience (Hiebert & Carpenter, 1992; U.S. Department of Education, 1994). Moreover, pedagogy should build on the students' conceptions. Yackel, Cobb, Wood, Wheatley, and Merkel (1990) provided insight into this constructivist perspective:

> We contend that not only are children capable of developing their own methods for completing school mathematics tasks but that each child has to construct his or her own mathematical knowledge. That is, in our view, mathematical knowledge cannot be given to children. Rather, they develop mathematical concepts as they engage in mathematical activity, including trying to make sense of methods and explanations they see or hear from others. The implications of this view for instruction are that children should be provided with activities that are likely to give rise to genuine mathematical problems. Accordingly, we developed instructional activities designed to foster children's construction of relatively sophisticated concepts of procedures, such as place value and computational algorithms. (p. 13)

Should the paradigmatic shift in mathematics education from behaviorism to constructivism be reflected in the opportunity-to-learn framework?

Constructivism and the measurement problem. The paradigmatic shift to constructivism should be reflected in an opportunity-to-learn framework. Although it is possible to provide instruction guided by principles of constructivism, traditional mathematics achievement tests are built on principles of behaviorism (Bloom, Hastings, & Madaus, 1971). The disadvantage of the traditional approach to assessment is that it encourages teachers to focus on superficial forms of learning.

Wilson (1992) recognized the limitation of the behaviorist approach to mathematics assessment. He pointed out the challenge is to find out enough about student understanding in mathematics to design performances and construct assessment strategies that reflect this understanding. Wilson stated, "Even in domains where much research has been done, it may be the case that important subgroups of students give responses that do not match our expectations well" (1992, p. 217).

In sum, current forms of mathematics assessment do not reflect constructivist principles of learning. Efforts to employ opportunity-to-learn frameworks that build on behaviorist approaches to assessment and learning impede rather than support opportunity to learn.

Fiscal Condition of Schools

The question, which school districts can afford to implement new mathematics standards? is a critical issue in the opportunity-to-learn debate. A 1990 national assessment of eighth-grade mathematics programs found a strong relationship between students' economic status and the level of resources provided for their classroom experience. More than 80 percent of teachers in schools with middle- to upper-class students received all or most of the materials or resources they requested for instructional purposes. In stark contrast, only 41 percent of teachers in schools with the largest concentrations of poor students received all or most of the instructional materials they requested (Educational Testing Service, 1991). Further, the students whose teachers reported having limited materials or resources had lower mathematics achievement than those whose teachers indicated their materials or resources were sufficient. The group of students with lower mathematics achievement was disproportionately African American (National Center for Education Statistics, 1993).

The call for new mathematics standards represents an epistemological shift in school mathematics from a shopkeeper (basic skills) philosophy of mathematics pedagogy to a constructivist, technology-driven vision of mathematics instruction (Devaney, 1991; Friske, 1988; Romberg, 1992; Smart, 1987). The fiscal appeal of a basic-skills mathematics curriculum is the low implementation cost. However, the technology-based vision of school mathematics requires urban schools to (1) reallocate funds and/or seek additional funding to improve teachers' mathematics qualifications, (2) update instructional materials (e.g., textbooks, science laboratories, and computer facilities), (3) provide summer mathematics programs, and (4) enhance the quality of many other resources (e.g., deteriorating classrooms and buildings) (Clune, 1993; Entwilse & Alexander, 1992; Kozol, 1991; NCTM, 1989).

Clune (1993) argued that the standards-based approach to educational policymaking requires rethinking fiscal policy. He contended funding should shift from fiscal equity to adequacy, and from discussions of financial inputs to emphasis on standards-based outcomes as the goal of both educational policy and finance. For example, in mathematics education, implementing a policy of fiscal adequacy would require each school district to (1) adopt a set of mathematics standards, (2) identify the resources necessary for achieving these standards, (3) formulate a long-term plan for developing an instructional program that incorporates the standards and for allocating the aligned resources, (4) have an implementation plan in place before money is spent, and (5) adopt the necessary structural changes to maximize cost-effectiveness (Clune, 1993; O'Day & Smith, 1993; Odden, 1992; Verstegen, 1994; Wong, 1994).

Policy proposals linking fiscal adequacy and opportunity-to-learn standards to the new mathematics standards have faced political opposition (see discussion by Porter, 1993). The Clinton administration supported the removal of amendments to the *Goals 2000* plan that would have linked federal education aid to local school districts' opportunity-to-learn standards (Kondracke, 1993). Also, the administration supported eliminating the fiscal connection between proposed mathematics performance assessments and opportunity-to-learn standards. The administration's decision to remove fiscal considerations from federal mathematics education reform proposals is linked to its philosophy of governance. Piliawsky provided insight into this philosophy:

> Clinton's "New Covenant" acceptance speech to the 1992 National Convention provides a useful guide to the Democratic Party's current political philosophy. Clinton called for a compact "between the people and their government" that makes "opportunity" contingent on "responsibility" and "restore[s] America's founding values" of "family, community" and "hard work." The Democrats claim that their approach represented an alternative to conservatives' coldhearted policy of laissez-faire capitalism and the liberals' knee-jerk belief in government spending as the solution to every problem...In reality, the Democrats' "third way," the so-called post-liberal consensus, is profoundly conservative. The primary stress is on

individual "responsibility," a word that appeared over twenty times in Clinton's address. What is sacrificed in this new vision is the liberal Democratic tradition of public assistance for disadvantaged people. (1994, p. 4)

The drawback of the Clinton administration's call for new mathematics standards without provisions for fiscal adequacy may be illustrated with a simple analogy (Tate, 1995). If drivers are to benefit from a toll road, they must be able to afford the fee. Similarly, those school districts that want to adopt the new mathematics standards must be able to afford the implementation costs. Many urban school districts are hampered by local fiscal constraints that impede mathematics reform (Kozol, 1991). Without significant federal financial support and local fiscal restructuring, many urban school districts will lack the capacity to reform. Thus the question is, should efforts to create opportunity to learn for African American students in urban schools be based on the toll road principle or on fiscal adequacy?

The need for fiscal support. An opportunity-to-learn framework that fails to include an appropriate fiscal adequacy component cannot fully support the adoption and implementation of high-level mathematics standards. The authors of the *Curriculum and Evaluation Standards for School Mathematics* (NCTM, 1989) recognized the new costs associated with preparing students to use mathematics in authentic contexts. Romberg provided insight into the thinking of the standards' authorship team:[iv]

> As the Standards were being developed, we were aware that change
> is costly. In fact, we felt that the primary costs would occur in the professional reeducation of teachers. Our strategy was to create a demand for new products (text materials, software, tests, teacher preparation programs, and in-service programs). (1992, p. 435)

To be effective, an opportunity-to-learn framework must address fiscal support.

Cultural Factors in Mathematics Education

What type of mathematics pedagogy, curriculum, and assessment practices must an African American student in an urban school negotiate to be successful? Traditionally, mathematics pedagogy has emphasized whole-class lectures, with teachers modeling one strategy for solving a problem and students listening to the explanation. Generally, this is followed by students working alone on a large set of problems from a worksheet or textbook (Fey, 1981; Porter, 1989; Stodolsky, 1988). The intent of this teacher-directed model of instruction is to prepare students to produce correct answers to narrowly defined problems. The curriculum often includes a tracking system, with many African American students being selected to participate in compensatory mathematics programs such as Chapter 1. The focus of these back-to-basics-type programs is the mastery of low-level computational skills (Strickland & Ascher, 1992). Typically, these programs portray mathematics as disconnected from the learner and void of real social context (LeTendre, 1991). Woodson (1933/1990) described the presentation of abstract and disconnected mathematical facts as a "foreign method" incapable of preparing the African American student for life in the U.S.

Today, the foreign method of mathematics education delineated by Woodson erects barriers to equity in school mathematics such as (1) persistent tracking, (2) fewer opportunities for African American students to learn from the best-qualified mathematics teachers, (3) less access to technology in school mathematics, and (4) cultural discontinuity between school mathematics and African American student life outside of school (National Science Board, 1991; Oakes, 1990; Piller, 1992; Stanic, 1991). The first three of these barriers to equity, which can be captured with statistical methods, are considered "acceptable" evidence of unequal conditions within the traditional paradigmatic boundaries of mathematics education. In contrast, the fourth barrier—cultural discontinuity—cannot be objectified with numbers and is subtler.

Stiff and Harvey (1988) reported that African American students who incorporated discussions of their lives and experiences within mathematics classroom discourse risked being dismissed from the communication process for digressing on and belaboring "extraneous matters." Similarly, Glaser and Silver (1994), Silver, Smith, and Nelson (1995), and Tate (1994) discussed how a group of African American middle-school students who integrated their out-of-school experiences into mathematical problem solving were penalized. The students were asked the following question on a district-wide test: "It costs $1.50 each way to ride the bus between home and work. A weekly pass is $16.00. Which is the better deal, paying the daily fare or buying the weekly pass?" The district's assessment group designed the test item on the assumption that students who solved the problem correctly would select the option to pay the daily fare. Implicit in the design of the assessment task is the notion that all people work five days a week. It is also assumed that the worker has one place of employment. These assumptions are closely associated with an "idealized White middle class" reality (Apple, 1979).

Yet these assumptions are not consistent with the daily lives of many African American students (Darity & Meyers, 1989). Thus, in retrospect, it seems appropriate that a large percentage of the students in this particular middle school selected the option "buy the weekly pass." When teachers and administrators questioned the students about their selections, they discovered many students had centered themselves in the solution process. These students transformed the "neutral" assumptions of the problem—all people work five days a week and have one job—into their own realities and perspectives. For example, the students stated that more than one family member could use the weekly pass. They also mentioned the opportunity to use the weekly pass on weekends. In the households of many African American students, the economic providers may hold several jobs—both on weekdays and weekends. For these children, selecting the weekly pass was financially correct and, thus, mathematically logical.

Understand the point here. It is not to suggest that all African American students have the same experiences and perspectives. In fact, African American students bring multiple experiences and realities to classrooms. However, the underpinnings of the school mathematics curriculum, assessment, and pedagogy are often more closely aligned with the idealized experience of the white middle class (Anderson, 1990; Baugh, 1994; Berlak, 1992; Garcia & Pearson, 1994; Stanic, 1991). Moreover, this alignment is subtle and often difficult to diagnose (King, 1991; Lawrence, 1987).

Despite its subtlety, the disconnection of mathematics classroom practice from the experiences and traditions of African American students represents a loss of opportunity to learn mathematics. Current proposals for opportunity-to-learn standards use combinations of engaged time and content coverage as central variables. These proposed models would not detect the missed opportunities to learn mathematics that result from cultural discontinuity. Should future research and development on opportunity-to-learn standards in mathematics include cultural factors as a construct?

The need for cultural congruence. Opportunity-to-learn models that only examine the overlap of content taught and content tested ignore the influence of cultural factors on student learning. This is problematic if equity in school mathematics is the intent of an opportunity-to-learn framework. Future research and development on the opportunity-to-learn concept should begin with recommendations found in the *Professional Standards for Teaching Mathematics* (NCTM, 1991), which call for mathematics pedagogy to build on (1) how students' linguistic, ethnic, racial, gender, and socioeconomic backgrounds influence their learning; (2) the role of mathematics in society and culture; (3) the contribution of various cultures to the advancement of mathematics; (4) the relationship of school mathematics to other subjects; and (5) the realistic application of mathematics to authentic contexts. Together these recommendations suggest opportunities to learn mathematics should build on African American students' thinking and should link to authentic contexts of society (King, 1995; Ladson-Billings, 1990, 1994; Stanic, 1991).

Conclusion

The purpose of this article is to examine the appropriateness of opportunity-to-learn standards as an equity framework for African American students in school mathematics. The importance of such an equity framework to guide and assist teachers, policymakers, administrators, and researchers is beyond question. Scholars who have employed opportunity-to-learn frameworks in their research have provided important descriptions of classroom practice and suggestions for more equitable pedagogy. Many proponents of opportunity-to-learn frameworks define equity as the overlap of curriculum content and testing content (Stevens, 1993a, 1993b; Winfield, 1993). They claim this method of gauging equity is simple. A strength of this method is that administrators, teachers, and researchers can conduct mathematics program evaluations by examining the overlap between mathematics content covered in classes and content covered in tests. However, this simplistic approach fails to adequately address many of the realities and needs of African American students seeking a mathematics education in urban schools.

Four questions that emerged from this analysis are relevant to future research and evaluation of African American students' opportunity to learn mathematics: (1) Should the opportunity-to-learn framework be consistent with the rapid growth and changes in the mathematics curriculum and the changing role of mathematics in our society? (2) Should the opportunity-to-learn framework reflect the paradigmatic shift in mathematics education from behaviorism to constructivist principles of learning and teaching? (3) Should efforts to create opportunity to learn for African American students in urban schools build on the concept of fiscal adequacy? And (4) should the opportunity-to-learn framework provide insight into cultural factors that influence mathematics learning?

I argue the answer to each of these questions is "yes." Moreover, administrators and policymakers could benefit from opportunity-to-learn standards that address these questions. First, most school administrators are charged with providing the instructional vision for their school. Opportunity-to-learn standards grounded in research on mathematics curriculum and pedagogy provide an important framework to assist in setting program goals and guiding instructional practice. Second, an opportunity-to-learn framework provides a standard to measure the accomplishments and shortcomings of the mathematics instructional program. More specifically, opportunity-to-learn standards can provide insight into the experiences of African American students in school mathematics. This insight can serve as a guide to administrators seeking to improve African American achievement in mathematics.

An opportunity-to-learn framework can be a barrier or springboard to mathematics reform. If it is designed on outdated theories of learning and teaching and without a fiscal component, it will surely be a hindrance to creating equitable opportunities to learn for African American students.

References

Anderson, S. E. (1990). Worldmath curriculum: Fighting Eurocentrisin in mathematics. *Journal of Negro Education, 59,* 348–359.

Apple, M. W. (1979). *Ideology and curriculum.* London: Routledge & Kegan Paul.

Apple, M. W. (1992). Do the standards go far enough? Power, policy, and practice in mathematics education. *Journal for Research in Mathematics Education, 23* (5), 412–431.

Baugh, J. (1994). New and prevailing misconceptions of African American English for logic and mathematics. In E. T. Hollins, J. E. King, & W. C. Hayman (Eds.), *Teaching diverse populations: Formulating a knowledge base* (pp. 191–206). Albany, NY: SUNY Press.

Bell, D. (1987). *And we are not saved. The elusive quest for racial justice.* New York: Basic Books.

Bell, D. (1992). *Faces at the bottom of the well: The permanence of racism.* New York: Basic Books.

Berlak, H. (1992). The need for a new science of assessment. In H. Berlak, F. M. Newmann, E. Adams, D. A. Archbald, T. Burgess, J. Raven, & T. A. Romberg (Eds.), *Toward a new science of educational testing and assessment* (pp. 181–206). Albany, NY: SUNY Press.

Bloom, B. S., Hastings, J. T., & Madaus, G. F. (1971). *Handbook on formative and summative evaluation of student teaming.* New York: McGraw-Hill.

Brophy, J., & Good, T. (1986). Teacher behavior and student achievement. In M. Wittrock (Ed.), *Handbook of research on teaching* (pp. 328–375). New York: Macmillan.

Carey, D. A., Fennema, E., Carpenter, I. P., & Franke, M. L. (1995). Cognitively guided instruction: Equitable classrooms in action. In W. G. Secada, E. Fennema, & L. Byrd (Eds.), *New directions for equity in mathematics education* (pp. 93–127). Cambridge: Cambridge University Press.

Carpenter, T. P., Fennema, E., Peterson, P. L., & Carey, D. A. (1988). Teachers' pedagogical content knowledge of students' problem solving in elementary arithmetic. *Journal for Research in Mathematics Education, 19* (5), 385–401.

Carpenter, T. P., Fennema, E., Peterson, P. L., Chiang, C. P., & Loef, M. (1989). Using knowledge of children's mathematics thinking in classroom teaching: An experimental study. *American Educational Research Journal, 26* (4), 499–532.

Carpenter, T. P, & Moser, J. M. (1983). The acquisition of addition and subtraction concepts. In R. Lesh & M. Landau (Eds.), *The acquisition of mathematical concepts and processes* (pp. 7–14). New York: Academic Press.

Carroll, J. B. (1963). A model of school learning. *Teachers College Record, 64,* 723–733.

Clime, W. H. (1993). The shift from equity to adequacy in school finance. *The World and I, 8,* 389–405.

Cobb, P., Yackel, E., & Wood, T. (1992). A constructivist alternative to the representational view of mind in mathematics education. *Journal for Research in Mathematics Education, 23* (l), 2–33.

Cohen, P. C. (1982). *A calculating people: The spread of numeracy in early America.* Chicago: University of Chicago.

Collins, P. H. (1991). *Black feminist thought.* New York: Routledge.

Council of the Great City Schools. (1992). *National urban education goals: Baseline indicators,* 1990–91. Washington, DC: Author.

Darity, W. A., & Meyers, S. L. (1989). *The problem of family structure, earnings, inequality, and the marginalization of Black men.* College Park: University of Maryland, Departments of Economics and African American Studies.

Davis, R. B. (1992). Reflections on where mathematics education now stands and on where it may be going. In D. A. Grouws (Ed.), *Handbook of research on mathematics teaching and learning* (pp. 724–734). New York: Macmillan.

Devaney, R. L. (1991). Putting chaos into the classroom. In M. J. Kenney (Ed.), *Discrete mathematics across the curriculum, K–12* (pp. 184–194). Reston, VA: National Council of Teachers of Mathematics.

Dossey, J. A., Mullis, I. V. S., Lindquist, M. M., & Chambers, D. L. (1988). *The mathematics report card: Are we measuring up?* Princeton, NJ: Educational Testing Service.

Educational Testing Service. (1991). *The state of inequality: A policy information report.* Princeton, NJ: Author.

Elmore, R. F, & Fuhrman, S. H. (1993). Opportunity to learn and the state role in education. In S. L. Traiman (Ed.), *The debate on opportunity-to-learn standards* (pp. 73–102). Washington, DC: National Governors' Association.

Entwisle, D. R., & Alexander, K. L. (1992). Summer setback: Race, poverty, school composition, and mathematics achievement in the first two years of school. *American Sociological Review, 57* (l), 72–84.

Ernest, P. (1991). *The philosophy of mathematics education.* London: Falmer Press.

Fennema, E., & Franke, M. L. (1992). Teachers' knowledge and its impact. In D. A. Grouws (Ed.), *Handbook of research on mathematics teaching and learning* (pp. 147–164). New York: Macmillan.

Fennema, E., Franke, M. L., Carpenter, T. P., & Carey, D. A. (1993). Using children's mathematical knowledge in instruction. *American Educational Research Journal, 30,* 555–584.

Fey, J. T (1981). *Mathematics teaching today: Perspectives from three national surveys.* Reston, VA: National Council of Teachers of Mathematics.

Floden, R., Porter, A., Schmidt, W., Freeman, D., & Schwille, J. (1981). Responses to curriculum pressures: A policy-capturing study of teachers' decisions about context. *Journal of Educational Psychology, 73,* 129–141.

Frankenstein, M. (1995). Equity in mathematics education: Class in the world outside the mathematics class. In W. G. Secada, E. Fennema, & L. Byrd (Eds.), *New directions for equity in mathematics education* (pp. 165–190). Cambridge: Cambridge University Press.

Friske, J. S. (1988). Using computer graphing software packages in algebra instruction. In A. F. Coxford (Ed.), *The ideas of algebra, K-12* (pp. 181–184). Reston, VA: National Council of Teachers of Mathematics.

Fuhrman, S. H. (1993). The politics of coherence. In S. H. Fuhrman (Ed.), *Designing coherent education policy* (pp. 1–34). San Francisco: Jossey-Bass.

Garcia, G. E., & Pearson, P. D. (1994). Assessment and diversity. In L. Darling-Hammond (Ed.), *Review of research in education* (pp. 337–391). Washington, DC: American Educational Research Association.

Glaser, R., & Silver, E. (1994). Assessment, testing, and instruction: Retrospect and prospect. In L. Darling-Hammond (Ed.), *Review of research in education* (pp. 393–422). Washington, DC: American Educational Research Association.

Goals 2000. Educate America Act, H.R. 92, House of Representatives, January 5, 1993.
Hiebert, J., & Carpenter, T. P. (1992). Learning and teaching with understanding. In D. A. Grouws (Ed.), *Handbook of research on mathematics teaching and learning* (pp. 65–100). New York: Macmillan.
Hilliard, A. (1991). Do we have the will to educate all children? *Educational Leadership, 49*, 31–36.
Husén, T. (Ed.). (1967). *International study of achievement in mathematics. A comparison of twelve countries.* New York: Wiley.
Irvine, J. (1990). *Black students and school failure.* Westport, CT: Greenwood.
Jefferson, T. (1954). *Notes on the state of Virginia.* New York: Norton. (Original work published in 1784.)
Joseph, G. C. (1987). Foundations of Eurocentrism in mathematics. *Race and Class, 28*, 13–28.
Keitel, C. (1991). *Implicit mathematical models in social practice and explicit mathematics teaching by applications.* Paper presented at the International Conference on the Teaching of Mathematical Applications, Nordwijkerhout, The Netherlands.
Kilpatrick, J. (1992). A history of research in mathematics education. In D. A. Grouws (Ed.), *Handbook of research on mathematics teaching and learning* (pp. 3–38). New York: Macmillan.
King, J. K. (1991). Dysconscious racism: Ideology, identity, and the miseducation of teachers. *Journal of Negro Education, 15*, 145–153.
King, J. K. (1995). Culture-centered knowledge and research in the African American intellectual tradition: Its nature, production and uses in multicultural education. In J. Banks & C. Banks (Eds.), *Handbook for research in multicultural education* (pp. 265–292). New York: Macmillan.
King, J. K., & Mitchell, C. (1990). *Black mothers to sons: Juxtaposing African American literature and social practice.* New York: Peter Lang.
Kondracke, M. (1993, September 29). Hanging tough on education. *The Dallas Morning News,* p. 27A.
Kozol, J. (1991). *Savage inequalities: Children in America's schools.* New York: Crown.

Ladson-Billings, G. (1990). Like lightning in a bottle: Attempting to capture the pedagogical excellence of successful teachers of Black students. *Qualitative Studies in Education, 3,* 335–344.

Ladson-Billings, G. (1994). *The dreamkeepers: Successful teachers of African American children.* San Francisco: Jossey-Bass.

Ladson-Billings, G. (1995). Making mathematics meaningful in cultural contexts. In W. O. Secada, E. Fennema, & L. Byrd (Eds.), *New directions for equity in mathematics education* (pp. 126–145). Cambridge: Cambridge University Press.

Ladson-Billings, G. & Tate, W. F. (1995). *Toward a critical race theory of education. Teachers College Record, 97,* 47–68.

Lawrence, C. (1987). The id, the ego, and equal protection: Reckoning with unconscious racism. *Stanford Law Review, 39,* 317–388.

Lee, S. M. (1993). Racial classification in the U.S. Census: 1890–1990. *Ethnic and Racial Studies, 16,* 75–94.

Leinhardt, G. (1983). Overlap: Testing whether it is taught. In G. F. Madaus (Ed.), *The courts, validity, and minimum competency testing* (pp. 153–170). Boston: Kluwer-Nijhoff.

Leinhardt, G., & Seewald, A. (1981). Overlap: What's tested, what's taught? *Journal of Educational Measurement, 18* (2), 85–96.

LeMahieu, P., & Leinhardt, G. (1985). Overlap: Influencing what's taught, a process model of teachers' content selection. *Journal of Classroom Interaction, 21* (1), 2–11.

LeTendre, M. J. (1991). The continuing evolution of a federal role in compensatory education. *Educational Evaluation and Policy Analysis, 13,* 328–334.

Mack, N. K. (1990). Learning fractions with understanding: Building on informal knowledge. *Journal for Research in Mathematics Education, 21,* 16–32.

Madaus, G. F., West, M. M., Harmon, M. C., Lomax, R. G., & Viator, K. A. (1992). *The influence of testing on teaching math and science in grades 4–12.* Boston: Boston College, Center for the Study of Testing, Evaluation, and Educational Policy.

Massell, D. (1994). Setting standards in mathematics and social studies. *Education and Urban Society, 26,* 118–140.

McDonnell, L., Burstein, L., Catterall, J., Ormseth, L., & Moody, D. (1990). *Discovering what schools really teach: Designing improved coursework indicators.* Santa Monica, CA: Rand.

Mellin-Olson, S. (1987). *The politics of mathematics education.* Dordrecht, Holland: D. Reidel.

Moses, R. P. & Cobb, C. E. (2001). *Radical equations: Math literacy and civil rights.* Boston: Beacon.

National Center for Education Statistics. (1993). *Youth indicators 1993.* Washington, DC: U.S. Government Printing Office.

National Council on Education Standards and Testing (1992). *Raising standards for American education: A report to Congress, the Secretary of Education, the National Goals Panel, and the American people.* Washington, DC: U.S. Government Printing Office.

National Council of Teachers of Mathematics. (1980). *An agenda for action: Recommendations for school mathematics of the 1980's.* Reston, VA: Author.

National Council of Teachers of Mathematics. (1989). *Curriculum and evaluation standards for school mathematics.* Reston, VA: Author.

National Council of Teachers of Mathematics. (1991). *Professional standards for teaching mathematics.* Reston, VA: Author.

National Council of Teachers of Mathematics. (1995). *Assessment standards for school mathematics.* Reston, VA: Author.

National Council of Teachers of Mathematics. (2000). *Principles and standards for school mathematics.* Reston, VA: Author.

National Governors' Association. (1993). *The debate on opportunity-to-learn standards.* Washington, DC: Author.

National Research Council. (2001). *Investigating the influence of standards: A framework for research in mathematics, science, technology education.* Washington, DC: Author.

National Research Council. (1999). *How people learn: Brain, mind, experience, and school.* Washington, DC: Author.

National Science Board. (1991). *Science & engineering indicators (NSB 91-1).* Washington DC: U.S. Government Printing Office.

Oakes, J. (1985). *Keeping track: How schools structure inequality.* New Haven, CT: Yale University Press.

Oakes, J. (1990). Opportunities, achievement, and choice: Women and minority students in science and mathematics. In C. B. Cazden (Ed.),

Review of research in education (Vol. 16, pp. 153–222). Washington, DC: American Education Research Association.

O'Day, J. A., & Smith, M. S. (1993). Systemic reform and educational opportunity. In S. H. Fuhrman (Ed.), *Designing coherent education policy: Improving the system* (pp. 250–312). San Francisco: Jossey-Bass.

Odden, A. R. (1992). School finance and education reform: An overview. In A. R. Odden (Ed.), *Rethinking school finance: An agenda for the 1990's* (pp. 1–40). San Francisco: Jossey-Bass.

Paige, R. (2001, February 15). *No child left behind: A blueprint for education reform.* Testimony before Senate Committee on Health, Education, Labor, and Pensions.

Piliawsky, M. (1994). Racism or realpolitik? The Clinton administration and African Americans. *The Black Scholar, 24* (2), 2–11.

Piller, C. (1992). Separate realities. *MACWORLD, 9* (9), 218–231.

Porter, A. C. (1989). A curriculum out of balance: The case of elementary school mathematics. *Educational Researcher, 18*(5), 9–15.

Porter, A. C. (1993). Defining and measuring opportunity to learn. In S. L. Traiman (Ed.), *The debate on opportunity-to-learn standards* (pp. 33–72). Washington, DC: National Governors' Association.

Pullin, D. C. (1994). Learning to work: The impact of curriculum and assessment standards on educational opportunity. *Harvard Educational Review, 64* (1), 31–54.

Robitaille, D. F., & Travers, K. J. (1992). International studies of achievement in mathematics. In D. A. Grouws (Ed.), *Handbook of research on mathematics teaching and learning* (pp. 687–709). New York: Macmillan.

Rock, D. A. & Pollard, K. M. (1995). *Mathematics course-taking and gains in mathematics achievement (Statistical Analysis Report NCES 95-714).* Washington, DC: National Center for Education Statistics.

Romberg, T. A. (1992). Further thoughts on the standards: A reaction to Apple. *Journal for Research in Mathematics Education, 23,* 432–437.

Secretary's Commission on Achieving Necessary Skills. (1991). *What work requires of schools: A SCANS report for America 2000.* Washington, DC: U.S. Department of Labor.

Secretary's Commission of Achieving Necessary Skills. (1992). *Learning a living: A blueprint for high performance.* Washington, DC: U.S. Department of Labor.

Secada, W. G. (1991). Agenda setting, enlightened self-interest, and equity in mathematics education. *Peabody Journal of Education, 66* (2), 22–56.

Secada, W. G. (1992). Race, ethnicity, social class, language, and achievement in mathematics. In D. A. Grouws (Ed.), *Handbook of research on mathematics teaching and learning* (pp. 623–660). New York: Macmillan.

Seligmann, J., & Sulavik, C. (1992, April 27). Software for hard issues. *Newsweek,* p. 55.

Silver, E. A., Smith, M. S., & Nelson, B. S. (1995). The QUASAR project: Equity concerns meet mathematics education reform in middle school. In W. G. Secada, E. Fennema, & L. Byrd (Eds.), *New directions for equity in mathematics education* (pp. 9–56). Cambridge: Cambridge University Press.

Smart, J. R. (1987). Implications of computer graphics applications for teaching geometry. In M. M. Lindquist (Ed.), *Learning and teaching geometry, K-12* (pp. 32–36). Reston, VA: National Council of Teachers of Mathematics.

Smith, A. (1937). *An inquiry into the nature and causes of the wealth of nations.* New York: Random House.

Stanic, G. M. A. (1991). Social inequality, cultural discontinuity, and equity in school mathematics. *Peabody Journal of Education, 66,* 57–71.

Stevens, F. (1993a). *Opportunity to learn: Issues of equity for poor and minority students.* Washington, DC: National Center for Education Statistics.

Stevens, F. (1993b). Applying an opportunity-to-learn conceptual framework to the investigation of the effects of teaching practices via secondary analyses of multiple-case-study summary data. *Journal of Negro Education, 62,* 232–248.

Stevenson, H., & Stigler, J. (1992). *The learning gap: Why our schools are failing and what can we learn from Japanese and Chinese education.* New York: Summit Books.

Stiff, L. V., & Harvey, W. B. (1988). On the education of Black children in mathematics. *Journal of Black Studies, 19,* 190–203.

Stodolsky, S. (1988). *The subject matters: Classroom activity in mathematics and social studies.* Chicago: University of Chicago Press.

Strickland, D. S., & Ascher, C. (1992). Low income African American children and public schooling. In P. W. Jackson (Ed.), *Handbook of research on curriculum* (pp. 609–625). New York: Macmillan.

Suter, L. E. (2000). Is student achievement immutable? Evidence from international studies on schooling and student achievement. *Review of Educational Research, 70* (4), 529–545.

Tate, W. F. (1994, February). Race, retrenchment, and the reform of school mathematics. *Phi Delta Kappan, 75,* 477–484.

Tate, W. F. (1995). Economics, equity, the national mathematics assessment: Are we creating a national tollroad? In W. G. Secada, E. Fennema, & L. Byrd (Eds.), *New directions for equity in mathematics education* (pp. 191–208). Cambridge: Cambridge University Press.

Tate, W. F. (1997 a). Race-ethnicity, sex, gender, and language proficiency trends in mathematics achievement: An update. *Journal for Research in Mathematics Education, 28,* 652–679.

Tate, W. F. (1997 b). Critical race theory and education: History, theory and implications. In M. Apple (Ed.), *Review of research in education* (pp. 195–247). Washington, DC: American Educational Research Association.

Thomas, G. E. (1992). Participation and degree attainment of African American and Latino students in graduate education relative to other racial and ethnic groups: An update from the Office of Civil Rights Data. *Harvard Educational Review, 62* (1), 45–65.

Tranquanda, R. E., & Glassman, P. A. (1992). Providing health care for the uninsured and underinsured in Los Angeles County. In J. B. Steinberg, D. W. Lyon, & M. E. Vainana (Eds.), *Urban America: Policy choices for Los Angeles and the nation* (pp. 307–328). Santa Monica, CA: Rand.

U.S. Department of Education. (1991). *America 2000. An education strategy.* Washington, DC: U.S. Government Printing Office.

U.S. Department of Education. (1994). *Issues of curriculum reform in science, mathematics and higher order thinking across the disciplines.* Washington, DC: U.S. Government Printing Office.

Van Sertima, L. (Ed.). (1988). *Blacks in sciences: Ancient and modern.* New Brunswick, NJ: Transaction Books.

Verstegen, D. A. (1994). Reforming American education policy. *Educational Administration Quarterly, 30*, 365–390.

Welch, W. W., Anderson, R. E., & Harris, L. J. (1982). The effects of schooling on mathematics achievement. *American Educational Research Journal, 19* (l), 145–153.

Williams, P. J. (1991). *The alchemy of race and tights: Diary of a law professor.* Cambridge, MA: Harvard University Press.

Wilson, M. (1992). Measuring levels of mathematical understanding. In T. A. Romberg (Ed.), *Mathematics assessment and evaluation: Imperatives for mathematics education* (pp. 213–241). Albany, NY: SUNY Press.

Winfield, L. F. (1987). Teachers' estimates of test content covering in class and first-grade students' reading achievement. *Elementary School Journal, 87*, 438–445.

Winfield, L. F. (1993). Investigating test content and curriculum content overlap to assess opportunity to learn. *Journal of Negro Education, 62*, 288–310.

Winfield, L. F., & Woodard, M. D. (1994). Assessment equity, diversity in reforming America's schools. *Educational Policy, 8*, 3–27.

Wiske, M. S., & Levinson, C. Y. (1992). *Coordinated support for improving mathematics education.* Cambridge, MA: Harvard University, Educational Technology Center, Harvard Graduate School of Education.

Wong, K. K. (1994). Governance structure, resource allocation, and equity policy. In L. Darling-Hammond (Ed.), *Review of research in education* (Vol. 20, pp. 257–289). Washington, DC: American Education Research Association.

Woodson, C. G. (1990). *The mis-education of the Negro.* Trenton, NJ: Africa World Press. (Originally published in 1933.)

Yackel, E., Cobb, P., Wood, T., Wheatley, G., & Merkel, G. (1990). The importance of social interaction in children's construction of mathematical knowledge. In T. J. Cooney (Ed.), *Teaching and learning mathematics in the 1990s* (pp. 12–21). Reston, VA: National Council of Teachers of Mathematics.

Yoon, B., Burstein, L., Gold, K., Chen, Z., & Kim, K. (1990). *Validating teachers' reports of content coverage: An example from secondary school mathematics.* Paper presented at the annual meeting of the National Council of Measurement in Education, Boston.

---

[i] Many of the issues addressed here are applicable to other racial and cultural groups. However, my intention is to move beyond a general analysis of traditionally underserved students in mathematics education to a more specific analysis about the experience of one group of students—African Americans attending urban schools. The tendency by some scholars is to discuss African Americans, Native Americans, Hispanics, and other cultural groups as one minimizes the "plurality of difference" that exists between these groups (King, 1995).

[ii] The author was a member of the state committee that assisted with the process.

[iii] Mathematizing is the use of numbers to model or approximate the relationship between elements of a social or physical situation.

[iv] Thomas Romberg was the chair of the Commission on Standards for School Mathematics for the National Council of Teachers of Mathematics.

ACE AND CHANGE IN EDUCATION: TOWARD A SEMIOTICS OF CURRICULUM

Garrett A. Duncan

In an article on race, gender, and violence in urban educational research, I described some of my experiences teaching for the first time a course titled "Literacy in the Schools" at Washington University, a major research university in the Midwest (Duncan, 2000). The course was designed to provide students with an intense experience in combining theory and practice in an ethnographic study of how children develop academic literacy and social skills. It had as its field site an after-school computer club, located in an elementary school in the nearby city. In the aforementioned article, I discussed the emphasis that student researchers in the course placed on the putative pathologies of the child participants in the computer club, and the ease with which the students conflated violence with the concept of masculinity. In addition, I discussed how the students, who were all white, generally spoke and wrote in ways that reinforced racist stereotypes and thus supported a link between their whiteness and the innocence with which racism is reproduced and given normal status in society (Morrison, 1993; Schick, 2000; Thompson, 1998).

Of course it is unremarkable that, given the racist nature of the U.S. hegemony, the students in the course would use damage imagery to depict the children of the predominantly black school, and to do so in ways that presented these views as self-evident. As Stanfield (1999) notes:

> [i]n a society such as America, racialism has become so routinized through many generations, that thinking and acting racially is normative on the part of all who are born in this country or have lived here for more than a few years. It is in this sense that racism organizes everyday life in America, shapes the moral character of Americans, and determines whom we associate with and whom we do not associate with in marriage, church, neighborhood, and school. (p. 420)

Further, given the students' liberal values and concern with equity, it is also unsurprising that they for the most part were willing to engage the issues of race and racism that I highlighted in our written assignments, seminar discussions, and work in the computer club. For example, early in the course, when I was attempting to help students understand how their views of the elementary school neighborhood could be at odds with those of the people who lived in it, I read from Langston Hughes's *Black Misery*. "Misery," Hughes wrote, "is when you heard on the radio that the neighborhood you live is a slum but you always thought that it was home" (1967/1994, p. 1). The following week, Karen, a twenty-one-year-old women's studies and English major returned to class with "Nikki-Rosa," a poem by Nikki Giovanni (1979) that concludes with: "And I really hope that no white person ever has cause to write about me because they never understand that Black love is Black wealth and they'll probably talk about my childhood and never understand that all the while I was quite happy" (p. 59).

Literary sources, or the work of those whom Andrew Billingsley (1973/1998) called "the more 'creative' black writers—including novelists, poets, essayists, biographers, and lyricists," contain perceptive insights that "move beyond art toward science" (p. 448). Billingsley argued that literature and art could do what white and black social scientists often failed to do: provide a rich and varied depiction of black culture and life in the U.S. However, despite the addition to the course of these enriched literary resources, the students' default views of black culture and life remained pretty much unaltered from what they were when the students began the course. This became clear late in the semester when students proposed final paper topics. Without exception, topics focused on the purported failings or problems of the children in the computer club. I was flawed in my assumption that with a little information everyone in the course would be on the same page, so to speak. It soon became clear, though, that our shared vocabularies masked basic differences in how we understood our work. On the one hand, I saw the research problem mainly in terms of the oppressive role of a broader white supremacist culture in undermining the human potential of the children in the research setting. The student researchers, on the other hand, understood the injustices they saw mainly in terms of inequality, and their work as helping unfortunate, underprivileged children take advantage of the offerings of a fundamentally fair society. In this view, if academic or behavior problems persisted among students in the computer club, they had to be the result of shortcomings within the students, their families, and/or culture.

That the students remained ideologically committed to not seeing social injustice in terms of its systematic and institutional mechanisms, despite the material evidence that they themselves witnessed, supported W. E. B. DuBois's argument (1968/1997) that

> not simply knowledge, not simply direct repression of evil, will reform the world. In long, indirect pressure and action of various and intricate sorts, the actions of men [and women] which are not due to a lack of knowledge nor to evil intent, must be changed by influencing folkways, habits, customs, and subconscious deeds. (p. 222)

As suggested by DuBois, any approach to social change must take seriously the role of complex semiotic networks (e.g., the folkways, habits, customs, and subconscious deeds) in the maintenance of the U.S. racial hegemony. The experiences in that initial course, then, raised for me the pedagogical questions of how to render these networks explicit, so as to critique them and inform our approach to our work. In what follows, I describe how I addressed these questions and made fundamental changes to the course over subsequent semesters.

From "Literacy in the Schools" to "Race, Ethnicity, and Culture": A Semiotic Approach to Curricular Change

Specific questions informed certain changes to "Literacy in the Schools": What strategies do I employ to promote a shift in the way we understand race and the politics of difference? How does one go about thinking differently— in terms of both the content and structure of our project—so as to affirm the humanity of those among whom we work? Below, I focus on changes I made to "Literacy in the Schools" during 1998, the subsequent times I offered the course, and emphasize the strategies that I used to orient our work prior to entering into the field.

Urban ethnography in the context of African American Studies. In the spring of 1998, I changed the name of the course from "Education 250: Literacy in the Schools" to "Education 400: Race, Ethnicity, and Culture: Qualitative Inquiry in Urban Education I." A more significant change came later that year in the fall of 1998 when I moved the course from the education department to the African American Studies (AAS) program; the course retained both its number and title. Anthropologist Cheryl Rodriguez (1996) describes at length that the merging of research courses with Africana studies or, as in the case of my institution, AAS programs, allows for new epistemological considerations that challenge the disciplinary boundaries of social science. Thus, the course, now housed within the AAS program, was far more amenable to curricular change and, specifically, to a pedagogy driven by critical race theory (CRT), which I describe in greater detail below. Although I included CRT material in the course during the 1998 spring semester, it was limited to content, such as reading materials (e.g., Ladson-Billings & Tate, 1995). These materials challenged students in ways that the previous materials did not; however, like the literary additions before them, they provided only a partial illumination of the way race was normalized within the routines of our work and the field site. Moreover, it did little to challenge pedagogical practices that subjugated the student cultural knowledge. To effect changes in the class along these lines required that I make radical changes in the course. Before I describe these changes, there are two other results of housing the course in AAS worth mentioning.

First, housing the class in the AAS program and increasing the course number attracted a greater number of cross-listings with other programs in the university. In addition to education, the course is now cross-listed with the sociology and the American culture studies programs, and attracts students from anthropology, economics, political science, social work, engineering, and biology, as well as various areas in the humanities. Students receive either departmental credit to fulfill methods requirements or degree credit to meet general education requirements. The original number of 250 designated the course primarily as a sophomore-level class, although half of the first class was comprised of seniors. Increasing the course number to 400 identified it as an upper-division course and broadened its appeal, attracting graduate students and students who were not seeking degrees. Second, the change in the placement of the course increased the number of students and dramatically changed the cultural composition of subsequent classes. The number of students enrolled in the course increased from nine in the 1997 spring semester to twenty-one for the 1998 fall semester, which is one over the limit I eventually imposed. As I mentioned earlier, the initial course was comprised entirely of white students. In the fall of 1998, nine black, one Latina, and eleven white students enrolled in the course.

Based on the numbers and composition of students in my other AAS and education classes, I had anticipated that placing the course in the AAS program would result in changes in the number and composition of students in the course. Changing the composition of the class was of critical importance to me for a number of reasons, but especially because of the pedagogical changes I made to the course. Here, as Mari Matsuda (1996) points out, CRT "is explicitly derivative of the history and intellectual tradition of people of color" (p. 55). Thus, the further changes made to the course were directly related to the presence of students of color with whom a CRT perspective seemed to have a special resonance.

"But I think it's maybe a little more complex": theorizing race. Central to any CRT-driven project is first and foremost a concern with race. Such a concern is generally met with much resistance given that it is fashionable nowadays to downplay and even dismiss race as a factor irrelevant to the quality of life in the U.S., and instead to favor class- and gender-based approaches to understanding social oppression. This sentiment is expressed throughout my courses as students will acknowledge racism but at the same time declare, "Well, it's not *only* about race. I think it has more to do with class/gender." In fact, many students (and colleagues, I might add) take up the argument that to talk about race is the real problem because to do so either reinforces "socially constructed" myths or consumes time and intellectual energy that could be devoted to understanding "real" social problems. The irony here, though, is that students are attracted to classes such as AAS 400 precisely because they explicitly address race. This contradiction may reflect an assumption that race is self-evident and that the concept, itself, need not be made problematic. Ladson-Billings and Tate (1995), however, assert that unlike gender and class, race remains untheorized (p. 49). Consequently, as Omi and Winant (1993) argue,

popular, self-evident notions of race have epistemological limitations. Popular notions of race, they posit, generally fall under one of two categories: (1) an ideological construct, an imaginary force that "denies the reality of a racialized society and its impact on 'raced' people in their everyday lives" (Ladson-Billings & Tate, 1995, p. 48); or (2) an objective condition, a set of self-evident and rigid categories that fail to account for the problematic issues of social classification and genetic and cultural hybridity (Omi & Winant, 1993).

To facilitate an examination of race in AAS 400, I began the 1998 fall semester course by focusing on student commonsense understandings of the phenomenon. In previous classes, I glossed over a powerful semiotic force—folk wisdom—that students brought to bear on their reasoning about social matters, and I introduced the issue of race by way of critiquing its use in the social science literature. By doing so, I privileged academic definitions of race over commonsense ones and reproduced the dichotomy between academic *theories* and the *practices* of everyday life. In addition, by disregarding the points of view of students at the start of the course, I virtually assured that the commonsense notions they brought to the class about race would remain intact. These default understandings would in turn find their way into their approach to the more substantial aspects of their projects.

To place their understandings at the center of the course's inquiry, on the first day of class I asked students to provide me with (1) racial/ethnic profiles of the U.S. and (2) their definitions of race. These questions provided the opportunity to employ statistical and anecdotal evidence in the discussion of the subordinated status of people of color in the U.S. and to challenge the use of linear, intent-based notions of causation as explanations for racism (Matsuda, 1996). I anticipated that differences among students in their responses to the questions would complicate the idea of race in the U.S. Differences in viewpoints would also set the stage to facilitate the process by which we could engage multiple views in our analyses of urban public schools.

Responses to the first question indicated that students in the course, as a whole, believed that white people comprised about 45 percent of the U.S. population. People of color, it followed, comprised the majority of society in various proportions, although students believed for the most part that blacks comprised the largest U.S. "minority" group. After reviewing the current

U.S. census data that indicated that white people constitute the majority of the U.S. population, we discussed the social and political implications of the class's responses. Briefly, students commented that the gross underrepresentation of the U.S. white population directly related to the issue of power. On the one hand, some students observed that the belief that white people, as a group, were a numeric minority gave credence to the politics of white victimization. On the other hand, the belief that people of color comprise a larger part of the U.S. population than they actually do supports a view that we live in a fundamentally egalitarian society and that social injustice is primarily a matter of the unequal distribution of material resources and social capital. Justice conceived primarily as a matter of fairness or distribution favors class-based and gender-based responses to eliminating social problems. The actual demography of the U.S., though, points to *domination* as the central theme of societal injustice.

Responses to the second question (i.e., what is your definition of race?) reflected popular notions of race that Omi and Winant (1993) describe above. Students generally defined race as a self-evident entity (twelve responses), as an ideological construct (four responses), or some combination of the two (three responses). One student provided a definition of race that highlighted its political dimension, while another indicated that she was unsure of a definition. The following responses are typical of the view of race as a biological or cultural entity:

1. Race is confusing to me. I think of it as a kind of mixture of cultural and ethnic backgrounds. Usually, people (me too) associate race with skin color and facial features; but I think it's maybe a little more complex. (Ally, a twenty-one-year-old white female black studies major)

2. Race is a condition of which beliefs, along with the appearance of a person, on which he or she is categorized. (Ronnie, a twenty-one-year-old black male pre-occupational therapy/psychology major)

3. Race is a category based on a mixture of cultures, backgrounds, and physical features. It is a definition both chosen by an

individual and chosen for an individual. (Sandra, a twenty-one-year-old white female English and French major).

The following response captures a view of race as primarily an ideological construct:

> Race is a socially constructed phenomenon that forces people into different groups based on skin color, not necessarily ethnicity or origin. It generally fails to recognize people that have various backgrounds (cultural). (Marilyn, a twenty-one-year-old white female marketing and black studies major)

Departing from the rest of her peers, Robin, an eighteen-year-old black female with a triple major in printmaking, education, and philosophy, foregrounds the political dimension of race. She writes that race is "a concept created to categorize people for purposes of power distribution through social institutions and interactions." Robin's definition is consonant with that of the historian and political scientist Manning Marable (1994). According to Marable, "Race is first and foremost an unequal relationship between social aggregates, characterized by dominant and subordinate forms of social interaction, and reinforced by the intricate patterns of public discourse, power, ownership, and privilege within the economic, social, and political institutions of society" (1994, p. 30). In my view, Robin and Marable define race in ways that do more than just highlight the power relations embedded in the social construction of the idea. Both definitions also make explicit references to the fluid relationships that challenge the idea that race is a self-evident, unchanging entity, and to the concrete, material dimensions of the phenomenon that defy the idea that race exists "mainly in the head."

CRT as a Mediator of Reflexivity

The definitions of race given by Robin and Marable allowed me to bridge the distinction between unofficial and official knowledge in the class as well as to highlight the aspects of race that informed daily realities. However, to mount an effective challenge to deeply engrained notions of race required "indirect pressure and action of various and intricate sorts" to highlight and effect changes in the "subconscious deeds" (DuBois, 1968/1997 p. 222) of the students in the course.

Through reflexivity, we were able to foreground the values, premises, and assumptions that give meaning to our work. The very act of foregrounding allows us to understand our viewpoints for what they are—*perspectives*—thus prompting us to recognize that persons whom we choose to observe and write about also have perspectives and are fully capable of reading and critiquing our work (Rodriguez, 1996; see also Blauner & Wellman, 1973/1998; Gwaltney, 1993; Williams, 1974). Thus, the significance of reflexivity in fostering curricular change is in its contribution to making visible the invisible relationships that characterize racial oppression by redirecting the focus on our own perspectives; it fosters a consideration of the multiple viewpoints that may come to bear in the social construction of reality. To facilitate this practice of reflexivity among the students in the course, I provided specific resources which aided them in explicating subtle social relationships, and which raised disturbing questions about these relationships.

For example, within the first two weeks of the course, we read and discussed selections from DuBois's 1968/1997 *Dusk of Dawn: An Essay Toward an Autobiography of a Race Concept* and from Thompson and Tyagi's (1996) *Names We Called Home: Autobiography on Racial Identity*. After reading and discussing these texts, I asked students to compose autobiographical accounts of the race concept, that is, to write personal histories on how they "became" black, brown, or white. These autoethnographies were later integrated in the final course project in which students developed theoretical frameworks that concluded with questions to inform future research projects. For the most part, the autoethnographies recounted how individuals came to know who they were racially in relation to others. White students often mentioned incidents of racism, prejudice, and discrimination in their autoethnographies, especially regarding white people, usually family members, who directed specific attitudes toward people of color. Here, they generally used language that made indirect references and that rarely described racial dynamics in concrete terms. However, they used concrete language in those instances when they repositioned themselves as "minorities" and as the objects of discrimination and prejudice. This occurred on the several occasions when they wrote about their experiences outside of North America, in places such as South and Central America,

Asia, and Africa. The following excerpt from a theoretical framework developed by Mitchell, a twenty-one-year-old white economics and biology major, shows evidence of this phenomenon:

> My encounter with Cardinal originated from the class for which this framework is being written, Race, Ethnicity, and Culture: Qualitative Inquiries in Urban Education...I went into Cardinal expecting to tutor and play with minority children in an after school program designed to keep them off the streets of a ghetto area. My initial belief was that I would be a combination babysitter/tutor for these children until their parents could pick them up after work. I expected the area to be extremely run down with considerable amounts of crime in plain sight. I have owned "The Club" to lock my steering wheel for quite some time, however the first time that I actually used The Club was the first day I went to tutor at Cardinal, under the explicit instruction of my mother.
>
> My initial expectations of Cardinal were reflective of my family's racism. My early childhood was spent in Manhattan; I was isolated from minorities because I lived and went to school in a predominantly white area. I was familiar with the ghetto areas of Manhattan from the back seat of the car whenever we needed to drive outside the city. Upon passing these areas my parents would tell me to roll up the windows and lock the doors because we were entering a "black neighborhood." My early childhood clearly associated minorities, specifically black people, with crime and the ghetto area. Thus we see how my initial expectations of Cardinal were derived.

In contrast to their white peers, black students often made direct, concrete references to the fact of racism in their lives. For example, Delphine, a sophomore majoring in African American studies and education, originally struggled with the assignment but, through dialoguing with her black peers, recalled how her blackness became significant to her when her family moved into an integrated neighborhood in the southern town where she grew up. Laughing, Delphine recalled how she and her sister had to "put on good clothes and comb their hair" just to play in the front yard. In addition, no longer were they allowed to freely run about and "be as loud" as they were in their previous all-black neighborhood. Delphine's emerging autoethnography, like those of her black classmates, supported John Langston Gwaltney's (1993) assertion that the words of drylongso—that is, ordinary blacks—are plainly analytic and contain theory-building properties. The experiences of these students gave flesh-and-bone reality to concepts such as double consciousness (DuBois, 1903/1989) and biculturalism (Darder, 1991).

I am not suggesting that students responded to the course and especially to the computer club according to a rigidly prescriptive color-coded schema. On the contrary, for example, Jane, a twenty-one-year-old black female majoring in African American studies and English, describes below what she initially expected to encounter at the CECEC:

> The way that the packet described the site made it appear as though the students were just getting by in a neighborhood that threatened them as children growing up with "considerable 'baggage' that inhibited [their] academic success" and placed them "at-risk" (Cardinal Information Packet). I was scared to leave my car and my belongings in my car parked on the street in an area with "one of the highest rates of larceny, burglary, and destruction of property; high rates of robbery, aggravated assault, auto theft, and reported drug sales; and moderate rates of homicide" (Cardinal Information Packet). How was I supposed to make meaning of these statistics? Not only was someone going to break into my car and steal my radio, but they were also going to leave my car on cinder blocks, rob me on my way into the school after they had hit me over the head for looking at them funny, try to sell me some crack or weed (marijuana), and then kill me for just being in their neighborhood. These statistics are harrowing. Here I am, just a college student, wanting to positively affect some child's life, and before I can do so, I, just like these children, am being set up to fail, if not die.

Jane clearly echoes some of the sentiments found in Mitchell's comments above. However, it should also be noted that midway in the semester, Jane was responsible for calling her peers on their use of white talk, or the use of language in a way that insulated individuals from taking responsibility for racism (McIntyre, 1997). The point here is that reflexivity created the space, especially for students of color in the course, to contribute invaluable subjugated knowledge to the practice of qualitative research. At the same time, the practice also invited students of color to reflect on their own socialization in a white supremacist society and to consider what this meant in terms of their thinking about and work in their own communities.

As we moved closer to our initial visits to the CECEC, I asked students to begin identifying the critical attributes that defined the ways that race played out in their lives. To facilitate this discussion, we viewed a documentary of the life of Gregory Williams, whose story is told in *Life on the Color Line: The True Story of a White Boy Who Discovered He was Black* (Williams, 1995). Briefly, Williams, recently a law school dean and currently a college president, grew up believing that he was white until his parents separated during his youth. His family split up and Williams, along with his brother and father, left his white mother in Virginia and moved to Muncie, Indiana. In Muncie he discovered that his father was the son of a black woman and had, in Virginia, been "passing" as an Italian-American. Thus, as a result of the move to Indiana, where Williams's father's heritage was common knowledge and where racial categories were closely monitored and rigidly enforced, Williams went from being a white boy to a black boy, literally overnight.

Prior to viewing the documentary, though, I showed the class video footage containing fourteen photographs of individuals that, unknown to students, included two of Williams, one as a child and another as an adult. I asked students to identify individuals in each photograph according to how they might be designated by the U.S. Census Bureau. I also indicated to students that they could choose more than one census category to identify an individual. All students classified Williams as white, with no additional designations, both as a child and as an adult. After identifying Williams's photographs and viewing the video documentary of his life, I asked students how they would classify Williams in light his personal history. I was less concerned with how students classified Williams and more interested in how they talked about race in the context of his life. Of the twenty-one anonymous responses, five students described Williams primarily as a sociopolitical construct and in terms of the concrete power relationships that shaped his life. For example, one student stated that:

> Gregory is neither white nor black, he is both white and black. This is a perfect example of why I'll never believe those who say that race is a biological description or a physical description of someone. Race is a completely societal description— 100 percent. Those who knew (defined) him as white treated him one way, and those who knew (defined) him as black, another. He never changed his appearance nor his actions. People/society labeled him as one or the other race and responded to him because of that label.

Eleven students described Williams primarily in terms of how they viewed his subjective responses to his experiences while the remaining students described him mainly in terms of his perceived physical attributes or purported genetic composition. With respect to the former description, one student stated that Gregory Williams is black because he thinks he is black. Race today is so obscure that it is more a state of mind than a gene pool.

Despite the biological and/or psychological language that some of the students used to frame the way they made meaning of Williams's race, discussions of the documentary clearly indicated that we were beginning to destabilize the rigid ideas that initially informed the way we talked about race in the course. Finally, prior to entering the research field, we viewed the teleplay "The Space Traders" (Hudlin & Hudlin, 1994), adapted from the similarly titled racial parable by Derrick Bell (1992). In "The Space Traders" Bell uses a fictional story to bring into bold relief the racism that is ingrained in U.S. society. Specifically, in this tale Bell explores the responses of white Americans to an opportunity to accrue great social and personal benefit at the complete sacrifice of the basic rights of black citizens. Perhaps more than any other CRT-driven strategy, the viewing and ensuing discussion of the teleplay prompted students to turn inward and reflect on a number of disturbing questions. Interestingly, white students in the course for the most part raised the question of whether the events detailed in the essay and vividly rendered in the teleplay could occur in the U.S., while many black students concluded that "The Space Traders" described events already in evidence and directed the discussion toward identifying dynamics that supported this view. Among other things, students pointed to the passage of recent anti-immigrant propositions and to the general public's support of anti-affirmative action legislation to name but two recent examples of the involuntary sacrificial roles that people of color have played in national policies.

It is important to emphasize here that rather than engaging in a fruitless argument on the merits of "The Space Traders," students began to rethink the role of race in U.S. history and contemporary society. Students reflected on the meaning of race, both in the context of their own lives and also in the context of the course, specifically their ethnographic work in the computer club. Along these lines, CRT and the focus on reflexivity assisted students in developing a more complicated understanding of their work. For example, reflecting on her experiences in the class, Freda, a twenty-seven-year-old white graduate anthropology student writes:

> This course is a journey for me, or rather, part of a journey, a part which I find it hard to decide whether it's magnificent or insignificant. I find it increasingly hard to explain to anyone outside this classroom what it is I learn here, what its significance is. However, by now, I am also quite aware that those people I explain it too are white, and living in a social setting where the fact that they're white does not matter to them. Thus, when I tell them that one of the things that I learn in this class is that being white **does** matter, some of them balk, whereas the ones that don't, simply find this shift of mindset hard to grasp. And I still do too, sometimes, when caught up in the hegemony of my own whiteness. And yet, as I believe at this junction on my journey, this shift of mindset is no small thing, even if it is incomplete as yet. Probably insignificant when I look forward, but most magnificent when I look back...

However, being on this junction is not without risk. McIntyre (1997, p. 138) stated that "a little whiteness could be dangerous," in that the discomfort that comes with this growth process can actually bring a person to flee back into perpetuating the system instead of critically challenging it.

Similarly, Ronnie reflects on his role at the CECEC:

> It was the fifth week of classes and we were about to start making the weekly trips to Cardinal. I had no idea what to expect. Dr. Duncan told us not to go in there thinking from the Cardinal information packet. I was not trying to read that packet because I know what goes into those packets. Usually, all you will find is a bunch of hasty conclusions about people that the criticizer doesn't even know...Anyway, with this information in my head now I am really hyped up. I want to see the children. I want to help the children. Why do I want to help the children, I asked myself? Who said these children need my help? Who am I? Obviously some hearsay has entered into my thoughts. I heard that these children were in need of help—an obvious misunderstanding of what was suggested in class. Apparently, these children here at Cardinal have been labeled at risk and they are not testing as well as the other public schools. This is what motivated me at first. That was when I was sorely ignorant. In other words, I wasn't hip to the game. So I figured if I just go in there and help one of these kids every week they would be better. I thought this—can you believe it?
> You see, now I can laugh at this thought, because it proves my high-priced intelligence can lead me to become ignorant at times...Cardinal Elementary has been labeled a problem or diagnosed with a problem and they asked for help. But not just us: there are at least seven other major groups of people representing at Cardinal. Yet, there is still a problem? And not to get on a different tangent, but what does high-risk mean? What are these kids at risk for? I was in too deep, and I could not turn back. But at this point I did not want to.

Not unlike most of their peers, Freda and Ronnie describe being at a crossroad, both in their thinking about race and in their assessment of their work. These junctures are made possible by the students' examining their value orientations, considering multiple points of views about the meaning of race in society, and locating themselves within the webs of societal power relations.

Conclusion

Although I restricted my discussion in this chapter to the pedagogical strategies that I used with students prior to their participation in the field, this simply reflects the focus of this chapter. It is not to suggest that we did not apply the changes that I made in the course to our work in the computer club. Suffice it to say, though, that once in the field, changes made to the course informed by concepts borrowed from CRT assisted students to comprehend the way that race permeates the daily interactions and processes involved in both the institution of schooling and in the enterprise of qualitative research. For example, students identified several dimensions of racialized time within the elementary school that sustained systemic violence through curriculum, pedagogy, and various state-, district-, and school-based educational policies. Racialized time refers to relationships between time and material conditions, such as resources and/or interactions between people, that adversely impact oppressed groups. A critical understanding of time is relevant for understanding how forms of race-related oppression are created and sustained in institutional settings.

In addition, students devised various categories of white talk (McIntyre, 1997) to analyze their notes and conversations about their work for the presence of language that interrupted their interrogation of race and racism, both in the field and in the framing of their work. The construction of these categories was particularly useful for raising self-awareness and promoting reflexivity. For example, one group of students constructed a category of white talk around "non-participation," defining it as "having opinions but not willing to face uneasiness and possible confrontation resulting from stated opinion." To illustrate their definition, the group provided the following example from their experiences in the field: "When Anne G. saw how Mr. Clark dismissed Ally W., she kept her mouth shut even though she had different opinions/ thoughts to say. She felt uncomfortable." Reflections such as these inspired students not only to reflect upon their multiple roles as students and researchers, but also to clarify their personal objectives for their work and to align their actions accordingly. Thus, changes to the course provided both new semiotic devices to rethink the race idea and to transform our approach to doing our work in tangible ways.

As indicated in the introduction, the purpose of this chapter is to describe how I addressed questions of pedagogy related to rendering explicit the folkways, habits, and customs that give race its normal status in the U.S. and to subject them to interrogation and transformation. The pedagogical strategies that I instituted helped to explicate the concrete, relational, and systemic character of racial oppression in ways that made it tangible and subject to intervention. Among other things, this chapter illustrates the power of CRT to bring into bold relief subtle forms of racial oppression in the U.S., and the power of reflexivity to lay the foundation for alternative ways to imagine and to conduct qualitative inquiry in urban educational settings.

References

America, R. (1998). The case of the racist researcher. In J. Ladner (Ed.), *The death of white sociology: Essays on race and culture* (pp. 451–467). Baltimore: Black Classic Press. (Original work published in 1973).

Bell, D. (1992). *Faces at the bottom of the well: The permanence of racism.* New York: Basic Books.

Billingsley, A. (1998). Black families and white social science. In J. Ladner (Ed.), *The death of white sociology: Essays on race and culture* (pp. 431–450). Baltimore, MD: Black Classic Press. (Original work published in 1973).

Blauner, R., & Wellman, D. (1998). Toward the decolonization of social research. In J. Ladner (Ed.), *The death of white sociology: Essays on race and culture* (pp. 310–330). Baltimore, MD: Black Classic Press. (Original work published in 1973).

Boler, M. (1999). *Feeling power: Emotions and education.* New York: Routledge.

Darder, A. (1991). *Culture and power in the classroom: A critical foundation for bicultural education.* New York: Bergin and Garvey.

Delgado, R. (1996). *The coming race war? And other apocalyptic tales of America after affirmative action and welfare.* New York: New York University Press.

DuBois, W. E. B. (1989). *The souls of black folk.* New York: Bantam Books. (Original work published in 1903).

DuBois, W. E. B. (1997). *Dusk of dawn: An essay toward an autobiography of a race concept.* New Brunswick, NJ: Transaction Publishers. (Original work published in 1968).

Duncan, G. (2000). Theorizing race, gender, and violence in urban ethnographic research. *Urban Education, 34* (5), 623–644.

Eaker-Rich, D., Van Galen, J., & Timothy, E. (1996). Conclusion. In D. Eaker-Rich & Van J. Galen (Eds.), *Caring in an unjust world: Negotiating borders and barriers in schools* (pp. 231–237). Albany, NY: SUNY Press.

Frankenberg, R. (1996). When we are capable of stopping, we begin to see. Being white, seeing whiteness. In B. Thompson & S. Tyagi (Eds.), *Names we call home: Autobiography on racial identity* (pp. 3–17). New York: Routledge.

Freire, P. (1996). *Pedagogy of the oppressed.* New York: Continuum.

Giovanni, N. (1979). *Black feeling, black talk/black judgement: Poems.* New York: Morrow Quill Paperbacks. (Original work published in 1968.)

Gwaltney, J. (1993). *Drylongso: A self-portrait of black America.* New York: New Press.

hooks, b. (2000). *All about love: New visions.* New York: William Morrow.

Hudlin, R., & Hudlin, W. (Producers), & Hudlin, R. (Director). (1994). "The Space Traders" [A teleplay by T. Ellis]. (Available from Home Box Office, 1100 Avenue of the Americas, New York, NY 10036.)

Hughes, L. (1994). *Black misery.* New York: Oxford University Press. (Original worth published in 1967).

King, M. (1986). *Testament of hope: The essential writings and speeches of Martin Luther King, Jr.* (M. Washington, Ed.). San Francisco: Harper Collins.

Ladson-Billings, G., & Tate, W. (1995). Toward a critical race theory of education. *Teachers College Record, 97* (1), 47–68.

Marable, M. (1994) Building coalitions among communities of color: Beyond racial identity politics. In J. Jennings (Ed.), *Blacks, Latinos,* and Asians in urban America: Status and prospects for politics and activism (pp. 29–43). Westport, CT: Praeger Publishers.

Matsuda, M. (1996). Where is your body? And other essays on race, gender, and the law. Boston: Beacon Press.

McIntyre, A. (1997). Making meaning of whiteness: Exploring racial identity with white teachers. Albany, NY: SUNY Press.

Morrison, T. (1993). Playing in the dark: Whiteness and the literary imagination. New York: Vintage.

Noblit, G. (1993). Power and caring. American Educational Research Journal, 30 (1), 23–38.

Noddings, N. (1999). Caring, justice, and equity. In M. Katz, N. Noddings, & K. Strike (Eds.), Justice and caring: The search for common ground in education (pp. 7–19). New York: Teachers College Press.

Omi, M., & Winant, H. (1993). On the theoretical status of the concept of race. In C. McCarthy & W. Crichlow (Eds.), Race, identity and representation in education (pp. 3–10). New York: Routledge.

Restak, R. (1984). Possible neurophysiological correlates of empathy. In J. Lichtenberg, M. Bornstein, & D. Silver (Eds.), Empathy I. Hillsdale, NJ: The Analytic Press.

Rodriguez, C. (1996). African American anthropology and the pedagogy of activist community research. Anthropology & Education Quarterly, 27 (3), 414–431.

Schick, C. (2000). "By virtue of being white": Resistance in anti-racist pedagogy. Race, Ethnicity, and Education, 3 (1), 83–102.

Stanfield, J. (1999). Slipping through the front door: Relevant social scientific evaluation in the people of color century. American Journal of Evaluation, 20 (3), 415–431.

Thompson, A. (1998). Not the color purple: Black feminist lessons for educational caring. Harvard Educational Review, 68 (4), 522–554.

Thompson, B., & Tyagi, S. (Eds.). (1996). Names we call home: Autobiography on racial identity. New York: Routledge.

Verducci, S. (2000). A conceptual history of empathy and a question it raises for moral education. Educational Theory, 50 (1), 63–80.

Williams, G. (1995). Life on the color line: The true story of a white boy who discovered he was black. New York: Dutton.

Williams, R. (1974, April). The death of white research in the black community. *Journal of Non-White Concerns in Personnel and Guidance*, 116–131.

Young, I. (1990). *Justice and the politics of difference*. Princeton, NJ: Princeton University Press.

This chapter is a revised version of an article that appeared in *Qualitative Inquiry*. The author wishes to thank Laurence Parker for his insightful comments on earlier drafts of this chapter and Frances B. Henderson for her research

assistance on this project.

EPILOGUE

"THE STRUGGLE CONTINUES..."

Geneva Gay

"The degree to which [B]lacks... succeed professionally is often a function of how well they handle the dissonance caused by race and racism" (Edwards & Polite 1992, p. 227)

The chapters in this book are compelling illustrations of this idea. They convey four very powerful messages, individually and collectively. The first is that race and racism are not merely theoretical constructs to be debated in academic circles. They are real, fundamental and shaping influences in the day-to-day lives of people. Second, racism is insidious and pervasive throughout society, including living and teaching in colleges and universities. They show how racism is manifested in a wide variety of ways by students, colleagues, and institutional policies and practices. Among these are the attitude and behaviors of European American students and professors toward African American instructors; curriculum content that excludes and/or distort sAfrican American contributions; negative reactions to learning activities and assignments, and to the scholarship of authors of color; the general climate of predominately white institutions (PWIs); and the frequency with which the competence, credibility, and credentials of African Americans in academia are questioned.

In examining racism the focus frequently centers on circumstances of the poorest segments of society, particularly undereducated and financially underresourced groups of color. The chapters in this volume shift the attention to the academically privileged by analyzing racism in college classrooms and the professional lives of African American academicians. The authors dispel the fallacious assumption held by many members of the

U.S. mainstream that social class and education nullify race and racism. They show why, as Edwards and Polite (1992) observed, African American "spend so much emotional energy dealing with race that it has become almost a visceral reflex," (p. 227). Yet it is not examined as thoroughly, deliberately, and often as it needs to be, particularly when it occurs among professionals. These authors, who are graduate students and professors at highly reputable mainstream colleges and universities, break this pattern by being very explicit in analyzing race and racism in their personal work spaces. Their revelations and related analyses make some significant contributions to the body of scholarship on these issues.

Third, this volume gives up-close and living testaments to how personal and institutional expressions and consequences of racism are deeply interconnected. They provide graphic evidence that racism is rampant in the hallowed halls of higher education—to the extent that the book might be titled, "Racism in the Academy." The use of autobiographical stories to convey this message makes it even more compelling and urgent. Readers who have "been there" relive the experiences, frustrations, anguish, and resolve who know deeply and unequivocal that the struggle against racism must continue wherever they are. This struggle is driven by the necessity of survival, not merely by a desire for a professional advancement.

A fourth telling message of the chapters in this volume is that the struggle of African Americans against racism has long historical roots. In some ways this is a very old message, and some might even argue that it is not worth being told yet again. But, the contributors to this book belie this jaundiced attitude by providing new analyses and perspectives on what is a perpetual problem for African Americans. By evoking historical records and scenarios, they also provide a valuable service to younger generations of African Americans who frequently do not have adequate knowledge about their historical legacies, and cannot place contemporary race-related dilemmas in appropriate historical contexts. Some even operate under delusions of racelessness. The authors are very effective in demonstrating that racism has a long *living* history, as do the responses of African Americans to it. Some valuable advice and viable techniques for resisting racism are embedded in their personal stories.

Power of the Test and Technique

These messages are at once disturbing and motivating. Most African Americans would hope that the need to deal with racism is obsolete, and they do not enjoy being reminded that this hope is still much more of a promise and a dream than a reality. Still they know that periodic reminders of the vicissitudes of racism and how they are exhibited in various places and platforms are a crucial part of the process of waging effective resistance. The chapters in this book do this for the reader. The illustrate, with haunting power and compelling persuasion, the suggestion made by Beverly Tatum (1997, p. 193) that

> We need to continually break the silence about racism whenever we can. We need to talk about it at home, at school, in our houses of worship, in our workplaces, in our community groups. But talk does not mean idle chatter. It means meaningful, productive dialogue to raise consciousness and lead to effective action and social change.

Sara Lawrence-Lightfoot (1994) offers similar advice in recommending that African Americans must "name the pain" in dealing with the "wounds of racism" (p. 635).

As a result, this book is disturbing, yet captivating to read. One is repulsed by the ugliness of the experiences with racism that are presented, and indignant by African Americans having to spend precious emotional, intellectual, and physical energy dealing with other people's crassness and cruelty. Yet, the reader is energized by the courage the authors exhibit in pushing past the psycho-emotional discomfort involved in these self-disclosures. They must have realized how important it is for readers, listeners, and observers to see and hear racism in their personal lives as a wake-up call to action, and a mandate for others to join them in the fight against it. Their testimonies give name, faces, and visibility to subtle forms of racism and, thus, facilitate recognition and resistance.

The stories these authors tell are galvanizing! They serve the functions that scholars attribute to narrative research. For example, Dyson and Genishi (1994) suggest that sharing stories provide opportunities for new relationships and interconnections among individuals to be forged. Witherell, Tran, and Othus (1995, p.42) add, even more convincingly, that narrative allows us to enter empathically into another's life and being—to join a living conversation. In this sense, it serves as a means of inclusion, inviting the reader, listener, writer, or teller as a companion along on another's journey. In the process we may find ourselves wiser, more receptive, more understanding, nurtured, and sometimes even healed.

Furthermore, in using story as a method and text for dealing with racism the authors of this book "speak" in cultural voice. They evoke two deeply rooted African American cultural traditions—storytelling and communal sharing. They simultaneously speak individually and collectively, and thus offer opportunities for the African American audience to join the discourse on multiple levels—reflectively, cognitively, experientially, morally, politically, viscerally, and most assuredly, kindredly. Historically, both techniques have been used to share experiences, to commiserate and strategize, to name causes and concerns, and to render calls to community. The power of the speaking styles used in this book and the effects they engender are similar to those produced by the participants in Lawrence-Lightfoot's (1994) study of six highly successful professionals that are reported in *I've Known Rivers*. She describes them as follows:

> The African-American legacy of storytelling infuses these narratives and serves as a source of deep resonance between us. Our cultural and historical roots have been given expression and meaning through stories. The slave narratives, for example, were elaborate tales of survival and cunning, but they can also be read as vehicles for individual empowerment, community building, and cultural transmission. In telling the story, the narrator defined his/her full humanity. A strong and persistent African-American tradition links the process of narrative to discovering and attaining identity. A more ancient source of story telling flows from the African continent, where stories were often embedded in tribal ritual, filled with entertainment, adventure, moral lesson, and cultural wisdom. I think of the storytellers in this volume as modern day griots, perceptive and courageous narrators of personal and cultural experience. They are working in an idiom steeped with tradition and cultural legitimacy, and, therefore, supportive of their personal revelations. (Lawrence-Lightfoot 1994, p 606)

Personal Agency for Resisting Racism

The narratives in this book prompted me to look within and across the chapters of common messages, and provoked my own thinking about what I, and others, might consider in constructing our own agendas for resisting racism. In the remainder of this discussion six key issues that should be part of this agenda are explained. Their emphasis on "personal preparedness" is not intended to suggest that institutions should not be held accountable for their own racist policies, or that their structures, programs and practices should not be transformed to eradicate racism. This is imperative. However, African American teachers, students, and staffs in academia need to develop their own agency for combating racism as well, least their personal experiences be dismissed by institutional representatives as merely "isolated cases," and "aberrant incidents." The underlying premises of the six ideas presented in this discussion are (1) "you've got to recognize and understand a problem before you can solve it," (2) "some things that look good on the surface are rotten at the core," and (3) "individuals can and should act to liberate themselves."

Preparation and Perseverance

Racism is a persistent presence in the lives of people in the United States. Whether they are the perpetuators, the benefactors, or the victims virtually everyone is personally affected by racism. However, the burdens and negative consequences are much more compelling for people of color. While education and economic privilege may temper these somewhat, they do not nullify or erase them. Regardless of their stations in life, African Americans do not have the luxury of wondering if they will ever encounter racism. Instead, they have to anticipate when and how it will happen. In their study of the "psychology of success" among 41 African Americans who came of age (regarding career development) during the Civil Rights Movement (in the 1950s to the 1970s) Edwards and Polite remind us that

> Success has always been a relative phenomenon in black America,... often measured as much by what has been overcome as by what has been achieved. For black achievement inevitably remains a triumph over odds, a victory over struggle. Whether it be in overcoming the debilitating effects of racism or the accompanying pathology of low self-esteem and self-hatred, black success is almost always the result of a peculiar kind of drama that gets played out first in the psyche. (1992, p. 3)

A good strategy for coping with racism is to be prepared for its eventuality. An essential part of this preparation is acquiring a thorough understanding of the various forms that racism takes, and developing personal endurance to deflect their negative effects. This understanding can be acquired by carefully examining subtle forms of racism exhibited by individuals and institutions, in informal and formal ways, and in contextually specific and general expressions within academia.

These suggestions resurrect the memory of an idea presented by Cobbs and Greer (1968) in their analysis of the rage against racism expressed by African Americans in the 1960s. They said, "Black people have shown a genius for surviving under the most deadly circumstances. They have survived because of their close attention to reality," (p. 175). African Americans in academia need to reactivate this genius, diligence, and close scrutiny of reality of their workplaces. Subtle forms of racism are the most insidious because the perpetuators often are not acting out of intentional viciousness; they are not consciously aware of what they are doing. The victims too can be blind sided and taken unaware, because they do not expect racism to occur so readily among the intelligentsia. African Americans want to believe that racial atrocities are actions committed by unintelligent people. Thus, *academic racism* can be a surprising and rude awakening for some African American students and professors in colleges and universities. It is almost as if they forget the lesson they know so well that education is not a neutralizer of racism. They begin to think that the educated know better and will do better by not being willing perpetrators of racism. Reyes and Halcon (1990) spoke about being lulled into this false sense of security for Latino academicians. Their observations are apropos for African Americans as well. They noted that

> As minorities, we know from personal experience that racism in education is vigorous and pointed. We realize that, in spite of bona fide college degrees, our credentials are challenged by pervasive racist attitudes, and our effort toward full incorporation into academic positions in institutions of higher education...are hampered by layers of academic stratification. We find that, even with earned Ph.D.s, the academic road is the beginning of another Sisyphean climb...
>
> ...as graduate students we believed that successful completion of our graduate programs would be our license to 'play in the big leagues'...we assumed—or maybe hoped—that the frequent encounters with racism which we experienced in schools were confined to the lower echelons of the educational ladder. We believed that our

Ph.D.s paved the way to an egalitarian status with mutual respect among professional colleagues, where the new rules of competition would be truly based on merit. We were wrong. Instead, we find that even in academia, we face the same racism under different conditions—the old wolf in new clothing. (p. 70).

In this case the best defense is a good offense—that is, not being taken by surprise, or being unaware and unknowing. African American students, teachers, and staff members should be continually on the alert and consciously looking for how racism is manifested in the day-to-day life of academia. That is, developing a particular "kind of perspective taking, a stance, an awareness...a self-protective watchfulness" (Lawrence-Lightfoot 1994, p. 635) that is necessary for healthy, productive, and creative survival. Once this consciousness is established then better decisions can be made about how to resist, deflect, and/or combat racism, and what levels of engagement one wants to invest in any given acts of resistance. It also places a person in a proactive rather than a reactive posture, which is itself a form of empowerment.

Another preparation of African American academics for resisting racism is building emotional, intellectual, and psychological stamina. This involves developing a wide repertoire of strategies for dealing with racism, and counteracting its corrosive effects. One useful strategy is to cultivate a strong sense of ethnic, cultural, and racial identity so that the denigration that is endemic to racism does not penetrate the inner core of none's self-concept and self-esteem. Edwards and Polite (1992) call these skills "self-reliance" and "self-acceptance" (pp. 252–262). They found that professional African Americans who have high levels of self-reliance are able to move independent and pursue constructive directions based on their own individual purposes and principles. They set their own courses; move to their own beat; and are not too much concerned about what others think of them. Instead, successful African Americans are driven by the urgency of their advocacies, and the desire to function according to their own standards of professional quality and personal integrity. Self-acceptance provides another kind of internal shield against racism. According to Edwards and Polite, it is

> The characteristic that gives you the ability to be yourself, to embrace who you are, and to bring forward to a work setting your natural strengths. This characteristic provides an internal gyroscope that allows successful [B]lacks to function in varying situations without getting emotionally or psychologically lost.

> Successful [B]lacks also operate from a position of racial strength. They are not trying to escape of play down either their socioeconomic background or their culture and history, nor are they trying to be or become someone who is not [b]lack. They not only accept the positive and constructive aspects of African-American heritage but integrate them into their professional lives...Blacks who have a positive sense of their own value and worth are much less likely to be disoriented by the vicissitudes of corporate cultures of the vagaries of corporate politicking (p. 258)

African American professors also can make acts of racism objects of research inquiry and scholarly analysis. Many of them are engaged in some form of social justice research and scholarship. Personal encounters with racism can be graphic and authentic examples of the issues that they are trying to reform and resolve. Turning these encounters into "data" can be personally therapeutic, generative for scholarly productivity, and a form of social activism. Minimally, these actions are opportunities for exposing the enemy—racism—and subjecting it to public and communal criticism, rather than allowing it to remain an individual and private struggle. The chapters in this book are illustrations of these ideas activated.

Yet another technique that African Americans need to develop for persevering in the face of racism is finding relief and renewal from oppression in the workplace. Developing networks and friendships with other African Americans (and individuals from other groups of color) who have "shared frames of reference" but live and work in other locations is critical. They are familiar with the issues but have enough distance from the local particulars to provide some fresh perspectives. Participating in hobbies and recreational activities away from the campus environment is helpful, too.

Finally, African Americans in academia need to accept the necessity, validity, and redemptive value of struggle. This acceptance enhances endurance and resilience. The perpetuity of the struggle against racism is unavoidably burdensome, but we cannot allow it to always be so. If that happens we can easily become bedraggled, bitter, incapacitated, and defeated. Instead, we have to make the struggle a creative challenge, and find within it potential for our individual and collective revitalization and recreation as African Americans.

We must realize that the ability to not just endure or even to overcome, "but to triumph in the face of obstacles, to make a way out of what appears to be no way, to wrest destiny from the seemingly arbitrary hands of fate, constitutes power that is transcendent, freedom that is supreme" (Edwards & Polite 992, p. 274).

My Intellect and Professional Position Are Suspect

Professors of color in PWIs face some obstacles in their classrooms that are unlikely to happen among their European Americans to a similar magnitude, or even at all. Mainstream students frequently question their intellectual depth, the validity of the information they present, and the merits of their disciplines. Scholars new to the academy are especially susceptible to these attacks on their intellectuality, as well as those whose specialities are Ethnic studies, Multicultural Education, Women's Studies, and related issues in other disciplines (such as Black Psychology, African American Literature, Asian American history, Ethnic Politics, or Social Work Services for Culturally Different Groups). These "challenging" students convey attitudes that suggest doubts about the competence of professors of color and their right to work in predominately white colleges and universities.

Many students (along with some collegial peers and administrators) assume that all African American professors (and graduate students) are "affirmative action hires," and that is used to frame discussions about affirmative action even before the content of the oppositional arguments is addressed. These skeptics are known to say things like, "we want to hire well qualified instructors, and admit capable students, not be governed by affirmative action dictates." They seem to think the two are incompatible. Yet, there is nothing in affirmative action policy statements that suggests admitting unqualified students or employing unqualified professors of color. The racist messages underlying these negative assumptions are that people of color cannot be as intellectually capable as their European Americans counterparts, and as such they do not deserve the dignity and respect that go with being members of academia. Thus, European Americans students challenge the intellectual integrity, competence, and rigor of professors of color at will, and using only their white privilege as the basis for their actions.

A case in point happened recently in one of my classes. In the midst of a discussion on African American cultural values a European American female student challenged the validity of the information I was presenting by declaring, "You are stereotyping," without revealing the bases of her "counter-knowledge." "When probed to explain the reasons for her claim, she offered no explanations beyond appealing to her "personal opinion," and "experience" of "knowing some African Americans who are not like that." Her presumption of white privilege superceded my scholarly expertise! These kinds of attitudes and behaviors are not rarities; they happen frequently. European American students try to refute an entire fund of knowledge and body of scholarship with only their personal experiences with one or a few African Americans, experiences that may not have been culturally authentic anyway. Sometimes the perpetrators are not even conscious of what they are doing, but the message is still deeply racist. What else could explain why untutored European American novices presume that they know more than learned African American scholar *in their own areas of specialization*!

Another expression of doubts about their intellectual capability that African American professors often encounter appears in the guise of compliments. They are frequently told, "You are so articulate," or "You speak so eloquently." This does not strike me as genuine praise for two reasons. First, why should something (speaking coherently) that is part of the routine behavior of being a professor merit special acknowledgment? Second, why is there a need to say this to African Americans when similar accolades are not offered to European Americans? Why is our normality considered exceptional? It seems to me that these individuals are surprised by the intellectual and verbal abilities of their African American peers. If that is so, then I have to wonder what else did they expect and why.

These attitudes and behaviors constitute a kind of racism that is perpetually present for professors of color in the academic workplace. At the least they are irritating and condescending, and at worst, demeaning and insulting. Dealing with these biases takes emotional and intellectual energy that could be used in more constructive pursuits, even if African Americans do nothing more than dismiss them as irrelevant nonsense. We have to always be on the alert for them, and not allow ourselves to be caught off guard to minimize the potential damage they can do to our psycho-emotional well-being and our academic productivity. To resist this resistance it is imperative for African Americans to develop deep convictions about and confidence in their advocacies and competencies; be well-grounded in their disciplinary knowledge and scholarship; and able to articulate how their particular issues exemplify broader concepts, principles, and theories.

Always On Stage

As a result of their under representation in the professorate and the suspicions that many of their colleagues and students have toward them, African American professors are conspicuous. They are always in the spotlight, and more often than not it is aimed to illuminate their shortcomings rather than praise their strengths. Everything they do is under close scrutiny. They are expected to be "exceptional"; being normal is a luxury that is denied to them. African Americans are expected to always be friendly, pleasant, agreeable, and accommodating. When they do not meet this expectation, they are accused of being stand-offish, and hard to get along with. If they speak too passionately about issues, and take opposing positions too frequently, they are chastised for being too emotional, overly sensitive, too personal, or too negative. They are expected to "represent their race," while simultaneously being penalized for being too racial or ethnic. These situations create disturbing dilemmas for some African American professors and students, especially those who are highly ethnically affiliated and are trying to find a way to live comfortably in two worlds—academia and their cultural/ethnic socialization.

In reflecting on her own efforts to make sense of the racist impositions academia impose on African Americans Jacquelyn Mitchell (1990) spoke poignantly about their negative effects. Many of us who also have "been there" readily identify with her portrayal of these consequences. She writes:

> It is of little consequence that we may be recognized and respected for our contributions and scholarship; our ever-present visibility never allows us to experience complete membership in White academia. At the same time, these marginal feelings begin to affect our ethnicity as well. We thus experience double marginality, belonging to and feeling a part of two worlds, yet never at home in either....Problems and stresses already inherent in being a minority and an academic become compounded when the ideologies of the two referent groups contradict and conflict. In an attempt to sustain a feasible balance between our cultural and social identities, we undergo feelings of strain, anomie, and alienation. We are in a no-win situation...(p.129)

Critics of the sociality of African American professors rarely address them directly on substantive issues and analytical thought. Publicly they use silence as a weapon of subterfuge, while privately pretending there are no problems. It is not a rare for African Americans and other professors of color to be misled into believing that they are doing well during their third-year probationary reviews, only to find out two or three years later at the time for tenure and promotion that their peers have serious problems with their work.

The various kinds of silences surrounding racism in academia must be unveiled, as the authors in this volume do. If they are not made visible and vocal they cannot be countered as effectively as they must be. Speaking out about racism can help us distinguish between real and illusionary progress in combating it, and to ensure our personal wellness in the face of racism. As Hidalgo, McDowell, and Siddle (1990, p. vi) explained,

> We cannot continue to remain silent about racism. We must acknowledge that the cloud of oppression and racial injustice has never left us, despite sporadic attempts, in times of national conscience, to create vehicles for the achievement of equality for all citizens. When the guardians of that conscience are displaced, however, any gains are undermined before real changes in the power structure,
>
> economic arena, or educational system can have a significant impact on the majority of people of color.

Who's Got My Back

Other dubious encounters that African American professors are almost certain to encounter from their European American peers is being expected to always be advocates of and responsible for race-related issues, to be experts on their own ethnic group regardless of their learned specialities, and to only and always teach race-specific content. Yet, when these expected expertise are actually claimed they become punitive. For example, advisors in my program frequently suggest that students take some classes that I teach to meet their cultural diversity requirement for applying to the teacher education program that are totally inappropriate. Because I do teach some classes in Multicultural Education these advisors falsely assume that *everything* else I teach will be acceptable as well. When confronted with these errors, they respond wit statements like, "But, you're so good with students that they will learn more about cultural diversity even in____ than in ____(the specific course on multicultural education), that is taught by_____."

Students often exaggerate the amount of attention African American instructors give to racial and cultural diversity, claim to be unduly intimidated if they express opposing points of view, and suggest that these professors practice, "reverse racism," and bashing of European Americans. Some colleagues who review the portfolios of African Americans for merit pay, tenure, and promotion express doubts about the significance and quality of their areas of study, and declare a lack of knowledge about them. Yet, they will proceed to cast votes on what they do not understand or value, thus making decisions based on ignorance. This seems to be a flagrant violation of academic ethos and claims of "objective and unbiased peer reviews."

Complicating matters further is the tendency for African American professors to be left standing alone in presenting arguments against racial inequities, without receiving any public support from their European American colleagues. The same individuals who remain silent and make no public declarations on the issues under discussion will approach African Americans privately, after the fact, or when the meeting is over to declare how much they agreed with or admired the points made and positions taken. Where was this support when it would have counted the most? There is little consolation in this empty compliment when a negative decision is rendered on the issue. These behaviors convey very graphical messages that avoiding the displeasure of other European Americans is more important than publicly endorsing issues advocated by African Americans. How are we to place any faith, trust, and respect in reactions like this, especially when they happensover and over again. African Americans learn early in their academic careers that support form European American colleagues for their causes may not be dependable or forthcoming at all. Consequently, they end up having to do battle alone, or recognizing the futility of battling at all, concede defeat, and retreat into silence.

It would not be surprising if European Americans interpreted this silence as victory for their viewpoints, or assume that the issues of concern to African Americans were not of major significance after all. Lisa Delpit (1998) called these non-engagements and their deleterious consequences on subsequent interactions "silenced dialogues." African American professors and students must resist being silenced by others or themselves for expressing viewpoints that are unpopular, disturbing, and "politically incorrect." Racism is not easy or pleasant to experience or to talk about. But, silence is not a viable response to this atrocity. Both its victims and their allies must continually scream the pains it inflicts, declare the urgency of resistance, and aggressively pursue its annihilation. If we do not talk about racism we become part of a "conspiracy of silence" (Hidalgo, McDowell, & Siddle 1990, p. v) that perpetuates racial inequalities, restrictions, and indignities, and reduce opportunities for reform.

It does not take long for recurrent encounters of ideological abandonment to generate distrust, which can have debilitating effects on the long-term feelings of collegiality of African American college professors toward their European American peers. Being habitually unsupported in discourse is a powerful form of intellectual and ideological marginalization, since African Americans are denied the mental engagement that can enhance their clarity, fluidity, and depth of thought, which is a normative expected from persons working and living in academia. Graduate students complain bitterly about this intellectual isolation, particularly those who are the "only ones" in their departments or programs of study. They point out (and rightfully so) that their intellectual development is being compromised when European American Professors and fellow students do not engage their ideas. Whatever the reasoning behind these avoidance behaviors, they constitute academic racism! Unless carefully monitored and held in proper perspective, this intellectual isolation can create a "victim mentality," incubating depression and paranoia.

What is the antidote for these forms and effects of racism in academia? One possibility answer is to force a public declaration of support from European Americans by using citations from their own scholarship and evoking previously recorded discourse (such as minutes of committee and faculty meetings) in arguing issues. This strategy can have some negative side effects as well. One is giving the impression that African Americans have to depend on European Americans to validate their viewpoints. Also, it may not be acceptable to some African Americans because it adds another burden to an already disproportionally heavy workload. A third drawback is it can interfere with African Americans refining their own thinking and promoting their advocacy from their own perspectives. Another resistance strategy to the racism inherent in intellectual isolation is to not depend on support from European Americans. If it is forthcoming, fine, but if it is not, African Americans should continue to persist with conviction and diligence in promoting their causes, concern, or issues. These reactions probably will not make African American professors popular with many of their European American peers and supervisors, but it will maintain their sense of personal and professional integrity. Lurking in the shadow, though, is the need to deliver these responses with finesse and a clear understanding of the calculated risks involved that may surface during tenure and promotion reviews under the guise of, "he or she is not a good community member?"

A third way to resist the resistance of silence and intellectual isolation is for African American professors to carefully study the ideological and political positioning of colleagues on issues of interest to them. This is useful information to have in determining how to position oneself in departmental politics, building allegiances with individuals who can be trusted to be supportive (both privately and publicly), and creating a means for receiving candid feedback on professional development on their local campuses and elsewhere.

My Advocacy Is Politics and Propaganda but Yours Is Research and Scholarship

Another persistent form of academic racism is conveyed through the skepticism many mainstream professors have about the research and scholarship of African Americans. They express doubts about the significance of the work, if it meets conventions of academic rigor, and whether African Americans are capable of studying anything other than race-related issues. As a result African Americans often have to defend the legitimacy of the work they do. Similar research and scholarship produced by European Americans are not perceived as being inherently flawed; nor is their validity automatically suspect because of their outsider perspectives. They affect recruitment, retention, tenure, and promotion reviews, and the long-term career development of African Americans.

Even in the research and scholarship paradigms that have emerged over the last 20 years or so which are more amenable to "personal presence," autobiographical narratives, and insider perspectives African Americans are frequently denied open access to these pejoratives. When not denied outright, the evocation of them leads to questions about whether they can study their own ethnic group's issues and experiences with a critical eye, analytical depth, and "academic objectivity." Or, will they merely engage in politicking and propagandizing instead of producing "scientific-based knowledge." The criticisms are particularly veracious in situations where mainstream presumptions of truth about African American experiences are challenged. A case in point is explanations about the achievement problems of African American students. It is a rare occurrence that mainstream scholars question the merits of attributing these problems broadly to poor academic stimulation in the homes, and parents who do not value education. They do not demand the frequent interjections of warning in these explanations "do not apply to everyone" nor do they insist in having proof that the proposed corrective strategies are successful with particular segments of African American students *before* they are applied them.

Such prerogatives are not granted to African American scholars who offer explanations that challenge these assumptions. They are asked to provide "guarantees for success," but when they are provided these guarantees are never acceptable. If the results of qualitative studies are given, the frequent reaction is they are too small-scale to be generalizable. The findings of larger-scale studies conducted by African Americans are dismissed as not appropriate for particular local situations. Or, the rigor of the research is questioned. Or, the evidence of success is simply ignored. When African Americans suggest, for example, that achievement problems may stem more from cultural characteristics and learning styles, and they elaborate the specificity of these features, they are accused of over-generalizing, stereotyping, or essentializing culture. Demands from African Americans (and other scholars of color) for the academic community to be more culturally attuned to ethnic and racial differences, and avoid perpetuating cultural hegemony and racism in its research and scholarship, are demeaned and converted into condescending responses about having to be "politically correct."

These attitudes and behaviors are rampant in academia. They create a work environment that is very unwelcoming and marginalizing. They demonstrate convincingly that as African Americans are working hard to acquire acceptable academic credentials and symbols of status, demonstrate competence, and to be judged by the merits of their productivity, they continually encounter "the quicksand of subtle exclusion" (Lawrence-

Lightfoot 1994, p. 10). It ties them to the periphery of the institutions and programs in which they work, and their outsider status is persistent even as they strive to claim an insider's place, such as moving up the professorial ranks, or into higher level administrative positions. Sometimes this marginality becomes even clearer as some African Americans appear to be closer to the centers of power (Lawrence-Lightfoot, 1994).

What is one to do about these troubling dilemmas? If African Americans ignore these attacks on their scholarship and continue within their own paradigmatic frameworks, they may find it difficult to get their work into mainstream publications. Fortunately, some windows of opportunity are now opening, and there are some publishers who are receptive to "innovative" scholarship. Another option for African Americans is to constrain the "ethnic nuances" in their scholarship and write in ways that are acceptable to mainstream publishers. This choice can be problematic, though, because it may be read by other African Americans as "selling out." Mainstream scholars may see these actions as tacit endorsements of their analyses and interpretations, regardless of how racist they are. Whichever choice is made, and whether in one's own or others' minds, many African American walk a thin and sometimes precarious line between ethnic authenticity and academic acceptability in conducting research and scholarship. Some find a way to successfully accomplish (and even integrate) both; many do not.

Mitchell (1990) provides graphic descriptions of these dilemmas that are very familiar to many African American academicians. She says "we are continually at risk, vulnerable to charges from either side of having sold out or of being written off as nothing more than an agitator rather than a serious academic" (p 130). We are burdened with the responsibility of representing our people's realities without misrepresentation, yet we are often penalized for doing what is expected of us. We are never given the benefit of the doubt. The "double jeopardy" causes us to sometimes be overtly cautious in our research and writing to ensure that we are not accused of being merely idiosyncratic; to accurately represent African American experiences in general; to prevent our information from being used to validate racial biases and distortions; and to make sure that we do not perpetuate hegemonic theories, methodologies, and premises in our won work. At times we even sacrifice our own intellectual autonomy, creativity, and voice (Mitchell, 1990). And, are we academicians who are African American, or just academicians? Sometimes it is provoked by ourselves, but most often it is imposed upon us by others. Whatever the sources, the question itself is symptomatic of the racism that haunts African Americans.

The most feasible way out of these dilemmas is for African Americans to strike a balance between these positionalities. But this is easier said than done. The contours of the challenges shift often, thus demanding careful monitoring and frequent changes in strategic responses. They place strain on intellectual creativity and psycho-emotional and physical stamina that stretch far beyond the normal demands of being teachers, researchers, and scholars in academia. When these situations are considered in concert with all of the other racist obstacles that African Americans encounter, it is not surprising that the academic careers of so many do not reach full potential in scholarly productivity, or by moving through the professorial ranks.

Extra Work But No Overtime Pay

Teaching in academia is hard work, intellectually and emotionally, under the best of circumstances. And as the authors in this volume demonstrate, many African American professors do not work under the best of circumstances. They do not have the luxury of simply fulfilling their professorial responsibilities. Other tasks, and the contexts in which they work, demand additional energy and efforts. This is not to say that African Americans are routinely assigned more courses to teach, students to advise, or committees on which to serve than their European American counterparts. The additional work usually appears as *tacit extensions* that take several different forms. It begins with simply being, on a daily basis, in predominantly white institutions without being seduced by them or being consumed by rage. Some more specific examples are useful in clarifying the meaning and nature of this extra work.

One of the ways in which African American professors work harder is apparent in the kinds of classes they are assigned to teach. As new members of the academic community their teaching assignments include frequently introductory, foundational, and/or required courses that have large student enrollments. Many of these courses have acquired negative reputations long before the African American instructors arrive. But, students do not make these distinctions. They often challenge the merits of the courses and link the negativism associated with them to the competence of the instructor. Consequently, African Americans are placed in positions where they have to justify the validity of these courses. Attending to this need can interfere with the substantive development of the course content, especially diversity; conferring with students beyond our own advisees on their study projects and research on issues of social justice; serving on committees and task forces because part of their charge has to do with racial and cultural differences; and having to be the voice of reason and recommendation on race, racism, and ethnic diversity because our European American colleagues "just don't understand, and don't know what to do." These declarations are even made by some European Americans who claim to be committed to promoting social justice, anti-racism, and educational equity. The demands they impose on our time are not in lieu of regular responsibilities, but in addition to them, and they usually are not accompanied by any reciprocity or compensation in kind. African Americans certainly would not have their jobs for long if they repeatedly publicly declared their incompetencies in areas of assigned responsibility, much less being rewarded for them. Yet there are no obvious sanctions imposed on European Americans who make these claims on issues related to racial, ethnic, and cultural diversity. Therefore, in real time and tasks, African Americans in academia work much harder then their mainstream counterparts.

Conclusion

Racism is a perennial presence in the lives of African Americans, including academics. However much we might wish it to be otherwise, it is not, and we can't help but deal with it in some form or another. And whatever that choice is—whether to try to avoid it, escape it, ignore it, bypass it, or confront it—it is emotionally, physically, psychologically, and intellectually demanding. To simply do our jobs means we have additional burdens to bear. Sometimes we are disheartened, anguished, and angered by the unfairness of these burdens. Sometimes we wonder if our efforts at resisting racism are worthwhile when so little progress seems to be made, and there is no relief from the struggle. We may even have fleeting flights of fantasy about giving up and walking away from it all. But, we cannot. And, if we could where would we go. If we could find a place to retreat, racism would be there waiting for us. There is no escaping racism since it is everywhere, permeating the entire fabric of all dimensions of U.S. society.

This does not mean we should develop martyr complexes (or accept impositions from others), feelings of helplessness, or concessions of defeat. It means, instead, that African American academicians must have a thorough understanding of the contextual realities of racism in academia, and fight it with all their might, and by whatever means at their disposal. This is necessary if they are to be personally healthy, more productive in their professional roles and responsibilities, and effective in their battles against racism. Unquestionably, institutional and structural changes must be made in combating racism, but we cannot wait for these to occur. Colleges and universities do not change easily, even when they support innovations; they are more resistant to change on issues that they do not perceive as imperative and urgent. This is the attitude of many of them toward racism. African Americans in academia have to press on in resisting racism in spite of having to operate in a climate of denial, ambivalence, or opposition. In the final analysis, each of us must take our own stand against racism.

African Americans in academia can find some consolation and affirmation in facing and fighting racism from Ralph Ellison's *Invisible Man*. After finally breaking the manacles of invisibility (which is analogous to racism) that resulted from being defined by white Americans the protagonist reflected:

> When one is invisible he finds such problems as good and evil, honesty and dishonesty, of such shifting shapes that he confuses one with the other, depending upon who happens to be looking through him at the time. Well, now I've been trying to look through myself, and there's a risk in it. I was never more hated than when I tried to be honest. Or when...I've tried to articulate exactly what I felt to be the truth. No one was satisfied—not even I. On the other hand, I've never been more loved and appreciated then when I tried to 'justify' and affirm someone's mistaken beliefs; or when I've tried to give my friends the incorrect, absurd answers they wished to hear....They received a feeling of security. But here was the rub: Too often, in order to justify *them*, I had to take myself by the throat and choke myself until my eyes bulged and my tongue hung out and wagged like the door of an empty house in a high wind. Oh, yes, it made them happy and it made me sick. So I became ill of affirmation, of saying 'yes' against the nay-saying of my stomach—not to mention my brain.

...I was pulled this way and that longer than I can remember. And my problem was that I always tried to go in everyone's way but my own. I also have been called nothing and then another while no one really wished to hear what I called myself. So after many years of trying to adopt the opinions of others I finally rebelled...
   Who knows but that, on the lower frequencies, I speak for you? (Ellison, 1952, pp. 559–560, 568).

As the "Invisible Man" came to realize, speaking his own mind and constructing his own identity as an African American was not easy or popular, but and absolute necessity. So too is fighting racism in academia for African American students, teachers, and staffs. The struggle is upon us, and it is urgent, continuous, and inescapable.

References

Delpit, L. (1998). The silenced dialogue: power and pedagogy in education other people's children. *Harvard Educational Review, 58* (3), 280–298.
Dyson, A. H. & Genishi, C. (Eds.). (1994). *The need for story: Cultural diversity in classroom and community.* Urbana, IL: National Council of Teachers of English.
Edwards, A., & Polite, C. K. (1992). *Children of the dream: The psychology of black success.* New York: Doubleday.
Ellison, R. (1952). *The invisible man.* New York: Vintage Books.
Grier, W., H., & Cobbs, P. M. (1968). *Black rage.* New York: Bantam Books.
Hidalgo, N. M., McDowell, C. L., & Siddle, E.V. (1990). Introduction. In N. M. Hidalgo, C. L. McDowell, & E.V. Siddle (Eds.), *Facing racism in education* (pp. v-vii),. Cambridge, MA: *Harvard Educational Review.*
Lawrence-Lightfoot, S. (1994). *I've known rivers: Lives of loss and liberation.* Reading, MA: Addison-Wesley.
Mitchell, J. (1990). Reflections of a black social scientist: Some struggles, some doubts, some hopes. In N. M. Hidalgo, C. L. McDowell & E. V. Siddle (Eds.), *Facing racism in education* (pp. 118–134), Reprint series No. 21. Cambridge, MA: *Harvard Educational Review.*

Tatum, B. D. (1997). *"Why are all the Black kids sitting together in the cafeteria?" And other conversations about race.* New York: Basic Books.

Reyes, M. d. l. L, & Halcon, J. J. (1990). Racism in academia: The old wolf revisited. In N. M. Hidalgo, C. L. McDowell, & E. V. Siddle (Eds.), *Facing racism in education* (pp. 69-83), Reprint series No. 21. Cambridge, MA: *Harvard Educational Review*. Imagination: taking the story to heart. In H. McEwan & K. Egan (Eds.), *Narrative in teaching, learning, and research* (pp. 39-49). New York: Teachers College Press.

About the Editors

M. Christopher Brown II is the Executive Director and Chief Research Scientist of the Frederick D. Patterson Research institute of the United Negro College Fund. He is on leave of absence from his appointment as Associate Professor of Education and Senior Research associate in the Center for the Study of Higher Education at The Pennsylvania State University. Dr. Brown earned a national reputation for his research and scholarly writing on higher education policy and administration meriting him both the ASHE (2001) and AERA (2002) early career research awards. His research addresses issues of higher education leadership and governance, postsecondary statutory and legal concerns, institutional history, and collegiate diversity. This scholarly agenda focuses on increasing effectiveness and efficiency, building organizational capacity, and assessing outcomes in campus settings. He is especially well known for his studies of historically black colleges, educational equity, and institutional culture. He is the author or co-author of more than 50 journal articles, book chapters, monographs, and publications related to education and society. Dr. Brown is the author/editor of *The Quest to define Collegiate Desegregation* (1999), *Organization and Governance in Higher Education* (2000), *Black Sons to Mothers* (2000, with James Earl Davis), and *Black Colleges* (2004, with Kassie Freeman). He is also co-author of one book forthcoming, *The Broken Cisterns of Brown* (with RoSusan Bartee and Tazewell Hurst). He has lectured and/or presented scholarship in various countries on four of seven continents – Africa, Australia, Europe, and North America. He has received research support from the Lumina Foundation, Spencer Foundation, AT&T Foundation, and the Pew Charitable Trusts.

Roderic R. Land is an Adjunct Assistant Professor at the University of Utah in the department of Educational Leadership & Policy, as well as the Department of Education, Culture, & Society. He is also an ICEOP Fellow at the University of Illinois Urbana-Champaign. Mr. Land's research includes the scholarly investigation of black faculty in predominantly white classrooms. This area of inquiry gives particular attention to the successful recruitment and retention of black faculty in postsecondary settings. Additionally, he has parallel research program in culturally relevant and critical pedagogy. Mr. Land's work in curriculum and pedagogy has posited African-centered approaches to improving the academic achievement of black student Pre-K through Ph.D. educational contexts. He is a regular presenter at the American Educational Research Association annual meeting. His research has also been disseminated at other education and sociology conferences both domestic and abroad.

Studies in the Postmodern Theory of Education

General Editors
Joe L. Kincheloe & Shirley R. Steinberg

Counterpoints publishes the most compelling and imaginative books being written in education today. Grounded on the theoretical advances in criticalism, feminism, and postmodernism in the last two decades of the twentieth century, Counterpoints engages the meaning of these innovations in various forms of educational expression. Committed to the proposition that theoretical literature should be accessible to a variety of audiences, the series insists that its authors avoid esoteric and jargonistic languages that transform educational scholarship into an elite discourse for the initiated. Scholarly work matters only to the degree it affects consciousness and practice at multiple sites. Counterpoints' editorial policy is based on these principles and the ability of scholars to break new ground, to open new conversations, to go where educators have never gone before.

For additional information about this series or for the submission of manuscripts, please contact:
        Joe L. Kincheloe & Shirley R. Steinberg
        c/o Peter Lang Publishing, Inc.
        275 Seventh Avenue, 28th floor
        New York, New York 10001

To order other books in this series, please contact our Customer Service Department:
        (800) 770-LANG (within the U.S.)
        (212) 647-7706 (outside the U.S.)
        (212) 647-7707 FAX

Or browse online by series:
        www.peterlangusa.com